Also by Simon Elmer

The Colour of the Sacred: Georges Bataille and the Image of Sacrifice

The Road to Fascism: For a Critique of the Global Biosecurity State

Virtue and Terror: Selected Articles on the UK Biosecurity State, Vol. 1

The New Normal: Selected Articles on the UK Biosecurity State, Vol. 2

Notes to Poetry

Fight and Flight: Poems, 2012-2023

and with Geraldine Dening

Architects for Social Housing, 2015-2022

The Truth about Grenfell Tower

Central Hill: A Case Study in Estate Regeneration

The Costs of Estate Regeneration

Inequality Capital

For A Socialist Architecture: Under Capitalism

Saving St. Raphael's Estate: The Alternative to Demolition

Simon Elmer

The Great Reset

Biopolitics for Stakeholder Capitalism

Published in Great Britain in 2023 by

Architects for Social Housing
Fairford House
Kennington Lane
London SE11 4HW
e-mail: info@architectsforsocialhousing.co.uk
website: www.architectsforsocialhousing.co.uk

ISBN 978-1-4467-2049-3 (clothbound)
ISBN 978-1-4467-2047-9 (paperbound)

Cover design by Architects for Social Housing

For the less deceived

Contents

'Cause we're going to wake up in the end-times,
We're going to be curled up in the wreckage
Thinking, yeah, life's going to happen
Whether we dismiss it or expect it.
So let me look into your eyes
And see my own eyes reflected,
I'm crying oceans into paragraphs
'Cause behind out backs our shadows laugh.

— Kate Tempest, *End Times*, 2009

Preface

'The technologies at the heart of the Fourth Industrial Revolution are connected in many ways — in the way they extend digital capabilities; in the way they scale, emerge and embed themselves in our lives; in their combinatorial power; and in their potential to concentrate privilege and challenge existing governance systems.'

— Klaus Schwab, *Shaping the Future of the Fourth Industrial Revolution*, 2018

The *Wikipedia* entry for the Great Reset, the first part of which is quoted in a blue panel as a corrective to any mention or discussion of this term on *YouTube*, reads as follows:

> The Great Reset Initiative is an economic recovery plan drawn up by the World Economic Forum (WEF) in response to the COVID-19 pandemic. The project was launched in June 2020, with a video featuring the then Prince of Wales Charles released to mark its launch. The initiative's stated aim is to facilitate rebuilding from the global COVID-19 crisis in a way that prioritizes sustainable development.

> The initiative triggered a range of diverse conspiracy theories spread by American far-right and conservative commentators on social media such as Facebook and Twitter. Such theories include that the COVID-19 pandemic was created by a secret group in order to seize control of the global economy, that lockdown restrictions were deliberately designed to induce economic meltdown, or that a global elite was attempting to abolish private property while using COVID-19 to enslave humanity with vaccines.

I am not an American, have never belonged to any far-right organisation, my views are not conservative with either a big or a little 'c', and I have published a number of articles arguing against the conspiracy theory of history; but I have also argued that a virus with the infection fatality rate of seasonal influenza never constituted anything approaching a 'pandemic'; that lockdown restrictions were imposed not to induce the 'meltdown' of the economy but, to the contrary, to insulate the real economy from the $12 trillion of quantitative easing created to bail out the collapsing financial sector between September 2019 and April 2022; and that, far from attempting to 'abolish' private property, the stakeholder model of capitalism promoted by the World Economic Forum and implemented by its corporate partners under the umbrella of 'sustainable development goals' is designed to privatise national assets, natural resources and, ultimately — as Klaus Schwab openly advocates — the existing system of governance in the West.[1]

In this respect, the *Wikipedia* entry is exemplary of how the accusation of 'conspiracy theory', illustrated with extreme or inaccurate or just plain ridiculous examples ('enslave humanity with vaccines') to which very few people subscribe, works to discredit and dismiss by association any and more rational criticisms of the global technocracies, international companies and national governments that, in the wake of multiple manufactured 'crises', have taken into their control the institutions, procedures and platforms by which a political, scientific and media consensus is reached.

Strange as it may seem, however, this grudging concession of the existence of a global economic plan, its origins in a corporate think-tank and its support by the now Head of State of the UK is an age away from the vociferous denials and mocking denunciations of being a 'conspiracy theorist' that were hurled at anyone who dared even to refer to the 'Great Reset' in the first year of lockdown. These only gradually diminished when someone pointed out that the term was openly used on the website of the World Economic Forum and had provided the title of the book published by its founder and Executive Chairman, Klaus Schwab, in July 2020, barely 4 months since the 'pandemic' was declared by the World Health Organization.[2] And while the accusation of conspiracy theory is still used to

---

1. See Simon Elmer, '*Cui Bono?* The COVID-19 "Conspiracy"' (19 February, 2021); and 'Lies, Damned Lies and Statistics: Manufacturing the Crisis' (27 January, 2021); both collected in *The New Normal: Selected Articles in the UK Biosecurity State, Vol. 2* (Architects for Social Housing, 2023), pp. 103-160 and 73-101; and 'Fascism and the Decay of Capitalism', Chapter 4 of *The Road to Fascism: For a Critique of the Global Biosecurity State* (Architects for Social Housing, 2022), pp. 61-80.

2. Compare Christopher Alessi, '"A golden opportunity" — HRH the Prince of Wales and other leaders on the Forum's Great Reset', *World Economic Forum* (3 June, 2020), and Klaus Schwab and Thierry Malleret, *COVID-19: The Great Reset* (Forum Publishing, July 2020), with, from across the Overton Window of UK politics, Hana Carter, '"Great Reset": Bizarre new Covid conspiracy theory as "Build Back Better" slogans around the world spark "fascist" regime claims', *The Sun* (20

silence anyone who attributes anything other than purely beneficent motives to the 1,200 banks, asset managers, information technology conglomerates, media corporations, energy utilities, industrial manufacturers and other companies that, on the same day the 'pandemic' was declared, formed themselves into a 'COVID-19 Action Platform', the term itself is now more or less openly used by politicians, civil servants, corporate CEOs, marketing executives, digital engineers, journalists, activists and other promoters of what the World Economic Forum calls 'stakeholder capitalism'.[3]

It's hard to say which term is more likely to attract censure and censorship when used by those not authorised to do so, but the most accurate description of the Great Reset — and the one most suppressed by those overseeing its implementation — is that it is the historical shift from the economic, political and social paradigm by which the West has been governed for the past forty years into stakeholder capitalism. As the emerging political economy of the West, this seeks to merge the separation of powers between executive, legislature and judiciary on which Western democracy has been founded into a technocratic form of governance that will signal the end of politics, properly speaking, insofar as politics designates — at least in principle — a space of debate, contestation, representation and accountability. For Schwab, whose latest book is titled *Stakeholder Capitalism*, this merger represents a revolution from shareholder capitalism, in which individual economies overseen by national governments were run for the benefit of company shareholders, into a global economy governed by the same companies, but ostensibly for the benefit of all, inclusively, sustainably, profitably.[4] The investment in which these multinational companies hold a stake, therefore, is the world itself. 'A global economy that works for progress, people and the planet' is the subtitle of Schwab's book, which like those preceding it doesn't lack in ambition, hubris and a complete disregard for anything one could

---

November, 2020); Jack Goodman and Flora Carmichael, 'The coronavirus pandemic "Great Reset" theory and a false vaccine claim debunked', *BBC News* (22 November, 2020); Quinn Slobodian, 'How the "great reset" of capitalism became an anti-lockdown conspiracy', *The Guardian* (4 December, 2020); and Naomi Klein, 'The Great Reset Conspiracy Smoothie', *The Intercept* (8 December, 2020).

3. See Peter Vanham, 'World Economic Forum launches COVID-19 Action Platform to fight coronavirus', *World Economic Forum* (11 March, 2020).

4. See Klaus Schwab with Peter Vanham, *Stakeholder Capitalism: A Global Economy that Works for Progress, People and the Planet* (John Wiley & Sons, 2021).

call democratic process, accountability or a mandate from those it claims to benefit.[5]

If we were to pick a starting date for this revolution in Western capitalism, whose economic forces lie in the neoliberal revolution of the late 1970s and the rise of finance capitalism as the dominant economic model of the West, it began in September 2019 with the spike in interest rates in the US repurchase agreement market that triggered the latest Global Financial Crisis, and to which the lockdown of the real economies of global capitalism in March 2020 was the concerted response.[6] My two collections of essays, *Virtue and Terror* and *The New Normal*, written between March 2020 and October 2021 when the UK was still ruled by emergency powers under lockdown restrictions, sought to describe this first phase of the Great Reset, its legislative frameworks and economic motivations. My argument in this book is that we have now moved out of the first phase of this revolution, whose trajectory and precedents I described in *The Road to Fascism: For a Critique of the Global Biosecurity State*, and into the second phase. In its sequel, *The Great Reset: Biopolitics for Stakeholder Capitalism*, I try to articulate what this new phase is and what it means for us. Hopefully — and what hope we have is one of the questions this book tries to address — by understanding this new phase of the Great Reset better, we will be able to offer more resistance to its enforcement than we managed in its first phase, which was met with almost universal credulity, compliance and collaboration.

1. From Legislation to Biopower

A lot of things have changed in the UK and across the Western World since, in March 2022, the coronavirus-justified restrictions on our human rights and civil liberties began to be lifted; but that doesn't mean, as too many opposed to lockdown initially thought, that the Great Reset of Western capitalism for which

---

5. Schwab's recent books include, with Thierry Malleret, *The Great Narrative: For a Better Future* (Forum Publishing, 2021); *COVID-19: The Great Reset* (Forum Publishing, 2020); with Nicolas Davis, *Shaping the Future of the Fourth Industrial Revolution: A Guide to Building a Better World*, with a foreword by Satya Nadella (Portfolio Penguin, 2018); and *The Fourth Industrial Revolution*, with an introduction by Marc R. Benioff (Portfolio Penguin, 2017).

6. See Fabio Vighi, 'A Self-fulfilling Prophecy: Systemic Collapse and Pandemic Simulation', *The Philosophical Salon* (16 August, 2021).

those restrictions laid the ground is over. Far from it. To emphasise how far from over the Great Reset is, I have referred to this new phase as the 'Four Horsemen of the Apocalypse'.[7] This is not only for dramatic effect but also because it gravitates around four apparatuses of biopower, not all of which are new, but which are being implemented simultaneously and are, indeed, dependent on each other for their implementation. Much of this book is about this interdependence, which Schwab refers to as their 'combinatorial power'.

But what is 'biopower'? It's a term I've been using since we were first locked in our homes on the justification of stopping the spread of the coronavirus, and I've made many attempts to describe it — which I shall continue to do, no doubt, because it is under its paradigm that the world is now governed and will be for the foreseeable future.[8] The term was first introduced into political discourse by the French philosopher and historian, Michel Foucault, who died in 1984. As Professor of the History of Systems of Thought at the Collège de France, Foucault explored its genesis in his lecture series of 1975-1979.[9] But he first used the term in his published work in *The Will to Knowledge*, where, in the pages titled 'Right of Death and Power over Life', Foucault described the movement from a juridical to a biopolitical paradigm of governance:

> Another consequence of this development of bio-power was the growing importance assumed by the action of the norm, at the expense of the juridical system of the law. Law cannot help but be armed, and its arm, *par excellence*, is death; to those who transgress it, it replies, at least as a last resort, with that absolute menace. The law always refers to the sword. But a power whose task is to take charge of life needs continuous regulatory and corrective mechanisms. Such a power has to qualify, measure, appraise and hierarchise, rather than display itself in its murderous splendour; it does not have to draw the line that

---

7. See Simon Elmer, 'The Four Horsemen of the Apocalypse: New Technologies of Biopower', PANDA Open Society Sessions, *YouTube* (2 June, 2023).

8. See Simon Elmer, 'Giorgio Agamben and the Biopolitics of COVID-19' (25 April, 2020); collected in *Virtue and Terror: Selected Articles on the UK Biosecurity State, Vol. 1* (Architects for Social Housing, 2022), pp. 3-20.

9. These lectures were published posthumously as Michel Foucault, *'Society Must Be Defended'* (1975-1976), *Security, Territory, Population* (1977-1978), and *The Birth of Biopolitics* (1978-1979); edited by Michel Senellart, English series edited by Arnold I. Davidson, translated by Graham Burchell (Palgrave Macmillan, 2003, 2007, 2008).

separates the enemies of the sovereign from his obedient subjects; it effects distributions around the norm. I do not mean to say that the law fades into the background or that the institutions of justice tend to disappear, but rather that the judicial institution is increasingly incorporated into a continuum of apparatuses (medical, administrative, and so on) whose functions are for the most part regulatory. A normalising society is the historical outcome of a technology of power centred on life.[10]

Foucault viewed the rise of biopower and the technologies of its implementation within a historical context that began around the time of the French Revolution of 1788, and which he associated with the First Republic's formulation of human rights. It was through these rights that the state first assumed its duty and its right to defend, but also to control, not only the life but also the quality of life of its citizens: our health, our bodies, our needs, our happiness — which have most recently been condensed into the new category of our 'well-being'. For Foucault, this represented a historical shift from the legislative power by which the sovereign and his government had authority over the life and death of his subjects, and within which laws have a purely punitive function that sets restrictions and obligations which, if broken, have penalties up to and including death, into a biopolitical paradigm, within which the technologies of power qualify, measure, appraise and hierarchise the life of the citizen.

This shift has parallels with what is happening now largely in the West under the banner of the Fourth Industrial Revolution, by which the new apparatuses of biopower and the technologies of which they dispose will qualify our access to what were previously the universal, indivisible and inalienable rights of citizenship; measure our levels of compliance with regulatory and corrective mechanisms that have not been written into any laws; appraise us through a system of surveillance and monitoring justified by 'crises' whose very existence it prohibits us from questioning; and, by doing so, will produce a new hierarchy of Social Credit rated according to our levels of obedience not only to the by-now familiar regulations

---

10. See Michel Foucault, 'Right of Death and Power over Life', part five of *The Will to Knowledge*, Volume 1 of *The History of Sexuality*; translated by Robert Hurley (Penguin Books, 1998), p. 144.

of the Global Biosecurity State but also to new actions of the norm extending into every aspect of our lives.

It's important to bear in mind that the shift Foucault described is an historical one that happened over several hundred years; but history does not move at an even pace, and at times of social and political revolution — such as the one the West entered in March 2020 — what might otherwise have taken a century to unfold can be implemented in a decade or less. We've seen this demonstrated most materially in the succession of industrial revolutions that the People's Republic of China has undergone in the space of 70 years, but which took the UK, by contrast, 250 years or more. Moreover, the shift from a juridical to a biopolitical paradigm does not happen all at once and definitively. Just as there are emergent social, political, legal and technological forces in any given society, so too there are residual elements formed under earlier economic models that continue to play a role. Under lockdown, for example, Western capitalism was governed — if we can use this word to describe the vast levels of theft of the future wealth of its populations — under a State of Emergency whose legal precedents can be traced back to the French Revolution.[11] But now, as we have emerged out of lockdown to be plunged into a biopolitical paradigm of governance, that juridical framework of human rights, legislative oversight, judicial appeal, media scrutiny of government and democratic accountability to the electorate — all of which utterly failed to defend what democracy we had — is being replaced — again, not completely but to a further and greatly expanded degree — by the technologies of biopower.

To recall, briefly, the juridical framework by which we were ruled for two years in the UK, and which continues to implement the biopolitical framework within which the apparatuses of biopower are being implemented, since March 2020 the following Acts and Statutes have been made into UK law:

- The Coronavirus Act 2020, whose 384 pages, 102 provisions and 29 schedules went through just one week of reading and three days of debate in Parliament before, according to a convention agreed to by Her Majesty's

11. See Giorgio Agamben, *State Of Exception*, Homo Sacer II, 1; translated by Kevin Attell (University of Chicago Press, 2005), pp. 1-31; and the pages titled 'Historical Precedents for Emergency Powers' in Simon Elmer, 'The New Normal: What Is the UK Biosecurity State. Part 1: Programmes and Regulations' (31 July, 2020); collected in *Virtue and Terror*, pp. 147-154.

Opposition, being 'nodded through' by MPs rather than approved by a democratic vote.[12]

- 580 coronavirus-justified Statutory Instruments made into law at a rate of 6 per week, 537 of which were only laid before Parliament after they came into force.[13]

- The Health and Care Act 2022, which furthered the privatisation and outsourcing of the National Health Service while granting the Secretary of State authority over its procurement.[14]

- The Police, Crime, Sentencing and Courts Act 2022, which empowers the police to impose conditions on demonstrations, effectively banning protest in the UK. It also permits the police to have access to our private education and health records, and criminalises trespass on privately-owned land.[15]

- The Judicial Review and Courts Act 2022, which empowered the law courts to suspend and limit challenges by UK citizens to the legality of, and redress for, the decisions and actions of the UK Government and other public bodies.[16]

- The Nationality and Borders Act 2022, which empowers the Home Secretary to revoke, without prior notification, the British citizenship of anyone who is not born in the UK, who is of dual nationality, who is judged to be a threat to national security, or whose behaviour is deemed to be 'unacceptable'.[17]

- The Elections Act 2022, which made voter ID a requirement for voting, setting another precedent for the implementation of a system of Digital Identity in the UK.[18]

- The Public Order Act 2023, which further increases the powers of police to criminalise protest through extending stop and search powers to allow police to search for and seize objects that may be used in the commission of a

---

12. See UK Public General Acts, 'Coronavirus Act 2020' (25 March, 2020).

13. See Hansard Society, 'Coronavirus Statutory Instruments Dashboard, 2020-2022' (4 March 2022).

14. See UK Public General Acts, 'Health and Care Act 2022' (28 April, 2022).

15. See UK Public General Acts, 'Police, Crime, Sentencing and Courts Act 2022' (28 April, 2022).

16. See UK Public General Acts, 'Judicial Review and Courts Act 2022' (28 April, 2022).

17. See UK Public General Acts, 'Nationality and Borders Act 2022' (28 April, 2022).

18. See UK Public General Acts, 'Elections Act 2022' (28 April, 2022).

protest-related offence; as well as issuing Serious Disruption Prevention Orders.[19]

- The Online Safety Act 2023, whose title, like that of most UK legislation, means the opposite of the powers it makes into law, and which in this case requires the providers of online platforms to censor and impose restrictions on what we can and cannot say, write, watch, read and hear online in compliance with the dictates of Ofcom, the UK Government and, ultimately, the transnational technocracies in which it has membership. Fines for non-compliance are set at up to £18 million or 10 per cent of global turnover.[20]
- The Energy Bill 2023, when made into law, will amend existing legislation to empower the Government to regulate and fine those responsible for the supply, transport, storage, safety, performance, consumption and disposal of energy for failing to comply with the restrictions consequent upon the drive to Net Zero carbon emissions by 2050. This include the installation of smart meters in all homes and businesses by the end of 2025, with non-compliance incurring a fine up to £15,000 or imprisonment for 1 year.[21]

Significantly, the bulk of these Parliamentary Acts, as distinct from the Statutory Instruments under which we lived during lockdown, were made as the regulations for the latter were revoked, with the remainder made into law this year. We haven't, therefore, moved out of a juridical framework — 'incorporated' is the word Foucault uses to describe this transition — and which is not, moreover, limited to the legislation I've listed here. But what I want to focus on in this book is the incorporation of the judicial institution, which this legislation is clearing the legal barriers to, into what Foucault called the regulatory apparatuses of biopower. These — my Four Horsemen of the Apocalypse — are:

- Digital Identity
- The United Nations' Agenda 2030
- The World Health Organization's Pandemic Treaty
- Central Bank Digital Currency

---

19. See UK Public General Acts, 'Public Order Act 2023' (2 May, 2023).

20. See UK Public General Acts, 'Online Safety Bill 2023' (October 2023).

21. See UK Parliament, 'Energy Bill 2023'.

Most citizens of the UK — if we can still call ourselves that — will have heard of some or all of these. It's safe to say that, after two years of lockdown and the threat of what were called 'vaccine passports', everyone in the UK will know something about Digital Identity. But few, perhaps, will be aware of the programme of eco-austerity imposed by the UN's Agenda 2030 and 2050, even though all will be familiar with the claims of the environmental activists that receive promotion in our media that only the world's richest individuals and institutions can buy. Fewer still will have heard of the World Health Organization's Pandemic Prevention, Preparedness and Response Treaty, or of the Bank of England's plans for a Central Bank Digital Currency. But the problem, as it was under lockdown, is that as soon as the plans and intentions of the so-called global elite become sufficiently public for opposition to them to gain critical mass, the media — both mainstream and social — first dismisses that knowledge as a conspiracy theory and then — as we saw with the leaked text messages of Matt Hancock about the Government's use of terror to enforce compliance from the British people — the actual import of those plans are displaced onto mundane concerns.[22]

As examples of which — and which I will discuss in greater detail in this book — what concerns there have been around the Pandemic Treaty and Central Bank Digital Currency have been about the UK's loss of national sovereignty, or elderly people who don't have a bank account or smartphone being excluded, or not being able to give spare change to beggars. Time and again we are told that CBDC is merely another form of digital payment and not appreciably different from existing bank cards; or that the WHO Treaty will simply make us more prepared for the next pandemic and therefore must be a good thing — except to those who denied the existence of the last one. Similarly, what concerns have been expressed about Agenda 2030 is that the corporate influence on the UN might be inhibiting its implementation of Net Zero rather than, as is the case, driving it to their own ends.

To use a word that is as abused as any other these days, this is 'disinformation', created and disseminated to inform the public just enough to allow us to inform ourselves no further, and to comfortably dismiss anyone who does as a conspiracy theorist. The truth, which this book sets out to demonstrate, is that these four regulatory apparatuses of biopower are going to fundamentally,

---

22. See 'The Lockdown Files', *The Telegraph* (1 March 2023).

and in certain aspects irreversibly, change the social contract between the British people and the state.

Crucially, in this book I show how all four of these regulatory apparatuses — the discourses justifying them, the institutions formulating them, the programmes implementing them, the legislation imposing them, the agendas requiring them, the treaties agreeing to them and the technologies enforcing them — are all interdependent on each other. Indeed, as instruments of the new totalitarianism I discussed in *The Road to Fascism*, they couldn't be other than part of a totalising system of surveillance, control and domination.[23]

The *Book of Revelation* was written around 90 A.D., almost two thousand years ago, and the Four Horsemen of the Apocalypse it announced appeared, respectively, wearing a crown, wielding a sword, carrying a scales and bearing the name of death. The emblems and technologies of power have changed since then, but the means by which the powerful seek to control us remain the same today: by conquest of a people, by waging war, by economic destitution, and by causing plagues and famine. The difference is, now it's being done, under the beneficent hand of stakeholder capitalism, 'for our own good'.

2. The Gateway of Digital Identity

As I devote a chapter of this book to each of the last three of these apparatuses of biopower — Agenda 2030, the Pandemic Treaty and Central Bank Digital Currency — I'm only going to discuss the first of them here, although it comes up throughout my book, because a system of Digital Identity is the gateway to the digital camp in which the other three will imprison us.[24] They all rely on it being in place for their own enforcement, and in this respect it is the most important and the one that has to be most resisted and defeated. Some form of Digital Identity has been talked about for some time, and although everyone appears to know what it is, there doesn't seem to be much opposition to its implementation in the UK, which I'd suggest indicates that in reality we don't understand it at all.

---

23. See Simon Elmer, 'The New Totalitarianism', chapter 9 of *The Road to Fascism*, pp. 183-227.

24. See Simon Elmer, 'The Camp as Biopolitical Paradigm of the State', chapter 8 of *The Road to Fascism*, pp. 153-181.

During the lockdown of the UK, Digital Identity was discussed in relation to the China Health Pass, which is now fully operative and linked to the Chinese system of Social Credit, and which like a traffic light has three signals of access to different aspects of the public realm and services: green for freedom of access; amber for limited access or only on condition of further proofs or acts of compliance (like taking a PCR test); and red for prohibition on everything from receiving a bank loan, accessing your bank account, using public transport, passing between zones of a city to being permitted to leave your home itself.[25] In Europe, a lot of the member states of the European Union universally or partially imposed — for instance, on members of certain industries, like health, education, police and other public services — the use of the EU Digital COVID Certificate, which was collectively known as the 'Green Pass'.[26] The technology for this was subsequently taken up by the World Health Organization, which in June 2023, in tandem with the European Commission, announced the WHO's Global Digital Health Certification Network, which it invited all member states — which includes the UK — to adopt and participate in developing.[27] In the UK itself, we had the NHS COVID Pass, which was never enforced as a requirement of employment except for care workers, but which private businesses were permitted and encouraged to enforce as a condition of employment, access to their premises and use of their services. In April 2022, as coronavirus-justified regulations were lifted in the UK, the Department for Health and Social Care awarded the £18 million contract to develop the NHS COVID Pass to the Danish IT firm, Netcompany Ltd. The specification for the project stated:

> The government may introduce a mandatory COVID Pass to access high-risk venues if the data suggests further measures are necessary to protect the NHS. In preparation for this eventuality, we have built the changes to support two levels of domestic passes. The functionality will be toggled off until required. This enables a quick response if/when the Government invokes mandate. If a citizen is fully vaccinated, medically exempt or has been in a clinical trial, they will be eligible

---

25. Drew Donnelly, 'China Social Credit System Explained — What is it and How Does it Work?', *NH Global Partners* (22 July, 2022).

26. See European Council, 'EU digital COVID certification'.

27. See World Health Organization, 'The European Commission and WHO launch landmark digital health initiative to strengthen global health security' (5 June, 2023).

for an 'all venues' (mandatory) pass. If a citizen only has natural immunity or negative test results, they will only be eligible for a 'limited venues' (voluntary) pass.[28]

In anticipation of this mandate and the functionality of Digital Identity being 'toggled on', in the first three months of 2023 the UK Government conducted a consultation on draft legislation for what it called — presumably in an attempt to distance it from the widely opposed 'vaccine passport' — 'identity verification'.[29] The consultation closed on 1 March, 2023; but the legal framework for a system of Digital Identity was first put in place by the Digital Economy Act 2017, which removed the legal barriers to data sharing in the UK.[30] It was initially anticipated that the Statutory Instrument implementing a system of Digital Identity in the UK would be made in July 2023, but we are still waiting for the Government mandate.

What will this system do? At present, the UK Government is promoting Digital Identity in terms of ease of access, greater convenience and increased safety. So, under the Online Safety Act 2023, Digital Identity will be a requirement of access to the internet, not in order to censor what we can see, read and write but to protect children from pornography and grooming gangs. Under the Elections Act 2022, it will be a requirement of voting, not in order to further discourage public participation in the electoral process but to stop illegal voting. It will be a requirement of receiving Universal Credit or, in the future, Universal Basic Income, not in order to force the immiserated and unemployed into obligatory retraining and work but to stop fraudulent benefit claims. It will be a requirement of gaining access to public transport, medical care, education and employment, not in order to control us whenever the World Health Organization declares a new pandemic but to protect the population from future health crises. It will be a requirement of travel and movement between nation states and within the UK, not in order to enforce the restrictions on our freedoms imposed by Agenda 2030 but to stop illegal immigration into the UK and save the planet from 'global boiling'. It will be

---

28. See Department of Health and Social Care, 'Specification COVID Pass Delivery Partner, Reference: C50516'; reproduced from its response to an FOI request in Richard Morgan, 'Vaccine Passports Are Alive and Kicking', *Daily Sceptic* (5 September, 2022).

29. See Cabinet Office, 'Consultation on draft legislation to support identity verification' (updated 26 June, 2023).

30. See UK Public General Acts, 'Digital Economy Act 2017' (27 April, 2017).

a requirement of opening a bank account, not to force us into opening a Digital Pound account but to stop financial crime.

And just as it is in China, the system of Social Credit that relies on Digital Identity for its enforcement will not be restricted to individuals, but will apply to both privately-owned companies and publicly-funded institutions. US asset managers like BlackRock, for example, have made it clear that adherence to the behaviours written into the UN's Sustainable Development Goals and the Environmental, Social and corporate Governance criteria by which they are enforced are now a condition of employment, bank loans, investment and other aspects of business formerly determined by the employment and trading laws of a sovereign state; and the monitoring and enforcement of compliance with these new norms will be increased exponentially with the development and expansion of systems of Digital Identity across the globe.[31]

This enforcement of the biopolitical requirements of citizenship outside of the juridical frameworks of nation states or international law is consistent with the way the NHS COVID Pass was employed in the UK during the two years of lockdown. The decision to require this pass was made by the UK Government, but it wasn't mandated through legislation, even in the daily coronavirus-justified regulations being made into law. Rather, the responsibility for the enforcement of the COVID Pass was passed onto the private sector. Ultimately, although we have been promised a Statutory Instrument making its requirement into law, I believe the UK's system of Digital Identity will be handed over to the UK's businesses, in both the public and private sectors, where it will be enforced as a condition of employment and custom by both employers and those who trade with and make loans to their businesses. As I will discuss in far greater depth in this book, once the requirements of citizenship are taken out of a juridical framework and become, as Foucault wrote, 'distributions around the norm', the more difficult those norms are to challenge. This is the goal of biopower.

The first question any public consultation on Digital Identity should be asking the British public is not — as it did — whether and to what extent it meets this or that objective required by the Digital Economy Act 2017, but rather whether the British public wishes for such a system. The Government has no mandate for its

---

31. See Aubrie Spady, 'BlackRock CEO slammed for "force behaviours" comment after 2017 interview re-emerges about DEI initiatives', *Fox Business* (5 June, 2023).

imposition in its election manifesto, and its failure to inform the British public about the system of surveillance and control of which Digital Identity is the key constitutes a dereliction of the duty of any elected executive body to receive informed consent before interfering with the rights and freedoms of those it has been elected to govern. The Government's sham consultation, to which I responded, provided none of the contexts necessary for the public to make such informed consent. Worse, it assumed the imposition of a system of Digital Identity as a *fait accompli*. Indeed, by couching its consultation in terms of undisclosed 'benefits' to the public and undefined and ideological terms like 'well-being', the consultation deliberately concealed the real import, reach and purpose of Digital Identity.

Contrary to what the Government has told us, a system of 'identity verification' does not benefit individuals of households or improve public services. We saw this with the UK Health Security Agency's proposals for the NHS COVID Pass that were nearly introduced in the UK on the justification of tracking and limiting the movements of UK citizens under lockdown.[32] What is more accurately called a system of Digital Identity only benefits those who wish to use such a system to monitor, regulate, correct and, when necessary, to punish those who do not comply with whatever new codes of behaviour, including our speech, the Government and the unelected international technocracies formulating those codes impose upon us. The 'Green Pass' introduced across Europe demonstrated that these will be imposed through prohibitions on our movements, sanctions on our consumptions, extra-legal fixed penalty notices and the removal of our human rights and civil liberties, all of which the Governments of the West have demonstrated they are willing to enforce with extraordinary and in many countries unprecedented levels of police brutality.[33]

Once it is imposed, however, the intervention of the police and the juridical framework within which they loosely act will become less and less necessary, as we move into the biopolitics of stakeholder capitalism. As the UK Government well knows, Digital Identity is not being implemented in isolation from, but in conjunction with, other technologies and programmes for the surveillance and

---

32. See UK Health Security Agency, 'Using the NHS COVID Pass to demonstrate COVID-19 status' (7 May, 2021).

33. For a brief summary of this brutality, see the pages titled 'The Biosecurity State in Practice' in Simon Elmer, *The Road to Fascism*, pp. 39-45.

control of the UK population, including Central Bank Digital Currency, 15-Minute Cities, the London Mayor's Ultra-Low Emission Zone, the requirements of Agenda 2030 and the enforceable obligations of the WHO's Pandemic Treaty. Currently being implemented as mere upgrades to the infrastructure of the UK state, these will fundamentally — and, as I have said, perhaps irreversibly — change the ability of the British people to scrutinise, influence or hold our rulers to account. And yet, few members of the British public are even aware of these programmes, let alone how they will be used. We certainly haven't voted for them. Nor, as the Government's sham consultation on 'identity verification' demonstrates, will we be asked to do so. Digital Identity is the gateway to this collective system of surveillance and control that truly deserves the description 'totalitarian'.

So little has been divulged about how it will function that it is difficult to say what it will contain; but as part of system of Social Credit, Digital Identity will certainly hold our credit history. It will almost undoubtedly hold our online browsing history. And as the World Health Organization's Global Digital Health Certification Network indicates, it will definitely hold our biometric data. It will equally certainly hold a record of our social compliance, and what we can learn from China is that social compliance will not only be with the regulations of biosecurity set by a juridical framework but also with the new norms of behaviour we have already so readily accepted and normalised since March 2020. These now include censorship of speech and opinions contrary to those espoused by our Government; increased conditions imposed on our previously inalienable rights and freedoms; and adherence to the dictates of technocracies over whose membership and decisions we have no influence. It will be used to monitor, limit and control our movement through and out of not just our countries but also the 15-Minute Cities currently being imposed on the justification of reducing everything from air pollution to global warming. To this spurious end, it will record and restrict our consumption of energy, heat, food and water. In practice, it will monitor and record our behaviour, opinions and compliance with the new orthodoxies of woke ideology. And in doing so, it will condition our access to everything from the internet, banking and employment to healthcare, welfare and education. One day, if the Bank of England has its way, it will be the condition of accessing the only kind of currency still in existence, over which it will have complete control.

3. A Camp With No Outside

Why, then, is the British public showing so little interest in, presenting so little opposition to, and demonstrating such passive acceptance of our enclosure in the biosecurity camp to which Digital Identity is the gateway? It's in order to try and answer this question that, in addition to writing about these new apparatuses of biopower, the second part of my book looks at what are not, properly speaking, technologies of biopower but, rather, the ideologies indoctrinating us into embracing its implementation as the dominant paradigm of governance in the West.

The first of these, of course, is the US proxy war in the Ukraine, which although started in February 2014 with the overthrow of the democratically elected Government, in the minds of most Westerners began in February 2022, as we were emerging from two years of lockdown restrictions. The transition, therefore, from the so-called 'war on COVID' to the war on Russia was an almost seamless one, and those obedient to the terms of the former have proven the loudest advocates of the lies of the latter, most obviously about when and why it began. In certain respects this is a new form of warfare, insofar as the US asset managers that have been driving US foreign policy for some time now are not using the lives of young US soldiers to enforce their interests, as they have in Syria, Iraq, Libya and Afghanistan, but are now using the lives of the citizens of foreign countries — in this instance hundreds of thousands of Ukrainian victims — to force the public assets, natural resources and even the economy of the Ukraine into their hands. It's a matter of indifference to them that, in doing so, they have reduced parts of the country to ruins, its people to poverty and its institutions to political impotence, except insofar as the carnage justifies them calling on even more US taxpayers' money to 'rebuild' what they have demolished.[34]

Ukraine is a bloody example and warning to the world of what can be done to a formerly sovereign state when the bodies and lives of its people are subject to a war whose goal is biopolitical control over an entire people. Indeed, Ukraine is the testing ground for the digital transformation of the infrastructure of an entire

---

34. See Lewis Pennock, 'Joe Biden is bankrolling Ukraine's 57,000 first responders — and even funding fashion stores, schools and farms — in $10bn aid package', *The Daily Mail* (25 September, 2023).

state, including online education and health services, Central Bank Digital Currency, so-called e-governance, including a civil service replaced by smartphone apps, COVID certification on the same, and a judiciary and military run by artificial intelligence.[35] As an image of its dystopian future drawn direct from Hollywood cinema — Ukraine's 32-year-old Deputy Prime Minister, Mykhailo Fedorov, has dubbed it 'Judge Dredd' — the country has already piloted an AI system that produces pre-trial and pre-sentencing reports that assess the risk of a suspect offending.

It's to the same end, although employing different means, that the orthodoxies of transgenderism have attained their now unquestionable status as part of the official ideology of stakeholder capitalism in the West in a period of time barely longer than it took to impose the equally official orthodoxies of the war in the Ukraine. Few appear to have considered why, in the middle of the vast upheavals we have undergone since March 2020, governments, corporations and public institutions otherwise struggling to save humankind from any number of manufactured 'crises' should suddenly devote so much time and effort and money to writing the orthodoxies of 'trans' into our laws, implementing them in our policies, promoting them in our media, indoctrinating them through our institutions of education and normalising them in our culture industries. It is my belief, for which a chapter of this book provides the argument and evidence, that the orthodoxies of trans are not incidental to the revolution in Western capitalism we are undergoing but, rather, instrumental to the new biopolitical paradigm of citizenship to which we will be expected to adhere — and compelled to obey by the technologies of biopower — in the Global Biosecurity State under construction.

Over the last few years I've written many times about the ideology of woke, which has now taken its place as the official ideology of stakeholder capitalism, having infiltrated the Cabinets of Western governments along with Klaus Schwab's Young Global Leaders, and with just as much brazenness and indeed pride.[36] In my penultimate chapter, I look at how the discourse of White racism

---

35. See 'Ukraine lays out plan to be "most digital" country', *Kyiv Post* (5 July, 2022); and Nimrah Khatoon, 'Ukraine to Become the World's First 100% Cashless Country by 2025, Says National Bank Official', *BNN* (7 September, 2023).

36. See 'Klaus Schwab of World Economic Forum boasting of his infiltration into governments', *Bitchute* (21 February 2021). For a list of the Young Global Leaders in the

developed by woke is being used not only to silence opposition to the regulations, programmes and technologies of the Great Reset of the UK, but also to force through the changes in attitudes, beliefs and behaviours they require for our acceptance and compliance with such blatant attacks on our freedoms. As with the apparatuses of biopower, therefore, my aim in the second part of my book is to show how the orthodoxies of woke — which now include dehumanisation of the Russian people and the Lysenkoism of transgenderism — are instrumental to the incorporation of the judicial institution, through which the limits of citizenship have until now been made in law, into a biopolitical paradigm, in which the requirements of citizenship in the Global Biosecurity State are normalised by technologies of power, as Foucault wrote, 'centred on life'.

Finally, the body of my book is topped and tailed by two short texts. The first introduces the book with the argument that one of the conclusions we can draw from the last three-and-a-half years is that the already questionable division of our parliamentary politics into Left and Right no longer has any descriptive or practical purchase on the paradigm of governance by which we are now ruled, and should be abandoned by anyone serious about forming opposition to it. The second text, in the absence of the comforting dreams with which the UK Left has rocked itself to sleep over the past forty years of neoliberalism, concludes my book by proposing one of the ways in which we can resist — initially at least — the construction of the digital camp being built not only around and between but also within us by the technologies of biopower.

In the UK, as across most of the Western World, we lived through an extreme two-year period of lockdown in which almost all our human rights and civil liberties were removed by wave after wave of legislation on the justification of combatting a respiratory virus which anyone who troubled to look at the statistics and the criteria by which they were produced knew had the infection fatality rate of seasonal influenza.[37] Even that's not quite accurate since, unlike influenza,

---

governments of the West, see the pages titled 'The Rise of Global Governance' in chapter 1 of *The Road to Fascism,* pp. 12-13. For earlier discussions of woke, see the pages titled 'The Global Safe Space' in *Virtue and Terror*, pp. 228-234; and 'The Ideology of Woke' in *The Road to Fascism*, pp. 109-121.

37. See Simon Elmer, 'Manufacturing Consensus: The Registering of COVID-19 Deaths' (1 May, 2020); collected in *Virtue and Terror,* pp. 21-54; and 'Lies, Damned Lies and Statistics: Manufacturing the Crisis' (27 January, 2021); collected in *The New Normal*, pp. 73-101.

coronavirus has no effect on the young, who despite being masked for two years, deprived of their education and injected with experimental gene therapies, are as statistically immune to COVID-19 as they are statistically vulnerable to the myocarditis, pericarditis and other damages to their health and immune systems caused by the messenger RNA sequencing the UK state injected into their arms as a vaccine.[38]

Now, however, the West has entered into a more generalised crisis carousel whose names change, week by week, from global boiling to Russian aggression to the cost-of-living to the resurrection of the threat of Islamic terrorism and, as I write, another made-to-order viral strain.[39] But whatever their ostensible cause, the ultimate goal of the technologies of biopower whose imposition these crises justify is to make permanent what were the temporary restrictions on our rights and freedoms under lockdown. Indeed, the best way to understand these crises is to ask how these new agendas, these new treaties, these new programmes and these new technologies make the State of Emergency under which we lived for two years permanent. Unfortunately, very few people are asking that question, of themselves or others. Under lockdown, thousands of people were forced into quarantine camps, most famously in China; but the digital camp into which we're being corralled now, and which is enclosing and dividing us even as we return to bickering about Brexit and immigration, is co-extensive with the space of the state itself.

How is it being built? As I've said, Digital Identity is the gateway to this camp, over which is written not *Arbeit Macht Frei* — for there is no escape from a space without an outside — but rather 'Freedom is Slavery'. And if we imagine this camp and try to visualise its structure, the Internet of Things, which includes the digital panopticon of quick response codes, facial recognition technology and now ULEZ

---

38. See Thomas E. Levy, 'Myocarditis: Once Rare, Now Common', *Orthomolecular Medicine News Service* (5 January, 2023).

39. As examples of this relentless fearmongering over just this summer, see Ajit Niranjan, '"Era of global boiling has arrived," says UN chief as July set to be hottest month on record', *The Guardian* (27 July, 2023); UK Government, 'Russian aggression and isolation continues: UK Statement to the OSCE' (21 September, 2023); Andrew Gregory, 'UK's cost of living crisis will cause thousands of premature deaths, study says', *The Guardian* (25 September, 2023); Lucy Fisher, 'Threat of terror attack in UK is "rising", home secretary warns', *Financial Times* (18 July, 2023); Robin McKie, 'As a new variant emerges, is Covid coming back to the UK?', *The Observer* (3 September, 2023).

cameras, and the Internet of Bodies to which it connects us, which as I argue in my conclusion includes smartphones, is the camp's system of surveillance.[40] 15-Minute Cities, which despite being proposed by the World Economic Forum — a corporate think-tank with no legislative authority over the populations of nation states — are being imposed on UK citizens by our local councils and metropolitan authorities, are the barracks into which the different areas of the camp are divided. Despite their vociferous denials to the contrary, as soon as a municipal authority or legislative body decides when, how, where, how often and in what its citizens can move about in their own country, you are on the road to fascism. 15-Minute Cities are the beginning of the transformation of the space of the state itself into a permanent spatialisation of the State of Emergency, which is why they are both justified as a means to 'save the planet' and denied as a 'conspiracy theory'.[41] And in case we're naïve enough — which the UK public has demonstrated itself to be beyond the dreams of even the most cynical globalist — to believe that the limits on our freedom of movement will only apply to cars, and are therefore a good thing, Transport for London has already proposed what it calls, with the ubiquity of one of the most powerful information technology companies in the world, 'smart transport'.[42] Employing not just facial recognition cameras but the AI technology within them, the purpose of smart transport is not merely to monitor our actions but also to learn from our behaviour, turning public transport into a vast training camp for the digital guards of our future. Finally, Central Bank Digital Currency, in this spatial visualisation of a digital structure, is the perimeter fence of the camp, which it renders impossible to escape; for once this fence is constructed there will no longer be a space outside its extent and reach, or at least, no space inhabitable by a human society larger than a small commune, and most likely nowhere in the West.

Although the Internet of Bodies is ready and waiting to insert its system of monitoring inside us, with the proto-cyborgs for the future already implanting computer chips under their skin and ingesting them into their bodies, these

---

40. See Xiao Liu, 'Tracking how our bodies work could change our lives', *World Economic Forum* (4 June, 2020).

41. See Laura Paddison, 'How "15-minute cities" turned into an international conspiracy theory', *CNN* (27 February, 2023).

42. See 'Exposed: London's Secretive "Smart Stations" Roll Out', *Winter Oak* (13 March, 2023).

technologies of biopower are, for the present, being implemented through the nation's smartphones. This includes, of course, a system of Digital Identity; but, initially at least, Central Bank Digital Currency wallets will also go through a smartphone software application. In anticipation of which, in March of this year the Government launched its Emergency Alert System, which was then tested the following month on the 82 million smartphones in the UK.[43] It has not been made public how many of their owners responded; but what the UK public needs to understand, and soon, is that when the technologies of biopower constituting the digital camp are in place, this alert will not be used to inform us of whatever crisis the Government has invented to terrorise us with next, but rather to instruct us in the operational status of mechanisms of compliance it will be impossible to disobey except at the cost of our liberty.

I say it again: once the legal framework for citizenship is incorporated into a biopolitical paradigm of governance administered by a continuum of regulatory apparatuses, then legislative, legal and political means of contestation will no longer exist except as spectacles of a democracy long since dismantled. In reality, Western democracy, for some time now, has only existed in the fantasies of an endlessly deceived electorate. But it's a measure of how far we have come since March 2020, how far we have declined as a citizenry worthy of the name, and how ready we are for the totalitarianism of biopower, that there was no protest and little outrage in response to this trial of our abject obedience. On the contrary, the same mouths and faces were wheeled out by the media to repeat the mantra of the unfailing obedient: 'Well, if it saves lives . . .'[44] This is the essence of biopower to which the politics of the West is being reset by stakeholder capitalism. And, somehow, the people of the West have to stop it, if we don't want to live in a camp with no outside.

— October 2023

---

43. See Tom Acres, 'Emergency alert test happens today — here's everything you need to know', *Sky News* (23 April, 2023); and Petroc Taylor, 'Number of mobile cellular subscriptions in the United Kingdom (UK) from 2000 to 2022', *Statista* (17 September, 2022).

44. See Rachel Russell, 'Emergency alert could be sound that saves your life, says deputy PM', *BBC News* (23 April, 2023).

The Great Reset

1. Another Right-wing Conspiracy Theory: or, How the Left was Won Over

I'll start with a question. Why is it that in the UK, which initially implemented the regulations and programmes of biosecurity under the most Right-wing Government in living memory — a cabinet of crooks led by the serial liar, Boris Johnson — the accusation made against anyone who questions the official justifications for our unquestioning obedience to its decrees continues to be that you are a 'Right-wing conspiracy theorist'? Previously, when a Western government and its media wanted to dismiss or delegitimise criticism of its actions, it did so by calling those who questioned its authority 'Loony Lefties' (in the UK) or 'Commies' (in the USA). This time, however, the loonies are officially 'Right-wing'.

It's equally true, of course, that the Western governments that enforced or voted for mandatory masking, lockdown restrictions and gene therapy with the greatest zealotry and enforced them with the most brutal violence — and are now pushing hardest for the implementation of a system of Digital Identity, the World Economic Forum's 15-Minute Cities, the World Health Organization's Pandemic Treaty and Central Bank Digital Currencies — have identified themselves to their electorates as either Left-wing or on the Left of Social Democratic or Liberal parties. These include the governments of Justin Trudeau in Canada, formerly of Jacinda Ardern in New Zealand, of Pedro Sánchez in Spain, António Costa in Portugal, formerly of Sanna Marin in Finland and now Lula da Silva in Brazil. But they also include opposition parties, such as the Labour Party of Keir Starmer in the UK, where the Labour-aligned trades unions also supported the lockdown of businesses and enforcement of 'vaccine' mandates for the workers whose rights they were elected to defend.

In doing so, the Left didn't hesitate to align itself with the Right-wing and anti-working-class governments of first Boris Johnson and now the globalist puppet Rishi Sunak in the UK; with the police state of Emmanuel Macron in France; of Giuseppe Conte, the first Western leader to impose lockdown restrictions, and then the former EU banker and architect of austerity, Mario Draghi, in Italy; of Sebastian Kurz and then Karl Nehammer, who made gene therapy compulsory for all adults in Austria; and of Viktor Orbán, who used the 'pandemic' to pass a Coronavirus Act which, much like that in the UK, enabled him to rule by decree in Hungary. Perhaps never before in the history of Europe since the division of our parliaments into Left and Right has there been such unanimity of purpose among our governments, such hegemony in our legislatures, and such violent suppression of opposed positions in our judiciaries and media.

All these governments, officially on both the Right and the Left of the almost closed Overton window of Western politics, together with nominally Liberal and Conservative governments in Germany, Poland, Belgium, the Netherlands and Greece, continue to describe those who oppose the regulations and programmes of biosecurity as 'Right-wing conspiracy theorists'. And this accusation isn't limited to governments and media aligned as never before across the political spectrum of the West, but is also made by transnational technocracies aspiring to form a World Government, including the United Nations, the European Commission, the World Health Organization and the World Economic Forum.[1] Why?

One of the consequences of this political hegemony between the nominally politically differentiated nation states implementing the Global Biosecurity State in the West is that those opposed to its authoritarianism and creeping totalitarianism from a broadly libertarian standpoint have described it as a form of 'communism' modelled on, if not actually instigated by, the People's Republic of China. We know that, in the UK, the lockdown of the population and businesses for the best part of two years, first tested with unexpected compliance in Italy, was explicitly modelled on that imposed in China by the Government of Xi Jinping.[2] However, not only does this commonly repeated accusation of a 'communist coup' fail to explain the Global Financial Crisis that began in September 2019 and is driving this revolution in Western capitalism from behind the cloak of various manufactured 'crises', but it also allows its architects and

---

1. See Francesco Farinelli, 'Conspiracy theories and right-wing extremism — Insights and recommendations for P/CVE', Radicalisation Awareness Network, European Commission (2021).

2. See Tom Whipple, 'Professor Neil Ferguson: People don't agree with lockdown and try to undermine the scientists', *The Times* (25 December, 2020).

ideologues to dismiss such a description of the Global Biosecurity State — with some accuracy — as a 'Right-wing conspiracy theory'.[3]

If you believe, as many libertarians appear to, that Bill Gates (the founder of Microsoft, global investor in vaccines and now agricultural land, and the world's most influential authority on health and climate change), Larry Fink (the CEO of BlackRock, whose $10 trillion of assets gives it something like state authority over the 500 largest companies on the US stock exchange, and which is currently 'co-ordinating' the €314.84 billion the West has invested in the Ukraine), Jerome Powell (Chair of the US Federal Reserve, which since September 2019 has injected $4.5 trillion into the collapsing financial sector), Klaus Schwab (Executive Chairman of the World Economic Forum that for years has worked to replace the democratic model of the nation state with a technocratic form of world government founded on 'stakeholder capitalism'), Agustín Carstens (General Manager of the Bank of International Settlements and the architect of Central Bank Digital Currency programmed with restrictions and limits on expenditure contingent on our biosecurity status, individual carbon footprint and social compliance) Tedros Adhanom (Director General of the World Health Organization responsible for the Pandemic Prevention, Preparedness and Response Treaty that will impose biosecurity restrictions on formerly sovereign states outside of any democratic process), Ursula von der Leyen (President of the European Commission and promoter of mandatory gene therapies and Digital Identity, who threatens economic sanctions against democratically elected governments), and the leaders of the G7 nations (Joe Biden, Fumio Kishida, Ola Scholz, Rishi Sunak, Emmanuel Macron, Giorgia Meloni and Justin Trudeau) are all covert communists in a secret alliance with Xi Jinping — then you probably deserve the accusation of 'Right-wing conspiracy theorist'.

However, beyond exposing the political naivety of libertarians, a far more important function of this accusation is its effect not only on Left-wing political parties but also on that wide diaspora of political organisations, unions, pressure groups and protesters that now constitute the Left.

When speaking of the Left, we should recall that the Left is a position taken by parliamentary parties in opposition to rivals in order to further their ambition to

---

3. See Fabio Vighi, 'Slavoj Žižek, Emergency Capitalism, and the Capitulation of the Left', *The Philosophical Salon* (24 May, 2021).

form a government. It is not a description of political principles. It began 230 years ago with the French Revolution, which was bourgeois, not socialist. There wasn't then, and there hasn't been since, anything inherently socialist in the Left. On the contrary, today the Left is Starmer, Trudeau, Lula. It is authoritarian, globalist, Zionist, environmentally fundamentalist, woke, trans, pro-capitalist, obedient to the World Economic Forum, to the World Health Organization, to the European Commission, to the United Nations, to the North Atlantic Treaty Organization and to the United States of America — any opposition to which it denounces as 'anti-Americanism' with the same unquestioning obedience that it denounces any criticism of the apartheid State of Israel as 'anti-Semitism'. Above all, the Left is at the forefront of enforcing the technologies and programmes of the Global Biosecurity State. That's the 'position' of the Left.

And while it occasionally identifies to varying degrees as 'socialist' when it suits it — and particularly when there's a chance to enact rituals of protest that had political mass in the Nineteenth Century but were already spectacles of democracy in the Twentieth Century — the Left in the Twenty-first Century is far more tightly unified by unquestionable values and ideas that are implicitly and sometimes explicitly opposed to the emancipatory principles of socialism. These include multiculturalism, political correctness, the orthodoxies of woke ideology and now so-called 'trans-rights', and above all by the radical conservatism of identity politics.

It is the unquestioned self-identification of large swathes of the Western middle-classes as 'Left-wing' that is the target of the cross-party accusation that anyone who questions the veracity of the various crises by which we are threatened — whether that's the coronavirus crisis, the environmental crisis, the energy crisis, the cost-of-living crisis or the geopolitical crisis — or opposes the regulations and programmes whose enforcement these crises are used to justify, is denounced and dismissed as a 'Right-wing conspiracy theorist'.

Whoever the architects of these manufactured crises were — and by now we know most of their names and all of their organisations — they accurately judged that those who identify as 'Left-wing' would rather inject their children with experimental gene therapies when ordered by their governments to do so, abandon their parents to die alone in hospitals and care homes, allow their jobs, businesses and standard of living to be destroyed by two years of lockdown and unprecedented levels of quantitative easing, watch passively as the social contract of the West built on human rights, democratic accountability and national sovereignty is torn up and discarded by unelected technocrats and international bankers, and collaborate willingly in its replacement by the digital infrastructure of the new totalitarianism — than be called 'Right-wing'. Anything has proven to be preferable to that. Because without that imaginary identity, the multi-cultural, politically-correct, woke-obedient, biosecurity-compliant populations of the West would be forced to confront the bad faith in which they live their increasingly illusory relation to finance capitalism.[4]

In March 2023, the UK experienced industrial action by the rail transport workers, London Underground workers, postal workers, junior doctors, nurses, ambulance staff, firefighters, civil servants, university staff and teachers.[5] The extent of their demands, however, was better pay and, by some unions, calls for more secure conditions of employment. Since coronavirus-justified restrictions on our human rights and civil liberties were largely revoked in March 2022, more workings days were lost to strike action last year than at any time since 1989.[6] Yet, not one of these unions went on strike in March 2020 when illegal lockdown restrictions were imposed on the mass of UK workers, nor when face masks were made mandatory for those still working or who returned to work that summer, nor when gene therapy was made a condition of continued employment first for care workers in November 2021 and then threatened for NHS staff in January 2022.[7] And as soon as the mandates were suspended for them, the thousands of nurses and junior doctors who joined the street protests against 'vaccine' passports and mandatory gene therapy in London in January 2022 went back to injecting the

---

4. See Simon Elmer, 'Whatever Happened to the Middle Classes? Bad Faith and the Culture Industry', *Architects for Social Housing* (10 May, 2019).

5. See Patrick Hollis, 'Strikes in March 2023: All the industrial action set to take place this month — including from the RMT', *London World* (28 February, 2023).

6. See Richard Partington, 'Number of days lost to strikes is highest since the Thatcher Era', *The Guardian* (14 February, 2023).

7. See UK Draft Statutory Instruments, 'The Health and Social Care Act 2008 (Regulated Activities) (Amendment) (Coronavirus) Regulations 2021' (11 November, 2021); NHS, 'Vaccination as a condition of deployment (VCOD) for healthcare workers' (8 February, 2022).

experimental gene therapies they had refused into British children as young as 6 months old.[8]

Today, not a single union leader or public figure on the Left has used the strikes and the media attention it has brought them to inform UK workers about the dangers of the UK 'vaccination' programme, or of the future uses of the Government's system of Digital Identity, or of the threat to national sovereignty of the World Health Organization's Pandemic Treaty, or about the implementation of 15-Minute Cities in accordance with the United Nation's Agenda 2030, or about the future threat of the Bank of England's Central Bank Digital Currency. The implications of these programmes, technologies, treaties and agendas for the UK public have not been discussed in Parliament or reported in the media, and the British public is largely unaware of their implementation or consequences.

Even beyond its willing collaboration with the Global Biosecurity State and the stakeholder model of capitalism implementing it, the Left's analysis of the power of government and state, like its outmoded model of industrial action and street protest, has no purchase on the new biopolitical paradigm of our governance. Indeed, the noise the Left generates in the media, like the noise generated by its activists and fellow travellers on its carefully curated demonstrations, serve one purpose: to drown out the imminence of the enforcement of the technologies of our governance by international technocracies whose very existence, let alone influence, the Left dismisses as 'conspiracy theories'.

This mostly urban and overwhelmingly middle-class Left has emerged from the 'pandemic' as the ideal citizen of the Global Biosecurity State: permanently and willingly masked; tracked and told what to do by their own smartphones; ready to pay for and download the next app for their surveillance, monitoring and control; tested regularly and at their own expense to establish their biosecurity status; injected as often and with whatever they're told to by international pharmaceutical companies; compliant with whatever regulations their national government imposes; happy to have their carbon footprint and record of social compliance uploaded into a system of Digital Identity; eager to open their Central

---

8. See Nick Clark, 'Anti-vax marches — a warning from the right', *Socialist Worker* (25 January, 2022); Medicines and Healthcare products Regulatory Agency, 'Pfizer/BioNTech COVID-19 vaccine authorised for use in infants and children aged 6 months to 4 years' (6 December, 2022).

Bank Digital Currency wallet; ready, at the twitch of a thread, to take to the streets to celebrate the Zelenskyy-puppet as a hero of democracy even as he submits the economy, resources and workers of the Ukraine to the Washington Consensus; but snug, too, in their 15-Minute Cities; doing their bit to 'save the planet'. Obedient. This Woke Left, which is a product of forty years of neoliberalism not only in our economy but in our politics, our media, our education industry and our culture industry, today constitutes a homogeneous force of compliance across the biosecurity states of the West. Its ideologues sit in our Parliaments, direct our media, curate our culture, run our universities, indoctrinate our children.

And it is they that were targeted, made compliant and quickly turned into willing collaborators with the Global Biosecurity State by the simple threat to their imaginary identity represented by the accusation of being a 'Right-wing conspiracy theorist'. Traditionally — at least in its own perception — it has been from the Left that the defence of human rights, opposition to the privatisation of public services, resistance to corporate capture of government and criticism of corruption of public institutions by global capital have come. All that has been reversed with the threat of an insult.

As a demonstration on the grandest scale of how identity politics works in practice, the mass compliance of the Left with the implementation of the infrastructure of the Global Biosecurity State will take some beating. With this threat, the globalists who run the United Nations, the European Commission, the World Health Organization, the World Economic Forum, the Intergovernmental Panel on Climate Change, the Global Alliance for Vaccines and Immunization and the Group of Seven nations managed to disarm, at a single stroke, the political parties, trades unions and civil institutions in which opposition to the Great Reset might have formed in Western nations.

What the three-and-a-half years of cowardice and collaboration since March 2020 have demonstrated, and that more decisively than any event in recent history, is that the residual and increasingly blurred division of our politics into Left and Right no longer has any descriptive purchase on the new paradigm of governance by which we are ruled today — except insofar as it promotes compliance with its implementation and divides opposition to the totalitarian future that is so nearly our present. More importantly, the Left offers neither a critique of stakeholder capitalism nor a model for overthrowing or even resisting the new totalitarianism with which it is complicit. Any such resistance must begin — already has begun — from a place outside this parliamentary position, which serves only to divide us. But who is this 'us'?

2. The Politics of Environmental Fundamentalism

'Of all tyrannies a tyranny sincerely exercised for the good of its victims may be the most oppressive. It may be better to live under robber barons than under omnipotent moral busybodies. The robber baron's cruelty may sometimes sleep, his cupidity may at some point be satiated; but those who torment us for our own good will torment us without end for they do so with the approval of their own conscience. They may be more likely to go to Heaven yet at the same time likelier to make a Hell of earth. Their very kindness stings with intolerable insult. To be "cured" against one's will and cured of states which we may not regard as disease is to be put on a level of those who have not yet reached the age of reason or those who never will; to be classed with infants, imbeciles, and domestic animals.'

— C. S. Lewis, *The Humanitarian Theory of Punishment*, 1949

In the decades that followed the Gulf War of 1990-1991 a single term came to dominate the foreign policy of the West and in particular of the United States of America. That term was 'Islamic fundamentalism'. This was used not only to justify the military invasion of sovereign states by US-led coalitions and the theft of their assets and resources by Western corporations, but also to demonise the occasional attempts at resistance by their defeated populations as 'terrorism'. We heard less during this time about Christian fundamentalism, even though every war instigated by the USA was accompanied by the cry of 'God Bless America'. Nor did we hear about the fundamentalism of a global market which, under forty years of neoliberalism, has made money the measure of every value in our societies, to the extent that the high priests of finance capitalism no longer speak of 'profit margins' but of 'value creation'.

More recently, however — although its genesis is coextensive with this period in Western geopolitics — the predations of Western capitalism have adopted a new strategy. The term that best describes this has not been coined by the propagandists in Washington or Brussels or even in Downing Street, but rather by those of us who recognise a continuity not only in purpose but also in means between the destabilising and pillage of the Middle East and the global aspirations of the emerging New World Order. This new term is 'environmental fundamentalism'. I use this term in a technical sense to describe this latest strategy of Western imperialism, because whether their God is called Jehovah, Mammon or Nature (with a capital 'N'), the mechanisms of all fundamentalisms are the same:

1. To identify sacred texts whose Truth cannot be questioned;
2. To authorise and impose a single interpretation of those texts;
3. To dismiss all other interpretations and all contradictory texts as heresy;
4. To silence and punish heretics;
5. To attain and defend power on the basis of the enforced orthodoxy, which in Western societies we call a democratic or scientific 'consensus'.

These overtly religious aims might seem at odds and even incompatible with the politics of an ostensibly secular West in the third decade of the Twenty-first Century; but in this chapter I'm going to show how and why the tenets of environmental fundamentalism serve the ends for which they've been formulated, sanctified and enforced as part of the new ideological orthodoxies of the Global Biosecurity State. By this, I mean the nexus of unelected technocracies, treaties, agendas, regulations, programmes, technologies and ideologies that have emerged from the revolution in Western capitalism being implemented on the justification of responding to multiple manufactured 'crises' — including the health crisis, the energy crisis, the cost-of-living crisis, the geopolitical crisis and, ultimately, the environmental crisis.

1. The Economics of Fear

As the restrictions and obligations of biosecurity have mostly but not entirely been lifted since March 2022, their replacement by their equally fundamentalist environmental equivalents has shown the arbitrariness of the crises on which the Global Biosecurity State is being imposed — and their shared end. Last year's COP27, the United Nations Climate Change Conference 2022, is a demonstration and model of how the forms of global governance that have assumed so much power over our lives on the justification of responding to numerous manufactured 'crises' will operate outside of any democratic representation or accountability. Held from 6-18 November 2022 in Sharm el-Sheikh, Egypt, COP27 was the twenty-seventh such conference held annually since the first United Nations climate agreement in 1992. This led to the Kyoto Protocol of 1997 and the Paris Agreement of 2015 that committed participating nations to unquestionable orthodoxies.[1] These included what it called the 'scientific consensus':

1. That global warming is occurring to a degree that threatens all life on the planet; and
2. That man-made emissions of the carbon dioxide molecule (CO_2), a compound of one carbon atom bonded with two oxygen atoms that is the primary source of life on Earth is causing this warming, primarily from the burning of fossil fuels.

The effect of this political agreement is that anyone, including climatologists, meteorologists, geologists, biologists or chemists, who asserts or presents evidence contrary to these assertions or the conclusions derived from them is categorised and branded as a 'climate-change denier' — exactly as those who question the equally authoritarian and unquestionable orthodoxies of the coronavirus 'crisis' are branded as 'COVID deniers'.[2]

Among numerous voices excluded from this 'consensus' are members of the Global Climate Intelligence Group, whose *World Climate Declaration: There is no climate emergency*, published in October 2022, has been signed (as of September 2023) by 1,609 scientists and energy industry professionals from 60 countries around the world.[3] One of the most outspoken signatories to this declaration is Professor Ian Plimer, a geologist, director of numerous mineral exploration and mining companies, former Professor of Mining Geology at the University of Adelaide, current Professor Emeritus of Earth Sciences at the University of Melbourne, Fellow of the Australian Academy of Technological Sciences and

---

1. See United Nations, 'What is the Kyoto Protocol?' and 'What is the Paris Agreement?'

2. See World Economic Forum, 'Is climate denialism dead?' (15 August, 2022); and European Commission, 'Identifying conspiracy theories' (12 August 2020-19 February, 2021).

3. See Global Climate Intelligence Group, *World Climate Declaration: There is no climate emergency* (October 2022).

Engineering, the Australian Institute of Scientists and the Australasian Institute of Mining and Metallurgy, and Honorary Fellow of the Geological Society of London, who has published more than 120 scientific papers, a dozen books, is one of three editors of the *Encyclopaedia of Geology*, and the recipient of numerous awards and medals. His knowledge, therefore, is vast, academic and practical. He is also, despite this, branded a 'climate-change denier' by such luminaries in the field as the *Guardian* columnist, George Monbiot, who called him 'a purveyor of 24-carat bafflegab.'[4]

I don't know what this childish insult means, but it presumably includes Plimer's observations that man-made emissions of CO_2 constitute only 3 per cent of total carbon emissions on earth; that the remaining 97 per cent of emissions come from ocean degassing from 300 hydrothermal vent sites in 60,000 kilometres of mid-ocean ridges and eruptions from over a million submarine volcanoes, 5,000 of which are still active; that CO_2, which makes up just 0.04 per cent of the earth's atmosphere, is not a pollutant but the food of life; that during the Second Ice Age, which occurred between 2.45 billion and 2.25 billion years ago when the ice caps had reached the equator, the carbon dioxide content of the atmosphere was around 20 per cent, 500 times the level it is now; and that the temperature of the planet is not controlled by its 100 kilometre-high atmosphere but, to the contrary, the atmosphere is controlled by the temperature of the 12,742 kilometer-wide planet, which is determined by plate tectonics, the orbit of the Earth round the Sun and the Sun itself.[5]

But perhaps what has triggered the fury of environmental fundamentalists the most is that Professor Plimer points out that the Intergovernmental Panel on Climate Change, an agency of the United Nations whose advisory board is appointed and funded by the member states, is not a scientific organisation but a political one that suppresses the data produced by earth-scientists and cherry-picks the evidence it needs, which it then feeds into predictive mathematical models to support its agenda. In other words, the IPCC works exactly like the other corporate-funded organisations that, at the request of their governments,

---

4. See George Monbiot, 'This professor of denial can't even answer his own questions on climate change', *The Guardian* (14 September, 2009).

5. See Ian Plimer, *Heaven and Earth: Global Warming — The Missing Science* (Quartet Books, 2009); and *Green Murder: A Life Sentence of Net Zero with No Parole* (Connor Court, 2021).

produced equally inaccurate justifications for locking down the populations of the West for two years because if they didn't 50 million people would die.[6]

Parties to these fundamentalist and therefore fundamentally unscientific orthodoxies, and the economic obligations and policies to which they commit them, include — by order of the size of their economy — the USA, China, Japan, Germany, India, the UK, France, Brazil, Italy, Canada and 182 other countries — which is to say, almost the whole world. To address what it melodramatically calls the 'existential threat' of climate change, the UK Government has committed to spending £11.6 billion of British taxpayers' money on international climate finance, with funding for what it calls 'climate adaptation' tripling from £500m in 2019 to £1.5 billion in 2025.[7] £150 million of that funding will go to 'protecting' rainforests, including in the Amazon and the Congo Basin, which happen to be the sites of some of the world's largest reserves of the copper and cobalt required for electric batteries. £65 million is earmarked for the Nature, People and Climate Investment Fund in Egypt, with a focus on hydrogen and wind power; and a further £2 billion to the UK-Kenya Strategic Partnership for 'clean and green' investment in geothermal, solar energy and hydroelectric power projects.[8]

All this public funding will go to private companies selected by the international technocracies formed to do so in accordance with the United Nations' Sustainable Development Goals, a Miss-World list of humanitarian objectives ranging from abolishing world hunger, poverty and inequality to peace, justice and gender equality that was adopted by the United Nations in 2015 under the rubric of Agenda 2030.[9] In reality and practice, however, Sustainable Development Goals allocate the flow of global capital, bank loans, investment and

---

6. See John P.A. Ioannidis, Sally Cripps and Martin A. Tanner, 'Forecasting for COVID-19 has failed', *International Journal of Forecasting*, Vol. 38, Issue 2 (April-June 2022), pp. 423-438.

7. See Prime Minister's Office, 'UK announces major new package of climate support at COP27' (7 November, 2022).

8. See Climate Investment Funds, 'Egypt' (2023); and British High Commission Nairobi, 'Climate finance to flow to Kenya as UK Prime Minister agrees with President Ruto to fast-track KES 500 billion of British investment' (7 November, 2022).

9. See United Nations, 'Sustainable Development Goals: 17 goals to transform our world'; United Nations Department of Economic and Social Affairs, 'Transforming our world: the 2030 Agenda for Sustainable Development'.

preferential treatment to governments and corporations according to their compliance with the Environmental, Social and corporate Governance criteria.[10]

Despite their United Nations branding, these are formulated and imposed by immensely wealthy international corporate asset managers, the most powerful of which, BlackRock, the Vanguard Group and State Street Global Advisor, between them hold 20 per cent of shares and with it something like government authority over the 500 largest companies on the New York Stock Exchange.[11] Far from saving the planet from exploitation by predatory corporations, Sustainable Development Goals are designed to increase the monopoly of wealthy Western economies and international companies able to meet their criteria over poorer countries.

In doing so, Sustainable Development Goals have created the financial framework for purchasing their United Nations-assigned quota of emissions in carbon credits, which is one of the 'market-based mechanisms' written into the Kyoto Protocol.[12] In practice, this means that, in order to offset their obligations to meet goals on carbon emissions, wealthier countries, companies and even individuals can buy and, indeed, sell carbon credits from poorer countries or companies. Since carbon emissions are a product of greater productivity, the carbon credit market is a mechanism for increasing inequality between already wealthy companies and nations and those forced to sell their carbon credit. Balancing this up and on the same justification, developing countries will be loaded with debt by financial organisations like the World Bank and the International Monetary Fund in order to fulfil these Sustainable Development Goals, and those unable to meet repayments through increased taxation and

10. See Cabinet Office, Department for International Development and Foreign, Commonwealth and Development Office, 'Corporate Report: Implementing the Sustainable Development Goals' (updated 15 July, 2021); and Department for Work and Pensions, 'Environmental Social Governance (ESG) and responsible investment' (6 June, 2019).

11. See Gibson Dunn, 'BlackRock, Vanguard and State Street Update Corporate Governance and ESG Policies and Priorities for 2022' (25 January, 2022); and Olúfẹ́mi O. Táíwò, 'How BlackRock, Vanguard, and UBS Are Screwing the World', *The New Republic* (7 March, 2022).

12. See Jason Hickel, 'The World's Sustainable Development Goals Aren't Sustainable', *Foreign Policy* (30 September, 2020); and United Nations, 'United Nations Carbon Offset Platform'.

spending cuts for their already impoverished populations will be compelled to hand over their land and natural resources to their creditors.[13]

Indeed, both Sustainable Development Goals and Environmental and Social Governance criteria are predicated on monetising the natural world, which has recently been estimated by the New York Stock Exchange at $4 quadrillion ($4,000,000,000,000,000).[14] Monetised nature is the basis of a new form of corporation called a Natural Asset Company, the purpose of which is to maximise what it calls 'ecological performance' and the production of 'ecosystem services', over the management of which these corporations will, of course, have legal rights and financial authority.[15] Behind their loudly-proclaimed 'green' credentials, therefore, both these programmes, like those implemented on the justification of the coronavirus 'crisis', are instruments of stakeholder capitalism.

As of March 2023, the total value of contracts awarded to companies by the UK Government in response to the coronavirus 'crisis' was £47.8 billion.[16] This included £22.8 billion on the utterly useless 'Test and Trace' programme; £14.7 billion on largely unusable or undelivered personal protection equipment; £4.1 billion on medicines and the almost entirely unused 'Nightingale' hospitals; £5.1 billion on 'other' supplies and services; and £1 billion on the totally useless and increasingly dangerous gene therapies injected into the British people as 'vaccines'.[17] This vast expenditure of public money on the justification of combatting a manufactured threat to public health that never existed is a microcosm of how the United Nations' Sustainable Development Goals, on the justification of combatting global warming, will allocate the national wealth of the countries party to its obligations to the international companies able to meet the

---

13. See Iain Davis and Whitney Webb, 'Sustainable Debt Slavery', *Unlimited Hangout* (13 September, 2022).

14. See Ellen Brown, 'Conservation or Land Grab? The Financialisation of Nature', *The Web of Debt* (5 November, 2021).

15. See Intrinsic Exchange Group, 'Be Invested' (2023).

16. See Henry Thompson, 'Latest Updates on UK Government COVID-19 Contracts and Spending', *Tussell* (15 March, 2023).

17. See Andrew Woodcock, 'Scathing report blasts 'unimaginable' £37bn cost of coronavirus test and trace system', *The Independent* (10 March, 2021); Gareth Iacobucci, 'Covid-19: Government writes off £10bn on unusable, overpriced, or undelivered PPE', *BMJ* (3 February, 2022); and Benn Quinn, 'What has happened to England's seven Nightingale hospitals?', *The Guardian* (8 October, 2020).

criteria they themselves have imposed. In this respect, the trillions of dollars to which the workers of the West have been placed in debt by their governments on the justification of combatting a 'pandemic' declared by the World Health Organization — an agency of the UN funded by Western governments and private companies, subject to lobbying from both, and under the Pandemic Treaty empowered to unilaterally declare pandemics and impose biosecurity restrictions on signatory nations — is an example and model of how the equally manufactured environmental 'crisis' is designed to impoverish their populations and enrich the architects of both this crisis and the power grab it is enabling.[18]

We should recall that, here in the UK, which is still the sixth largest economy in the world, all this vast expenditure, which is loading still more debt onto the future of our children, is being implemented at a time when the UK public is facing £60 billion in tax rises and spending cuts; when National Insurance contributions have been increased by 10 per cent; when the price cap on annual energy costs for a typical household has been set at £3,000, and has pushed 3.26 million households into fuel poverty by energy companies making record-making profits; when there has been a 19 per cent rise in food prices over the past year, the highest rate since at least 1977, resulting in nearly 3 million people having to use a food bank last year in order to eat; and when, as a result 8.9 million British citizens and 3.3 million of our children are living in absolute poverty.[19]

2. The Chimera of Net Zero

Creating public compliance for this transfer of billions of pounds from the national taxpayer to international corporations without mandate from the electorate or

---

18. See Katheryn N. Russ, Phillip Baker, Manho Kang, and David McCoy, 'Corporate Lobbying on U.S. Positions Toward the World Health Organization', *Science Digest* (19 May, 2022).

19. See HM Treasury, 'Policy Paper: Autumn Statement 2022 HTML' (17 November, 2022); Rachel Pugh, 'National Insurance rates are set to rise by 10% from April', *Manchester Evening News* (3 February, 2022); Paul Bolton and Iona Stewart, 'Domestic energy prices', *House of Commons Library* (13 March, 2023); Department for Energy Security and Net Zero, 'Annual Fuel Poverty Statistics in England, 2023 (2022 data)' (28 February, 2023); 'United Kingdom Food Inflation', *Trading Economics* (2023); D. Clark, 'Number of people receiving emergency food parcels from Trussell Trust foodbanks in the United Kingdom from 2008/09 to 2022/23', *Statista* (3 May, 2023); Brigid Francis-Devine, 'Research Briefing: Poverty in the UK: statistics', *House of Commons Library* (6 April, 2023).

oversight of how it is spent, by whom or on what, has been achieved by a vast international campaign of propaganda. One of the forms this has taken is the protests by environmental fundamentalist groups like Extinction Rebellion, Insulate Britain and Just Stop Oil, all of whom are funded by The Climate Emergency Fund, an organisation established in 2019 to fund such promotional activities with the largesse of US billionaires, including the heiress to the Getty family oil fortune.[20]

They also have the support of our new head of state, King Charles III, who as the Prince of Wales spoke as far back as 1992 at the annual meeting of the World Economic Forum, for whom he has since become the obedient puppet of the corporate membership as it has master-minded the globalist coup that only began to be revealed with the coronavirus 'crisis'. Indeed, at the annual meeting of the World Economic Forum in June 2020, three months after the World Health Organization announced the 'pandemic', Prince Charles was chosen to launch what was dubbed the 'Great Reset'.[21] As a result of this backing from the corporate sector and its public shills, our Government, municipal authorities and police forces have granted these groups freedom to shut down UK roads for hours, and the antics of a handful of their 'activists' receive millions of pounds of media coverage denied to the millions of UK citizens who marched in protest against illegal lockdown and 'vaccine' mandates.

I am not claiming that these activists are hired actors or not sincere in their infantile beliefs. The best salesman is someone who believes in their product, and there is no need to hire crocodile tears when a generation of lachrymose kids and apocalyptic 'greens' will shed theirs for free. Indeed, Just Stop Oil's imperious declaration on its website that 'If you are not in resistance you are appeasing evil' is typical of the religious rhetoric of these environmental fundamentalists, and as authoritarian as Black Lives Matter's motto that 'silence is violence', or Extinction

---

20. See Simon Elmer, 'Extinction Rebellion: Socialist Revolution', *Architects for Social Housing* (24 April, 2019); Insulate Britain, 'We all want to just stop oil' (2023); Just Stop Oil, 'What if the Government doesn't have it under control?'; Climate Emergency Fund, 'Our 2022 grantees disrupted normalcy and created breakthroughs: Funding Disruptive Climate Protest in the US' (2022).

21. See World Economic Forum, 'Great Reset | HRH Prince of Wales | We have no alternative' (3 June, 2020).

Rebellion's demand for 'zero carbon'.[22] Only a demographic as politically naive as the Western middle classes could believe that the globalists, international bankers and corporate CEOs implementing Agenda 2030 will 'save the planet'; but their absolutist rhetoric makes it clear that they are willing to impoverish the rest of the world to realise their fundamentalist religious beliefs.

Of course, we've seen this before, and I don't mean the suicide bombers and iconoclasts of Islamic fundamentalist groups. There are parallels between the stage props in the global theatre of biosecurity (masking, social distancing, lockdown, PCR tests, gene therapy, 'vaccine' passports) invented to 'combat' the virus and the equally fanciful 'solutions' proposed to avert the imminent prospect of environmental disaster.

In April 2022, the Intergovernmental Panel on Climate Change declared that annual greenhouse gas emissions must be reduced by 43 per cent by 2030 and reach Net Zero emissions by 2050.[23] This will supposedly be achieved not only by enforced restrictions on our energy and food consumption but also through our embrace of highly inefficient technologies like wind turbines, solar panels and electric batteries, in the illusory belief that, over the next three decades, these supposedly renewable sources of energy, which currently provide just 2 per cent of global energy, can replace coal, petroleum and natural gas, which provide 82 per cent. The problem is, unlike the silicon technologies that have transformed computer power exponentially over the past decades, the energy required to move people, drive machines, produce heat or grow food is determined by properties of nature whose boundaries are set by the laws of gravity, inertia, friction, mass, and thermodynamics. Even the vast resources of propaganda disposed of by the United Nations, the European Commission, the World Economic Forum and Big Oil cannot overcome the realities of energy production and storage. These realities, which are both physical and economic, include the following:

---

22. See Just Stop Oil, 'Campaign Background'; Alan Hudson and Ania Calderon, 'Silence is Violence: Black Lives Matter', *Global Integrity* (5 June, 2020); Extinction Rebellion, 'Enough is enough . . . How are our governments letting us down?', *Emergency on Planet Earth*.

23. See Paul Collins, 'IPCC climate report 2022 summary: The key findings', *Selectra Climate* (7 April, 2022).

- Hydrocarbons, the energy components of fossil fuels (that is, crude oil, natural gas and coal), which insofar as they have been produced by solar energy in ancient seas and forests are 100 per cent 'organic', today supply over 80 per cent of the world's energy, while solar and wind today supply less than 2 per cent. The small 2 per cent decline in the share of hydrocarbons in world energy-use entailed over $2 trillion in cumulative global spending on alternatives over that period.

- If the four billion poor people in the world increased their energy use to just one-third of Europe's per capita level, global demand would rise by an amount equal to twice the total consumption of the USA, which consumes 16 per cent of the world's energy.

- Replacing US hydrocarbon-based electric generation over the next 30 years would require a construction program building the grid at a rate 14 times greater than at any time in history. Eliminating hydrocarbons to make US electricity would leave 70 per cent of US hydrocarbon use unaffected.

- For security and reliability, an average of 2 months of national demand for hydrocarbons are in storage at any time in the US. Today, barely 2 hours of national electricity demand can be stored in all utility-scale batteries plus all batteries in the 1 million electric cars in the US.

- Batteries produced annually by Elon Musk's Tesla Gigafactory, the world's biggest battery factory, can store 3 minutes' worth of annual US electric demand. To make enough batteries to store 2 days' worth of demand would require 1,000 years of production by the Gigafactory.

- A 100x growth in the number of electric vehicles to 400 million on the roads by 2040 would displace just 5 per cent of global oil demand. Renewable energy would have to expand 90-fold to replace hydrocarbons in 2 decades. It took 50 years for petroleum production to expand just 10-fold.

- Storing the energy equivalent of 1 barrel of oil, which weighs 300 pounds, requires 20,000 pounds (and $200,000 worth) of Tesla batteries. It takes the energy equivalent of 100 barrels of oil to fabricate the batteries to store the energy equivalent of a single barrel of oil.

- As the history of road-building has demonstrated, efficiency doesn't reduce but instead increases the demand for energy. Since 1995, when global energy efficiency has improved by 33 per cent, total world energy use rose

21

by 50 per cent, an amount equal to adding two entire United States' worth of demand.

- Every $1 billion in aircrafts produced leads to $5 billion in aviation fuel consumed over 2 decades to operate them. Global spending on new jets is more than $50 billion a year and rising.

- Every $1 billion spent on the more than 8,000 data centres on which the technologies of the Fourth Industrial Revolution rely to monitor, control and restrict our consumption to Net Zero leads to $7 billion in electricity consumed over 2 decades.

- Global spending on data centres is more than $100 billion a year and rising. It has been predicted that, by 2025, communications technology will account for more than 20 per cent of global energy consumption and 5.5 per cent of carbon emissions.

- Over a 30-year period, $1 million worth of a utility-scale solar or wind facility produces, respectively, 40 million and 55 million kilowatt hours. By contrast, $1 million worth of shale well produces enough natural gas to generate 300 million kilowatt hours over 30 years.

- It costs roughly the same to build one shale well or two wind turbines. However, the latter, combined, produces the equivalent energy of 0.7 barrels of oil per hour, while the shale rig averages 10 barrels of oil per hour.

- Wind and solar machines produce energy an average of 25–30% of the time, and only when nature accommodates. Conventional power plants can operate nearly continuously and are available when needed.

- About 60 pounds of batteries are needed to store the energy equivalent of 1 pound of hydrocarbons. At least 100 pounds of materials are mined, moved and processed for every pound of battery fabricated.

- It costs less than 50 cents to store a barrel of oil or its equivalent in natural gas; while it costs $200 to store the equivalent energy of a barrel of oil in electric batteries.

- A battery-centric energy grid and electric-vehicle world would mean mining gigatons (that is, billions of metric tons) more of the earth to access lithium, copper, nickel, graphite, rare earths, cobalt, etc., and using millions of tons of oil and coal both in mining and to fabricate metals and concrete.

So, if the Intergovernmental Panel on Climate Change goal of Net Zero by 2050 is neither a 'challenge' nor an 'opportunity', as the attendees at this year's annual meeting of the World Economic Forum boasted, but — as these figures show — a physical and economic *impossibility*, we should be asking what the enforcement of the policies it has been used to justify will mean for us, to what end these restrictions are being put and to whose benefit?

In the interests of disclosure, this data was published in March 2019 by Mark P. Mills, a senior fellow at the Manhattan Institute and a faculty fellow at Northwestern University's McCormick School of Engineering and Applied Science, where he co-directs an Institute on Manufacturing Science and Innovation.[24] He is also a strategic partner with Cottonwood Venture Partners (an energy-tech venture fund). Previously, Mills was a technology advisor for Bank of America Securities, and before that he served in the White House Science Office. Early in his career, he was an experimental physicist and development engineer at Bell Northern Research, so he is very much an industry insider. However, until environmental fundamentalists can answer the questions this data raises with something more than denouncing Mr. Mills as a 'right-wing conspiracy theorist and climate-change denier', these questions will continue to hang over what he calls the 'magical thinking' of the so-called 'sustainable' energy economy.

Now, in reality, the energy produced by these new technologies is a new commodity, the promotion of which suppresses the fact that producing millions of electric vehicles to replace the existing ones taxed and fined out of use — as they are, for example, in London by the Mayor's Ultra-Low Emissions Zone — or erecting hundreds of thousands of wind turbines with a 20-year life-span, or demolishing hundreds of thousands of social and council housing homes to make way for so-called 'passive housing' market-sale properties, or mining the lithium, cobalt and copper for the vast increase in the number of batteries required to harness these energy sources, is far more destructive to our environment and the people who live in it but far more lucrative to the companies and governments with access to the technology and natural resources of other countries.[25]

---

24. Mark P. Mills, 'The "New Energy Economy": An Exercise in Magical Thinking', *Manhattan Institute* (March 2019).

25. See Iain Davis, 'SDG7: The Impossible Energy Transformation', *Unlimited Hangout* (6 January, 2023).

The refusal to see the environmental, social, economic and even political costs of the total cycle of extraction, manufacture, construction, transportation, demolition and disposal within which these new technologies operate 'sustainably', and to stare instead with blinkered eyes at the carbon cost of their operational performance alone, is part of the willing blindness with which the chimera of Net Zero has been conjured into being.[26] My own company, Architects for Social Housing, has extensive knowledge of this argument, which over the last decade have been used to justify the demolition of London's social housing in the middle of a crisis of housing affordability. To counter this argument, we commissioned environmental engineers to produce estimates of the carbon cost of the entire life cycle of housing estates, beginning with the extraction of the raw materials, their transportation, transformation and processing into building material, the construction of the buildings and infrastructure, the lifespan of their inhabitation and uses, their management and maintenance (or operational carbon), and, finally, the energy required to demolish, transport and dispose of them — and the conclusion is clear. No matter how improved is the thermal performance of the new buildings, it is impossible for them to offset the total carbon cost of demolition, disposal and redevelopment within the 60-year predicted lifespan of the new developments.[27]

For the same reason, CO_2 emissions from the production of an electric car are 70 per cent higher than for the manufacture of a petrol-driven car, because of the resources consumed in the production of lithium ion batteries.[28] It's worth recalling that, contrary to the fantasies of environmental fundamentalists, electricity is not a source of energy but a means by which it is stored and transferred. Before it is used, it must first be generated, and in the UK 44 per cent

---

26. See Simon Elmer and Geraldine Dening, 'Lecture 3. The Economic Sphere: Part 1. Environmental Principles', *For a Socialist Architecture: Under Capitalism* (Architects for Social Housing, 2021), pp. 87-103.

27. See Simon Elmer and Geraldine Dening, 'Part Two: The Alternative to Demolition. 9. Comparative Environmental Costs', and 'Appendix B. Embodied Carbon Assessment by Model Environments', in *Saving St. Raphael's Estate: The Alternative to Demolition* (Architects for Social Housing, 2022), pp. 104, 157-165.

28. See Rob Hull, 'Volvo says emissions from making EVs can be 70% higher than petrol models — and claims it can take up to 9 years of driving before they become greener', *This is Money* (5 November, 2021).

of electricity comes from fossil fuels, rising to 57.84 per cent globally.[29] It is also extremely volatile, as the incidents of electric vehicles spontaneously combusting are demonstrating to a public coming to the realisation that they are not a replacement for petrol-driven cars but the means by which we will be deprived of their ownership and, eventually, their use.

Like the figures I quoted on so-called 'sustainable' energy sources, these are empirically-verifiable givens, and cannot be explained away by environmental fundamentalists, no matter how much their corporate backers use their financial clout to silence those who raise them. The truth is, 'sustainable energy' and the resources of which it disposes constitutes a newly emergent market requiring new relations of production, new rights of ownership, new regulations of distribution and new controls of consumption enforced by an authoritarian reduction not only of our standard of living but also of our rights and freedoms, and with them the sovereignty of governments over their national wealth, assets and resources.

3. The Ideology of Science

It's unclear what the environmental fundamentalists hope to achieve with their demands, which if realised will condemn hundreds of millions in the global south to starvation and billions more to increased poverty and hunger. About half the world's current population relies on fertilisers and pesticides to produce the food it needs to eat, and as the recent example of Sri Lanka demonstrated, eliminating the fossil fuels on which these agricultural aids are dependent will have devastating consequences. Under Net Zero agricultural policies imposed in April 2021 in the guise of that favourite illusion of Western consumers — 'going organic' — rice production in Sri Lanka in 2022 dropped by more than 50 per cent and domestic prices increased by 80 per cent.[30] Inflation reached 54 per cent, 90 per cent of the population were forced to skip meals, and in May 2022 Sri Lanka defaulted on its debt repayments.[31] That's what Net Zero achieved in a year in a country previously referred to as the 'rice bowl of the East'. The following month,

---

29. See Hannah Ritchie and Pablo Rosado, 'Electricity Mix', *Our World In Data* (10 July, 2020).

30. See Richard Lindzen and William Happer, 'Challenging "Net Zero" with Science', *CO2 Coalition* (February 2023), pp. 35-37.

31. See Krishnan Francis and Elaine Kurtenbach, 'Explainer: Why Sri Lanka's economy collapsed and what's next', *AP News* (11 July, 2022).

April 2022, a creditor group began to 'restructure' the country's £12 billion debt.[32] This included accepting loans from the International Monetary Fund conditional upon the Government imposing fiscal austerity on its already impoverished population and, to cover the cost of not allowing them to starve, the privatisation of state industry and assets. The largest creditor is BlackRock. Sri Lanka is an object lesson in how Sustainable Development Goals export debt.

Doubtless the environmental fundamentalists of the West know or care little about the material consequences of their religious dogma, but their naivety about the ends to which their beliefs are being put is the legacy of this generation. Born into austerity and identity politics, raised by iPhones and social media, in debt £30,000 for a degree nobody wants, graduated to masks, lockdown and gene therapy: they're so alienated from themselves and the world they experience through social media they don't know what sex they are, yet they think they can 'save the planet'. In reality, they're the New Compliant. The images of hysterical, weeping children, chained to bridges or glued to a painting, accusing an imaginary father-figure of stealing their future through the screens of smartphones, the footage from which is then sent around the world by international media companies promoting Agenda 2030, is the new model of citizenship in the Global Biosecurity State.[33]

Like all arguments that use the threat of a 'crisis' to justify coercive action by the forces of the state, the effect of environmental fundamentalism is to circumvent critical thinking, silence questions and pathologise disagreement as 'denial'. Indeed, the intended ideological reach of environmental fundamentalism over the British public is written out by chapter and verse in the report published by the House of Lords Environment and Climate Change Committee in October 2022, 'In our hands: behaviour change for climate and environmental goals', which I recommend to anyone who doubts the extent to which this fundamentalist

---

32. See Darini Rajasingham-Senanayake, 'Privatizing Sri Lanka ex-ante IMF Bailout of BlackRock', IDN-InDepthNews (26 August, 2022).

33. See Zoe Tidman, 'Just Stop Oil shuts parts of M25 as protesters climb gantries over motorway', *The Independent* (7 November, 2022); Gareth Davies, 'Just Stop oil protesters force Dartford Crossing to close after scaling bridge' *The Telegraph* (17 October, 2022); Damien Gayle, 'Just Stop Oil activists glue themselves to Turner painting frame in Manchester', *The Guardian* (1 July, 2022).

ideology has taken over our politics and civil liberties.[34] So that it's clear, the report is open about whose behaviour has to change. It isn't multinational corporations. It isn't our governments. It isn't the US military, the world's biggest institutional consumer of petroleum which, if it were a country, in fuel usage alone would be the 47th largest emitter of greenhouse gases in the world.[35] And it isn't the Lords, Ladies, Baronesses, Bishops and Duke who sit on the Committee. No, it's *our* behaviour they want to change: our consumption of food, our heating of our homes, our use of transport, our consumer goods, our leisure activities.

And also our cost of living. The total cost of capital spending on so-called 'green' projects required to reach Net Zero emissions by 2050, which include surface transport, energy networks, electricity supply, fuel supply, residential and non-residential buildings, manufacturing and construction, calculated by the Office for Budget Responsibility based on estimates by the Climate Change Committee, is £1.4 trillion, which is £1,700 a year for every UK household between 2020 and 2050.[36] Even this figure, though, has been called 'disingenous and dangerous', because it ignores the carbon emissions embodied in the UK's imports, so the actual cost to UK taxpayers is likely to be far higher. Like the equally manufactured health, energy, food and geopolitical 'crises' with which we are threatened today, the purpose of the environmental 'crisis' is to dismantle our institutions of democracy, erase our human rights, remove our freedoms, automate our jobs, bankrupt our businesses, empty our savings and mortgage our futures, leaving us impoverished and defenceless against the predations of capital, the authority of the state and the dictates of unelected, unaccountable and autocratic transnational technologies.

The full extent of our intended immiseration is made clear in *Absolute Zero*, a report commissioned by the Government and collectively produced by the universities of Cambridge, Oxford, Bath, Nottingham, Strathclyde and Imperial College London, the latter of which was responsible for the completely inaccurate

---

34. See House of Lords Environment and Climate Change Committee, '1st Report of Session 2022–23. In our hands: behaviour change for climate and environmental goals' (12 October, 2022).

35. See Neta C. Crawford, 'Pentagon Fuel Use, Climate Change, and the Costs of War', Watson Institute International and Public Affairs (13 November, 2019).

36. See Chris Giles, 'How much will it cost the UK to reach net zero?', *Financial Times* (3 November, 2021).

modelling that justified the lockdown of the UK for two years.[37] This report was published in November 2019, as the world entered its second and long-expected Global Financial Crisis in twelve years, and $11 trillion of quantitative easing was created to purchase collapsing financial assets in a little over 6 months, necessitating the suspension of trade to avoid the hyperinflation that would have ensued had these vast sums entered into enter the real economy.

	2020-2029	2030-2049	2050 Absolute Zero	Beyond 2050
Road vehicles				
Rail				
Flying				
Shipping				
Heating				
Appliances				
Food				
Mining material sourcing				
Materials production				
Construction				
Manufacturing				
Electricity				
Fossil fuels				

Source: University of Cambridge, Absolute Zero

But as we can see from the accompanying chart (*above*), the economic wreckage, ruined businesses and destroyed lives left by two years of lockdown is nothing compared to what the environmental fundamentalists have planned for us. By 2030, if they have their way, all airports in the UK will be closed; shipping will be reduced to zero; all new cars will be electric; all appliances will be electric and reduced in size to reduce power requirement; beef and lamb will be prohibited; fertiliser-use will be greatly reduced; cement, concrete, mortar, steel, plastic and fossil fuels will all be phased out. By 2050 it will be even worse. Road

---

37. See University of Cambridge, 'Absolute Zero: Delivering the UK's climate change commitment with incremental changes to today's technologies' (November 2019).

use will be reduced to 60 per cent of current usage; flying and shipping will both be banned (except, presumably, for the rich flying to Davos); heating, cooking and energy-use will all be reduced to 60 per cent of today; manufacturing will be reduced to 50 per cent; all fossil fuels will be banned and all energy — magically — will be electricity. Net Zero, quite clearly and openly, is a programme of global immiseration and disenfranchisement. Indeed, based on what happened in Sri Lanka in a single year, it's not too much to say that Net Zero is a genocidal programme of global depopulation.

So why aren't the populations Net Zero plans to reduce rising up against these plans? To try and answer this question, I want to look at just one of the numerous examples of how the discourse of environmental fundamentalism is used to silence and circumvent criticism off its dictates. On 9 May this year, 2023, there was a sudden downpour in the south of England, causing flooding in some areas.[38] One of the environmental fundamentalists to cite this as proof of climate catastrophe was Dr. Charlie Gardner, one of the more vocal members of Scientists for Extinction Rebellion. Posting footage of flooding in the village of Tipton St. John near Sidmouth in East Devon, he wrote: 'Can we please stop listening to the people saying there's no need to change anything?' I'll pass over, for the moment, that this is a statement that no scientist should be making; but in response I pointed out that such flooding is caused by building on flood plains, containing rivers in canals, overdeveloping land, laying tarmac and concrete over soil to prevent drainage, industrial mono-culture farming that dries out the soil so that it cannot soak up periodic increases in rainfall, and a myriad of other causes relating to land-use. It isn't caused by 'climate change'. What needs 'changing' is not to whom we should be listening — although we could certainly do with turning the volume down on environmental activists like Dr. Gardner — but how planning authorities financed by property developers and international investors use land in this country. Bringing that about, however, is achieved not by lying down in the road, but through real activism. As we know at Architects for Social Housing, this means difficult and unrewarded work with local communities to produce practical measures for beneficial change that don't involve impoverishing and disenfranchising the population to the benefit of corporate forms of governance.

---

38. See Richard Davies, 'UK — Evacuations After Floods in Devon and Somerset', *Floodlist* (10 May, 2023).

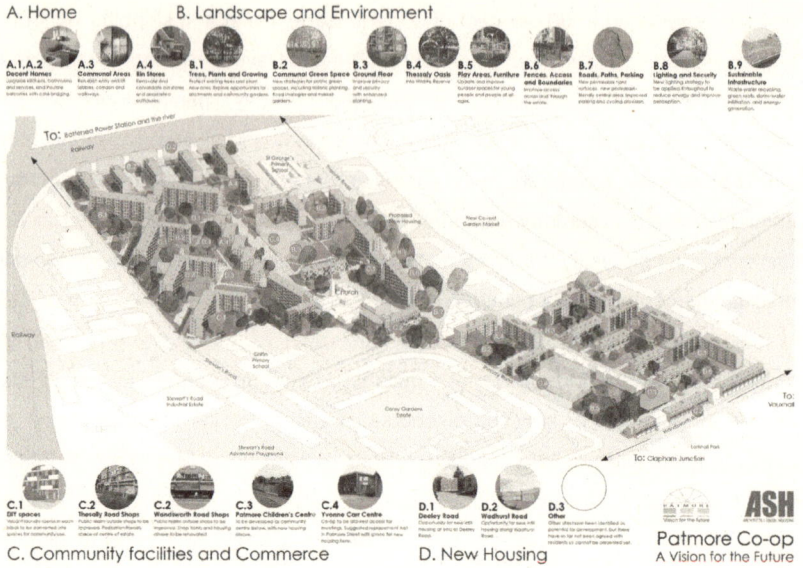

Source: Architects for Social Housing

In 2017, ASH started working with the housing co-operative that runs it to refurbish and improve the Patmore estate in South London.[39] Like the nearby Battersea Power Station, this is built on a flood-plain for the River Thames that was formerly marsh-land. Under the planning authority of the 'Vauxhall, Nine Elms, Battersea Opportunity Area', the regeneration of this industrial and residential part of London is one of the largest building sites in Europe, throwing up high-rise, high-priced, market-sale properties for investment. The environment, however, is a radical leveller in whom and what it effects, and rainwater doesn't stop falling at the edge of up-market gated communities. What many architects appear not to know and fewer developers want to hear is that the first consideration in any development is the management of water — not the water that is piped into the homes and offices of the occupants, but the rainwater that falls from the sky and, if not given a means of egress and proper drainage, can cause flooding.[40] This

39. See the pages titled 'Regeneration of the Patmore Co-operative Housing Estate' in Simon Elmer and Geraldine Dening, *For a Socialist Architecture: Under Capitalism* (Architects for Social Housing, 2021), pp. 79-81.

40. See Daniel Roehr, 'Vancouver's Housing Crisis: A Collaborative Opportunity for Planners and Architects', *Spacing Vancouver* (16 September, 2019).

can be ameliorated through green roofs that absorb flash flooding, maintenance of existing drainage, upgrading old sewer systems, increasing the permeability of the built landscape; but, first and foremost, by not building on flood plains in the first instance.

However, as an explanation of flooding and a challenge to change how planning legislation is made and planning approval is granted in a public sector captured by corporate finance, that's not as sexy as 'saving the planet' from yet another 'crisis', and is unlikely to attract thousands of youthful activists looking to change the world in a weekend's protest. A short bit of research on my part revealed that Tipton St. John is built on the flood plains between two bends of the River Otter, which accounts for its history of flooding, most memorably in the East Devon floods of 1968, long before we blamed such events on 'global warming'.[41] Perhaps the fact the average price of a residential property sold in the village is now £570,000 played a part in the local planning authority granting the developer permission; but I imagine the farmers on the hills either side who have watched the plain flood for decades had a laugh at the expense of the buyers.[42]

Unfortunately, Dr. Gardner and others like him wear their white coats like a priest wears his cassock, and with the same claim to be the keeper of an unchallengeable Truth. But what is clear from this example of his irresponsible and unscientific fearmongering is that donning a white coat doesn't mean you know what you're talking about, except perhaps in the eyes of a public bullied over the last three-and-a-half years into regarding doctors as the final arbiters of what we can and cannot do. But the absolutism of their statements are the exact opposite of the principles of scientific inquiry, which is based not on stopping people from asking questions but rather on asking the right questions and then working to produce the correct answers.

On the basis of this unscientific absolutism, the Government of the Netherlands, which is the second-largest exporter of agricultural goods in the world after the USA, is forcing its farmers to kill a third of their livestock to meet their Government's 'Zero-Carbon' commitments.[43] In Ireland, the Government is

---

41. See '50th anniversary of the devastating floods in East Devon', *Straitgate Action Group* (10 July, 2018).

42. See Zoopla, 'House prices in Tipton St. John' (September, 2023).

43. See Andy Bounds, 'Dutch farmers in uproar over plans to curb animal numbers to cut nitrogen emissions', *Financial Times* (3 August 2022).

planning to kill 200,000 cows to meet so-called 'emissions targets'.[44] While last year, the President of the European Commission, Ursula von der Leyen, proposed a mandatory target for reduced electricity-use during peak hours in order, as she expressed it with a by-now familiar justification, 'to flatten the curve'.[45]

And it doesn't stop there. At this year's annual meeting of the World Economic Forum held in Davos, Switzerland, the ideologues and architects of stakeholder capitalism, on the justification of responding to numerous manufactured 'crises', elected themselves to form an openly technocratic, authoritarian, World Government presiding over the new corporate-run economy they call stakeholder capitalism. This, in effect, is a rebranded fascism for the Twenty-first Century, and the political economy of the New World Order.

Satya Nadella, the Chief Executive Officer of Microsoft, reported that the company is producing software that, through what he calls 'carbon accounting', allows banks to measure the carbon footprint of small businesses before granting them loans.[46] Jim Hagemann Snabe, the Chairman of Siemens, the largest industrial manufacturing company in Europe, called not for a reduction in production but for 'a billion people to stop eating meat'.[47] Patricia Poppe, the Chief Executive Officer of the Pacific Gas and Electricity Corporation said that, in order to transition to an electric grid, an automated system will make it possible to turn off supply to 'smart devices, wi-fi and electric vehicles'.[48] Bastien Girod, a Green Party Member of the Swiss National Council and corporate sustainability advisor to a Swiss carbon finance consultancy, argued that governments should only buy from companies compliant with the Sustainable Development Goals of Agenda 2030, and that we should 'build environments' in which people not only

---

44. See Jude Webber, 'Irish farmers pressured to cull up to 200,000 cows to meet climate goals', *Financial Times* (11 August, 2023).

45. See European Commission, 'Statement by President von der Leyen on energy' (7 September, 2022).

46. See World Economic Forum, 'A Conversation with Satya Nadella, CEO of Microsoft | Davos 2023', *YouTube* (19 January, 2023).

47. See The New World Order, 'WEF 2023: Siemens Chairman Jim Hagemann Snabe on eating meat and sustainable food', *YouTube* (19 January, 2023).

48. See World Economic Forum, 'Mastering New Energy Economics | Davos 2023', *YouTube* (17 January, 2023).

cannot but do not want to use cars. He called this 'living in harmony with nature'.[49] And Al Gore, the former US Vice President, current Board Member of Apple and the World Economic Forum and senior advisor to Google, in a speech posted on Just Stop Oil's *YouTube* channel, threatened us with 'rain bombs', 'boiling oceans' and a billion 'climate refugees' that will take away our 'capacity for self-governance' — unless we 'ACT NOW!'[50]

As the Italian critic and political commentator, Umberto Eco, warned us nearly 30 years ago now, such bullying calls to action are the hallmark of fascist movements, which are ideologically opposed to the critical thought they do everything they can to censor, while slandering and dismissing those who dare to question their dogma.[51] What the young protesters of today don't know — and why they've been selected to promote environmental fundamentalism — is that the threat of imminent catastrophe has been made for decades by the United Nations and other institutions in order to increase their power over us.

In 1989, the UN predicted we had until the year 2000 to reverse global warming, otherwise melting ice caps would result in sea levels rising three feet, entire countries being submerged, millions of 'eco refugees', and other fantasies from the apocalypse factory of environmental fundamentalism.[52]

In 1995, a UN study produced by the Intergovernmental Panel on Climate Change predicted that rising sea levels ensured that 'most of the beaches on the East Coast of the United States would be gone in 25 years.'[53] That means in 2020, and they're still there.

In 2000, Dr. David Viner, a scientist at the Climate Research Unit of the University of East Anglia, predicted that, in a few years, UK children would no

---

49. See Nativa Economics, 'Open forum: In Harmony with Nature', *YouTube* (17 January 2023).

50. See Just Stop Oil, 'Al Gore | World Economic Forum', *YouTube* (9 February, 2023).

51. See Umberto Eco, 'Ur-fascism', *The New York Review of Books* (22 June, 1995); collected in *How to Spot a Fascist*; translated by Ricard Dixon and Alastair McEwan (Harvill Secker, 2020).

52. See Peter James Spielmann, 'U.N. Predicts Disaster if Global Warming Not Checked', *Associated Press News* (30 June, 1989).

53. See William K. Stevens, 'Scientists Sat Earth's Warming Could Set Off Wide Disruptions', *The New York Times* (18 September, 1995).

longer know what snow is.[54] It has snowed in the UK every year since, and British children are still playing in it.

In 2009, at a Copenhagen climate change summit, Al Gore said: 'There is a 75 per cent chance that the entire ice cap of the North Pole, during the summer months, could be completely ice-free within five to seven years.'[55] Twenty-four years later, the ice cap is still there.

In 2014, together with the US Secretary of State John Kerry (now US Special Presidential Envoy for Climate), the French Foreign Minister, Laurent Fabius, announced: 'We have 500 days to avoid climate chaos.'[56] Nine-and-a-half-years years later, the only chaos is being created by arsonists.[57]

In January 2019, 19 years after the deadline predicted by the United Nations 30 years earlier, the US Representative, Alexandria Ocasio-Cortez, predicted that 'the world is going to end in 12 years if we don't address climate change.'[58]

In 2019, in *No One Is Too Small to Make a Difference*, the 16-year-old high-school dropout, Greta Thunberg, claimed: 'Around 2030 we will be in a position to set off an irreversible chain reaction beyond human control that will lead to the end of our civilization as we know it.'[59]

As Professor Plimer laconically reminded us during a talk he gave in 2022: 'The laws of physics have not changed just because you're alive on planet earth.'[60] As these by turns apocalyptic and hubristic assertions demonstrate, environmental fundamentalism is, first and foremost, an anthropomorphism. This is why it appeals to children and the religious, who view the world as an extension

---

54. See Charles Onians, 'Snowfalls now are just a thing of the past', *Independent* (20 March, 2000).

55. See Frank James, 'Al Gore Slips On Arctic Ice; Misstates Scientist's Forecast', *NPR* (15 December, 2009).

56. See John Kerry, 'Remarks With French Foreign Minister Laurent Favius Before their Meeting', *U.S. Department of State* (13 May, 2014).

57. See Laura Gozzi and Sofia Bettiza, 'Are arsonists behind Italy's devastating wildfires?', *BBC News* (28 July, 2023); Chay Quinn, 'Wildfires in Tenerife blamed on arsonists by Spanish authorities after 12,000 evacuated in holiday spot', *LBC* (20 August, 2023); and 'Greece investigating whether organised arson groups to blame for deadly wildfires', *SkyNews* (23 August, 2023).

58. See Alexandria Ocasio-Cortez, '"People are dying": Ocasio-Cortez delivers fiery speech on climate inaction — video', *The Guardian* (27 March, 2019).

59. See Greta Thunberg, *No One Is Too Small To Make A Difference* (Penguin, 2019).

60. See Ian Plimer, 'Professor Ian Plimer on "Green Murder"', *YouTube* (27 April, 2022).

of their fears and sins. It is also why it employs figures like Greta Thunberg and Al Gore — scientific illiterates posing, respectively, as a saint and a prophet — to promote its orthodoxies.

All these predictions, which date back to the 1960s, were not wrong or out by a few years of decades.[61] They were and are lies, promoted to increase the power of unaccountable transnational technocracies and corporations over the populations of nation states. The trouble us, if someone keeps crying 'Wolf!' over and over again, eventually that wolf has to come, or people will come to the conclusion that the cryer is lying. So now we are being taught, as Orwell long ago predicted, to reject the evidence of our own eyes and ears.[62]

If we had actually lived through a viral pandemic that constituted a public health crisis, the UK state wouldn't have had to terrorise us with the propaganda, fearmongering and lies that it did. By the same logic, if we were really facing a climate catastrophe threatening life on earth, the state wouldn't need the current programme of propaganda, fearmongering, blatant lies and blanket censorship. In the same way that medical scientists funded by Big Pharma lied to us about a 'pandemic' that had the infection fatality rate of seasonal influenza, so too climate scientists at the Intergovernmental Panel on Climate Change in the pay of its corporate funders are lying to us about the threat of climate change. What the last three-and-a-half years of lies has demonstrated is that not only politicians but scientists, doctors and academics too will say *anything* if you promise them a grant or, conversely, threaten to withdrawn funding from their institution. Follow the money and you'll find 'The Science' to which we are being ordered to bow down and obey. We might reflect that, if every doctor, nurse and clinician in the UK was willing to inject experimental gene therapies into the UK public because serial liars like Boris Johnson, Matt Hancock and Sajid Javid told them to, what would they not say and do when even bigger and more powerful liars tell them to promote environmental fundamentalism and not ask questions?

---

61. See Myron Ebell and Steven J. Milloy, 'Wrong Again: 50 Years of Failed Eco-pocalyptic Predictions', *Competitive Enterprise Institute* (18 September, 2019).

62. George Orwell, *Nineteen Eighty-four*, Everyman's Library; with an introduction by Julian Symonds (Alfred A. Knopf, 1992), p. 84.

4. The Protest of the Elite

But that's not all. In addition to silencing critical questions, protest groups promoting the ideology of environmental fundamentalism also serve another function, of which the religious acolytes only too ready to offer themselves for arrest appear to be equally ignorant. Just as Black Lives Matter and Extinction Rebellion were cited as justification for the Police, Crime, Sentencing and Courts Act 2022, so the vandalism by Just Stop Oil and Insulate Britain, whose activists have apparently unimpeded access to the city with the highest level of security in Europe, are cited by the Government as justification for the Public Order Act 2023 that has removed even more of our freedoms.[63]

This is why environmentalist activists can park a pink yacht on Oxford Circus, shut down Westminster Bridge or Trafalgar Square, spray paint across the Houses of Parliament, shatter the windows of JP Morgan's City offices, empty milk bottles across the floor of the Harrods department store, or glue themselves to priceless works of art in the National Gallery, and the police refuse to arrest them; when a few months before UK citizens were carried off by the same police for holding a sheet of paper saying 'Not my King', and a few months before that violently assaulted for not wearing a mask or leaving their homes without permission.[64]

The Metropolitan Police Service is one of the largest, best equipped and well-funded police forces in the world, with 43,000 personnel and an annual budget of £3.8 billion. If it didn't want Just Stop Oil activists blocking roads in London, they wouldn't be able to do so. The UK also has the highest density of CCTV cameras

---

63. See UK Public General Acts, 'Police, Crime, Sentencing and Courts Act 2022' (28 April, 2022); 'Public Order Act 2023' (2 May, 2023); and Rebecca Speare-Cole, 'Just Stop Oil activists spray paint on Aston Martin showroom in London', *The Independent* (16 October, 2022).

64. See Damien Gayle, 'Extinction Rebellion protesters block Oxford Circus in London', *The Guardian* (25 August, 2021); Damien Gayle, 'XR protesters shut down central London bridges including Westminster', *The Guardian* (15 April, 2022); Mark Duell and Abbie Llewelyn, 'Police swoop on eco mob and arrest 32 activists who set up road blocks around Trafalgar Square as they demand new oil and gas projects are shutdown on sixth day of chaos', *Daily Mail* (6 October, 2022); Rachel Burford, 'Animal Rebellion: ten arrests as protesters spray Houses of Parliament with paint', *Evening Standard* (7 September, 2022); Lily Russell-Jones, 'Extinction Rebellion activists smash JP Morgan windows', *City A.M.* (1 September, 2021); Daniel Keane, 'Watch: Animal Rebellion protesters pour milk on Harrods shop floor', *Evening Standard* (16 October, 2022); Damien Gayle, 'Just Stop Oil activists throw soup at Van Gogh's Sunflowers', *The Guardian* (14 October, 2022); 'Arrest of UK anti-royal protesters raises free speech concerns', *Al Jazeera* (13 September, 2022).

in Europe, with 1 for every 10 of the population in London.[65] If the security of Goldman Sachs, the Royal Academy and Westminster Palace was so easy to circumvent, it wouldn't be these innocents who made their way inside, but organisations with a far greater reason to resent the UK state.[66] They can do so with such ease and lack of consequence because their protests are corporate-funded advertisements for Agenda 2030. They're there by invitation — of the London Mayor, who shares their environmental fundamentalism, under the protection of the Metropolitan Police Service and British Transport Police, with the support of the UK media, with the authorisation of the UK Government and, ultimately, in the service of the international technocracies composing the new World Government.

In stark contrast to which, the millions of UK citizens who, in the spring and summer of 2021, protested without trespass or vandalism against the illegal lockdowns, 'vaccine' mandates and 'vaccine' passports — on the imposition of which the environmentalists' 'Zero-COVID/Zero-carbon' demands are founded — received a very different welcome from the Metropolitan Police Service, who used extraordinary levels of violence to attack and arrest us, were universally censored by the media who refused to report marches of half a million UK citizens and more from all over the country; were ignored and ridiculed by those we have elected to represent us in Parliament; and were threatened by the Government with increased powers of police arrest, fines and criminal sanctions.[67]

The increasingly frequent scenes of members of the working public, infuriated not only by a handful of environmental activists blocking London's roads with impunity but also by the refusal of the Metropolitan Police Force to remove them, hides the fact that in doing so the police are not only not enforcing the law, but are actually interfering with the public's rights. Despite their consistently thuggish behaviour, the police do not have some extra-legal right over the British

---

65. See Richard Barker, 'How many security cameras are in London?', *Clarion Security Services* (2023).

66. See 'Goldman Sachs's European headquarters targeted by climate-change activists', *Reuters* (25 April, 2019); Ben Quinn, 'Leonardo would have backed gallery protest, say Just Stop Oil activists', *The Guardian* (8 February, 2023); 'Extinction Rebellion: Climate activists arrested after protest in Commons chamber', *BBC News* (2 September, 2022).

67. See Subject Access, 'Massive Anti Lockdown Protest — London', *YouTube* (20 March, 2021); and Simon Elmer, 'March for Freedom, 29 May, 2021', *Architects for Social Housing* (30 May, 2021).

people. They are, to quote the former Justice of the Supreme Court, Lord Sumption, 'citizens in uniform'.[68] And as citizens, we have as much right as they to see the law observed, although with different powers of intervention. Under Section 137 of the Highways Act 1980, it is an offence wilfully to obstruct free passage along a highway, and the offender is liable to a fine or imprisonment for a term not exceeding 6 months.[69] Whether or not our police forces refuse to enforce that law, under Section 24a of the Police and Criminal Evidence Act 1984, a UK citizen can carry out an arrest if he or she has reasonable grounds for believing it is necessary to prevent, under Section 4a), the person causing physical injury to himself or others.[70] Sitting in a busy road in Central London and impeding the passage of hundreds of furious drivers clearly constitutes such grounds. Any UK citizen clearing a road of a deliberate threat to safety and order is therefore acting within UK law.

Where does that leave the right to protest? The simple answer is that, just as Agenda 2030 isn't a popular 'cause' but a programme of the United Nations that has been formulated by and for the benefit of international corporations, so too the activities of environmental activists aren't protests but corporate-funded public relations stunts. Protest, by contrast — as exemplified by the marches against the illegal lockdown in the Spring of 2021 — is when a substantial body of people assert their right to occupy a public space, whether that's a municipal square, park, building or public highway, in order to bring public attention to their cause. If that means blocking a major road, that right should be balanced against the rights of the users of the road. Clearly, when several thousand people march along a street in order to draw attention to their 'cause', they should be allowed to do so. A measure of this balance is that drivers of the vehicles blocked by what they recognise as a protest — whether or not they agree with its 'cause' — do not get out of their cars and vans and start physically removing individual protesters from the road, because the mass of protesters makes that an impossible task.

In contrast, when tiny groups of half-a-dozen people are repeatedly blocking roads used by hundreds if not thousands of drivers on a weekly and increasingly a daily basis, their right to protest is infringing on the rights of the far greater

---

68. See Jonathan Sumption, 'Former Supreme Court Justice: "This is what a police state is like", *The Spectator* (30 March, 2020).

69. See UK Public General Acts, 'Highways Act 1980' (13 November, 1980).

70. See UK Public General Acts, 'Police and Criminal Evidence Act 1984 (31 October, 1984).

number of road-users to move about the city. It's clear that Just Stop Oil and their fellow activists are not blocking roads in order to draw attention to their corporate Agenda; rather, the point of their activity is to block roads, the use of which they have identified as an 'evil'; and that the Metropolitan Police have been given instructions by the same authorities to permit them to break the law. The incidents of police assaulting and arresting members of the public who try to clear the road themselves, as is their right, amply demonstrate that the police aren't upholding UK law.[71] In effect, the police are uniformed activists enforcing the dictates of the unelected globalists who want to take away the constitutional freedoms of the UK public on the justification of 'saving the planet'. Indeed, far outnumbering the handful of Just Stop Oil activists, it is the police who constitute the protest. So what's the goal?

Apart from their localised interference, these protests are habituating an outraged public to the permanent restriction of our freedom of movement. This is in the process of being imposed on a permanent basis by local and municipal authorities across the UK under the direction of the World Economic Forum's and its urban panopticon of 15-Minute Cities.[72] Like the systematic reduction in our standards of living, the closing of roads with physical bollards and the system of surveillance monitoring and enforcing these restrictions will fundamentally change the social contract in this country without consulting the people on whom it is being unilaterally imposed and certainly without our vote. And like the actions of these police-protected activists, these restrictions illegally interfere with our freedom of movement under Protocol No. 4, Article 2 of the European Convention on Human Rights.[73] As these widely-reproduced photographs of these protests show, the police are not policing these protests; they are part of them, and a part that, given that the police are operating above the law, the general public are prohibited from opposing. What we're seeing here is the emergence of a fully

---

71. See Danielle de Wolfe, '"If you do that it's a crime": Police warn motorists it's assault if they move Just Stop Oil protesters off road', *LBC* (25 April, 2023); and Barney Davis, 'Police detain man after Just Stop Oil activist shoved to ground on Blackfriars Bridge', *Evening Standard* (23 May, 2023).

72. See Lisa Chamberlain, 'The surprising stickiness of the "15-minute city"', *World Economic Forum* (15 March, 2022).

73. See European Court of Human Rights, 'Guide on Article 2 of Protocol No. 4 to the European Convention on Human Rights: Freedom of Movement' (updated on 31 August, 2022).

politicised police force that is operating beyond the law of the land and in contravention of our constitutional rights and freedoms.

And, of course, the enormous media coverage for such incidents increases the public's sense of political impotence over our own lives, of disenfranchisement from the law and its enforcement by both the police and the courts, of confusion about the motivations for permitting this apparently unending lawlessness, and of growing anger at changes to our lives and country for which we have not been consulted and certainly haven't voted. All of this renders the public even more susceptible to government and corporate propaganda. It is also exacerbating the class war that is being waged between the corporate 'elite' creating the regulations and programmes depriving us of our civil liberties and political agencies and the workers, households and communities at whom they are targeted. In this war, the middle classes — as they did with mandatory masking, illegal lockdowns and experimental gene therapies — are working for the ruling class from whom they derive their administrative power over the working class.

You don't have to be a sociologist to see the very clear divide between the lorry drivers, self-employed builders, electricians and plumbers, delivery men, parents dropping their children off at school before driving to work, and all the other Londoners trying to keep their heads above the spiralling cost of living in the capital, and the green-haired activists, performance artists and ageing hippies who have the time and money to sit in roads between university classes, designing banners in their Hackney Wick studios, working from their parents' suburban homes, or returning to their home-county cottages.

It's indicative of where their class allegiances lie — and where their financial support comes from — that Just Stop Oil never try to block access to 10 Downing Street or Whitehall, or Buckingham Palace, or the private residences of senior politicians or corporate CEOs. If they did, there is no doubt whatsoever that the police would enforce the law and have them off their feet not in the hour or longer it takes them when interfering with the freedoms of working men and women, but in seconds, and the charges they would face would not be dropped by the accommodating courts and pro-bono lawyers with a slap on the wrist. It's entirely in keeping with the class divisions being built into our supposedly human rights that the London Mayor's Ultra-Low Emission Zone, which now encloses the entire capital, is a fine-based restriction which unevenly restricts the freedoms of the working class over those able to afford the otherwise prohibitive rise in the cost of driving in the capital.

No-one appears to have asked why members of Just Stop Oil turned up, with both the media and the police apparently notified in advance, to protest at the recent coronation of King Charles, when he has been one of the key figures in popularising the politics of environmental fundamentalism in this country for decades, and before most of the youthful activists mouthing his credos were even born.[74] The answer, I would suggest, lies in the overcoming the paradox of this movement. The activists given free rein to interfere with our constitutional rights present themselves as young, radical, fearless, anti-establishment, oppressed by the police, standing up to corporate power. In reality, as I've tried to show, they are protected by the police, exonerated by the courts, given extraordinary freedoms to flaunt the authoritative legislation around public space and protest by our government and municipal authorities, and in every respect promoting the interests of corporate power.

The coronation of a king who is unpopular among the middle classes from which these activists are overwhelmingly drawn was an ideal spectacle to create and foster the appearance of being anti-establishment in the eyes not only of the public but, I would suggest, more importantly in the growing number of environmental activists. It was pointed out that, while the Just Stop Oil activists stopping the working men and women of London from going about their lives and work are protected by police who refuse to arrest them, those who turned up to the coronation were arrested before they got anywhere near their supposed protest. I would suggest that, rather than a protest, the arrests at the coronation were a recruitment drive for Just Stop Oil and their sister organisations. 'Down with the monarchy!' is far more likely to attract the support of the university students that fill their ranks than a detailed explanation of the structures of funding and influence between JP Morgan, the World Economic Forum, King Charles and Extinction Rebellion.

There is a reason why the spokesmen for environmental fundamentalism are drawn not from meteorologists but from young, articulate, privately-educated, upper-middle-class girls in higher education bred to a sense of entitlement denied

---

74. See Chloe Naldrett, 'Arrested for wearing a T-shirt? The coronation heralded a frightening slide towards authoritarianism', *The Guardian* (7 May, 2023).

to the workers they look down on with such contempt.[75] Protest has for some time now been a form of spectacle by which political parties and their corporate backers manipulate public opinion in their favour, but police arrest represents a more subtle and successful means of giving rise to powerful emotional responses that circumvent critical thinking and entrench the public more firmly in their allotted tribal identifications. Outrage and anger are the medium of environmental fundamentalism, because both are easier to yield to than the demands of critical thought. Confronted with the complexity of global geopolitics and the refusal of the media to produce an explanation more complex than that which a child could understand, protest has become a form of collective therapy for the confused, the angry and the frightened. Indeed, it is the role of the media to produce citizens who are all three: confused, angry and frightened.

Unfortunately, and perhaps understandably given their youth and ignorance of even recent history, the children elected to front this globalist coup don't understand that the media isn't there to report the news, it's there to make it. As a rule of thumb, if you're invited onto the BBC to discuss your 'cause', your protests are reported across the globe by the most powerful media corporations and information technology companies in the world, you have the legislative backing and police protection of every Western government, and your demands are echoed by US vice presidents, corporate CEOs and the King of the United Kingdom of Great Britain and Northern Ireland, it's safe to conclude that you don't represent a threat to their hegemony, but are in fact a part of it.[76]

That, however, is a difficult pill to swallow, particularly when experiencing your first taste of apparent power and influence, and your anger has become a sacred war — indeed, a *Jihad* of the Western middle classes from which the converts to environmental fundamentalism are drawn. And like all fundamentalisms, any disagreement with its dogma is rejected by its acolytes as denial, as the ignorance of unbelievers in their rapidly growing faith, into whose tenets it is their duty and mission to indoctrinate the rest of the population. Like the coronavirus 'crisis' that borrowed so much of its dogma — the most doctrinal of which was the command to 'Follow the Science!' — environmental

75. See GB News, 'Just Stop Oil's Phoebe Plummer argues "People are dying" in net zero clash with Jacob Rees-Mogg', *YouTube* (27 March, 2023).

76. See BBC Politics Live, 'I'm not a Criminal I'm a Scared Kid trying to Fight for my Future', *YouTube* (30 March, 2023).

fundamentalism is a religious movement formed to conceal and promote the very material and economic goals of a corporate globalist coup.

Despite their radical and apocalyptic rhetoric, therefore, and whether their activists know it or not, Just Stop Oil are the paid promoters of the United Nations' Agenda 2030. This is why their website, their professionally-printed banners and their media-covered protests combine the slick look of consumer advertising with the language of 'revolution'. Like Insulate Britain, Animal Rebellion, Extinction Rebellion, Black Lives Matter, The People's Assembly, Momentum and all the other ostensibly 'grass roots' movements that are in practice 'astro-turfing' for their political and corporate backers, Just Stop Oil has appropriated street protest for the political agenda of globalists.

At this year's annual meeting of the World Economic Forum, John Kerry, the United States Special Presidential Envoy for Climate Change, described the power of what he described as the 'select group' in Davos to 'save the planet' as 'extra-terrestrial'.[77] But behind these exaggerated and ludicrous claims, the actual goal of these US oligarchs is to financialise the natural world for their benefit, impoverish the populations of the West, dismantle what's left of our democracies, and remove — under a permanent state of environmental emergency — our human rights, civil liberties and political agency. In return for which, they have offered us the sad and pathetic spectacle of protests by people gluing themselves to the road, chaining their necks to railings with D-locks, pouring oil over their naked bodies, hurling paint at works of art, and, at the behest of billionaires, demanding the reduction in the standard of living not only of themselves but of everyone else in the world who isn't wealthy or influential enough to get into the same room as John Kerry. As C. S. Lewis warned us long ago, the goal of any tyranny exercised for the good of the people is to reduce that people to the status of 'infants, imbeciles and domestic animals'.[78] For some time now we have been behaving like infants and thinking like imbeciles; and if we believe that the cull of the global population to 'save the planet' will stop at animals — domestic and livestock — we are fatally mistaken about the lengths to which the environmental

---

77. See John Kerry, 'John Kerry at World Economic Forum: "Extraordinary" for "Select Group" to Discuss Green Mandates', *YouTube* (17 January, 2023).

78. C. S. Lewis, 'The Humanitarian Theory of Punishment'; collected in *Undeceptions: Essays on Theology and Ethics*; edited by Walter Hooper (Geoffrey Les, 1971), p. 287-288.

fundamentalists will go to inflict the genocidal consequences of the UN's Agenda 2050 on the world.

Between 2015 and 2019, I watched the UK Labour Party under the leadership of Jeremy Corbyn turn council estate residents protesting against the demolition of their homes into voters for the Party whose councils were demolishing them, and then blame Labour's neoliberal housing policies on Tory 'austerity'.[79] This is a similar lie but with far greater resources and on a global scale. Indeed, this nexus of environmental fundamentalism, biosecurity restrictions, woke ideology, corporate takeover of national governments and managed decline of our standard of living is what the governments of Western nations, only a few months into the 'pandemic', informed us was to be 'The New Normal' to which we would 'build back better'. What they didn't tell us is to what end. As more and more of the damned are beginning to understand, we are the carbon they want to reduce.

---

79. See Simon Elmer, 'Stand Up To Labour: The Denials of Momentum', *Architects for Social Housing* (10 October, 2019).

3. Contexts for Central Bank Digital Currency

No new technology is good or bad in itself, just as new technology comes into use outside of programmes for its use; and only its application can and will determine whether we should embrace or resist its implementation. I can't quite remember now how mobile phones were sold to us all those years ago beyond the promises of convenience, progress and a competitive edge; but I don't recall being told they would become the tracking devices for a system of surveillance and control that is becoming increasingly hard not to describe as totalitarian. Neither does the application of new technology exist in isolation from other technologies and other programmes, some of which are a condition of its own operability, others sharing the same goal. What I want to do in this chapter, therefore, is to discuss the contexts — economic, social, political and environmental — in which Central Bank Digital Currency is being — in the terminology used by UK governments when announcing programmes for which we haven't voted — 'rolled out'. The avid promoters of CBDC, which include our unelected Prime Minister, Rishi Sunak, say very little about its necessity, applications and benefits beyond similar claims to progress, fighting financial crime — which would be a first for the Bank of England and our Government — and, of course, sustainability, which is now the justification for every new removal of a human right or civil liberty.[1] But the wider and expanding contexts of what I call the Global Biosecurity State, I believe, give us a more accurate understanding of the real application of Central Bank Digital Currency and, indeed, of its intended purpose. To recall what I mean by this term, the Global Biosecurity State describes the nexus of organisations, treaties, agendas, regulations, programmes, technologies and ideologies that have emerged from the revolution into stakeholder capitalism being implemented on the justification of responding to multiple manufactured 'crises'. It is in the context of these 'crises' — health, environmental, cost of living, energy, geopolitical — and the solutions proposed to address them, that I want to situate Central Bank Digital Currency.

---

1. See 'New UK Prime Minister Rishi Sunak Pushes Heavily to Introduce CBDC', *Unlock* (25 October, 2022).

1. Is it Programmable?

CDC is digital or electronic money for households and businesses alike. The Bank of England, which calls it the 'Digital Pound', says CBDC is not a crypto-currency like Bitcoin, because it is not privately issued, but instead a 'liability' of the bank, and will therefore retain its value over time, rather than being subject to rapid fluctuations in value as happens with investments in crypto-assets.[2] Significantly, the Bank of England describes CBDC as the 'safest' form of money available — a value with the greatest currency in the Global Biosecurity State. If — or, more accurately, when — it is implemented, the Bank of England will make central bank money available to the public in digital form for the first time. As of last November, the Bank of England insists that CBDC will not replace but, instead, 'exist alongside cash and bank deposits'.[3]

The Bank of England published its first paper on CBDC in March 2020 — not coincidentally, the same month that lockdown restrictions were imposed on the UK, largely closing down the real economy for the next two years.[4] The Chancellor of the Exchequer, who at the time was Rishi Sunak — another coincidence — set up a CBDC Taskforce in April 2021, shortly after the second spike in UK deaths attributed to COVID-19.[5] This joint taskforce between the Treasury and the Bank of England is working with the central banks of other countries and states, as well as with the Bank for International Settlements — about which more later. The same month, the Bank of England set up two forums, one for CBDC technology, the other for CBDC implementation and operation. These include its use, functions, the role of the public and private sectors, its implications for data privacy, and what the Bank of England, with a nod to the newly enforced orthodoxies of woke, calls financial and digital 'inclusion'. By this they mean, not

---

2. See Bank of England, 'The digital pound' (last updated 1 June, 2023).

3. See Bank of England, 'Statement on Central Bank Digital Currency next steps' (9 November, 2021).

4. See Bank of England, 'Central Bank Digital Currency: opportunities, challenges and design' (12 March, 2020); and UK Statutory Instruments, 'The Health Protection (Coronavirus, Restrictions) (England) Regulations 2020 (26 March, 2020).

5. See Bank of England, 'Bank of England statement on Central Bank Digital Currency' (19 April, 2021).

how everyone will have access to this wonderful new advancement in digital technology, but rather how everyone is going to be forced to adopt it.

In June 2021, Tom Mutton, the Director of the Bank of England's Central Bank Digital Currency unit, addressed why we need another form of digital money to that already offered by the private sector.[6] One of the needs, apparently, is to avoid the risks presented by new forms of private money creation like Bitcoin. Another is improving the availability and usability of central bank money to all British citizens. Another is building a platform for better cross-border payments. Another is what he claimed is the greater efficiency of the Digital Pound when compared to the energy costs of Bitcoin, which the Agenda 2020-compliant G7 nations have said should be a core consideration in CDBC design. The rest were vague promises about meeting future payment needs in a digital economy and the apparently complete natural and not at all managed decline in the use of cash.

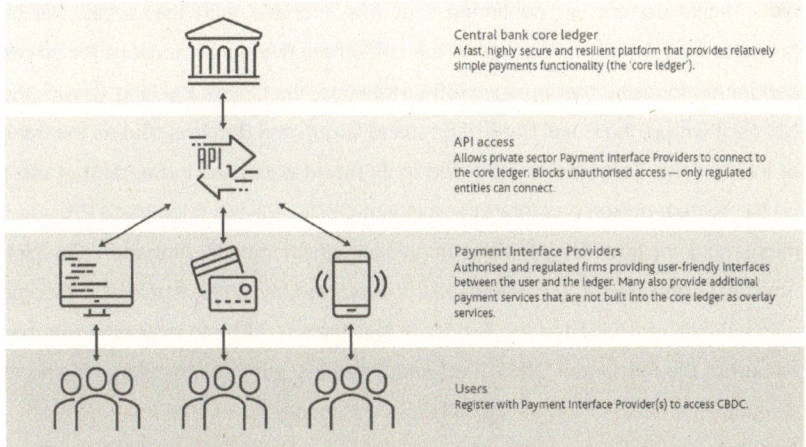

Source: Bank of England

Of more interest than his touting of these apparent benefits was his admission that CBDC 'could support wider public policy objectives', which is a new role for money. Germane to this new role as policy supporter is CBDC technology, which allows it to be 'programmable'. By this, Mutton means that

---

6. See Bank of England, 'Central Bank Digital Currency: An update on the Bank of England's work — speech by Tom Mutton' (17 June, 2021).

transactions using CBDC can occur (or not occur) automatically 'according to certain conditions, rules or events'. So how is this going to work? The proposed architecture of CBDC is that, at the top, 1) the Central Bank core ledger is accessed via 2) an Application Programming Interface (API) that regulates and authorises 3) private Payment Interface Providers (PIP), through which 4) registered users at the bottom can access Central Bank Digital Currency. Importantly, the API is different from a user interface, in that it connects computer programmes, not a computer to a person. It also hides the internal details of how a system works.

The Bank of England claims that it will not be able to programme our money or how we spend it. However, it adds that, if and when CBDC is introduced, the programmability features will be designed by the private sector companies providing the Payment Interface. Last July, the Deputy Governor of the Bank of England, Jon Cunliffe, who is overseeing the Bank of England's work on central bank digital currencies, confirmed that this inferface with the public will be provided by commercial banks.[7] In the UK, where five banks account for 90 per cent of all deposits, that means HSBC Holdings, the Lloyds Banking Group, the NatWest Group, the Royal Bank of Scotland Group and Barclays. But as the Bank of International Settlements indicated in its report published in September 2021 on the system design and interoperability of CBDC, Payment Interface Providers might also include 'Big Tech' companies, which means Alphabet (Google), Amazon, Apple, Meta and Microsoft.[8] Indeed, in May 2020, Apple and Google automatically downloaded an 'Exposure Notification' API into their smartphones as part of the misnamed 'NHS' Test and Trace programme they were helping to develop with £22.8 billion of British taxpayers' money.[9]

Passing the buck on what this will mean in practice, in June 2021 the Bank of England called on Government Ministers to decide whether CBDC should be 'programmable', and therefore giving the issuer control over how it is spent by the

---

7. See Reed Landberg, 'Bank of England Says Digital Punds Unlikely to Work Like Cash', *BNN Bloomberg* (6 July, 2022).

8. See Bank of International Settlements, 'Central bank digital currencies: system design and interoperability' (September 2021).

9. See Google, 'Exposure Notification API launches to support public health agencies' (20 May, 2020); and Department of Health and Social Care, 'Next phase of NHS coronavirus (COVID-19) app announced' (18 June, 2020).

recipient.[10] Mutton commented: 'There could be some socially beneficial outcomes from that, preventing activity which is seen to be socially harmful in some way; but at the same time it could be a restriction on people's freedoms.' Beyond a means to 'support' public policy objectives therefore, it appears CBDC will also be a means to 'prevent' actions of the public deemed to be harmful. As the last three-and-a-half years have demonstrated and the Online Safety Act has written into legislation, that includes questioning the Government on anything from the dangers of experimental gene therapies to the tenets of environmental fundamentalism. This is the context in which we should understand what a 'restriction' on our freedoms means. No wonder that an anonymous spokesman for the Treasury confirmed: 'Programmability is a potential feature of a Central Bank Digital Currency'. From what its designers and promoters have said, I'd say it was the primary feature.

Tom Mutton also highlighted that the problem of how users identify themselves — and in doing so ensure the 'inclusivity' of CBDC for every lucky citizen — would be solved by a system of Digital Identity. He framed this in terms of a 'trade-off' between the privacy of the users and the security of CBDC against financial crime. He admitted this will, regretfully but inevitably, entail sharing information about the identity of the users with the Payment Interface Providers, who would therefore be responsible for security and also for the privacy and uses of the user's personal data. We've already had numerous examples of where this leads — most famously demonstrated by the agreement between Facebook and the UK private intelligence company Cambridge Analytica — which is to the market sale of our private data by information technology companies to the highest bidder.[11]

It sounds very much, therefore, as if Central Bank Digital Currency cannot be implemented without Digital Identity, and that Digital Identity is being justified by, among other programmes, the joys and benefits of CBDC. It is not by chance that, in the same week the Government published its consultation on the Digital Pound,

10. See Tim Wallace, 'Bank of England tells ministers to intervene on digital currency "programming"', *The Telegraph* (21 June, 2021).

11. See Sascha Matuszak, 'Data Privacy and the Cambridge Analytica Scandal', *The Compliance and Ethics Blog* (27 March, 2018).

it also published its consultation on Digital Identity, neither of which actually asks the British public whether it wants either.[12]

As of September 2023, 130 currencies representing 98 per cent of global GDP are considering implementing CBDC.[13] It is being researched in 46 of them; in 33, including the UK, the USA, the European Union, Japan, Brazil, Canada, Indonesia and the Philippines, it is being developed; 21, including China, Japan, India, South Korea, Saudi Arabia, South Africa, Russia, Turkey, Australia, Belarus and the Ukraine, have a pilot scheme, and 11, including the Bahamas, Jamaica and Nigeria, have already launched it. In February 2023, the Bank of England and the Treasury together announced that a Central Bank Digital Currency will be launched in the UK this decade, and be operational by 2025 at the earliest.[14] Suggestively, it proposed limiting individual holdings of digital 'wallets' to between £10,000 and £20,000, with the former limit holding the existing balance, salary and bonuses of 75 per cent of the UK population, the latter limit 95 per cent.[15] This doesn't sound like a currency that will exist 'alongside' cash.

Finally, in the Consultation Paper jointly published by the Bank of England and the Treasury in February, and which stretches to over 100-pages, only one page mentions the question of 'programmability', where it states:

> We do not propose to develop a digital pound that enables government or central bank-initiated programmable money. . . . While it may be possible to program the digital pound so that it could only work in certain ways, this is not relevant to HM Treasury and the Bank's policy objectives for the digital pound.
>
> However, HM Treasury and the Bank would permit Payment Interface Providers and External Service Interface Providers to implement such functionalities themselves, but they would require user consent and not be at HM Treasury or the Bank's direction.[16]

---

12. See HM Treasury, 'The digital pound: A new form of money for households and businesses?' (7 February, 2023); and Department for Digital, Culture, Media and Sport, 'Digital identity and attributes consultation' (3 February, 2023).

13. See Atlantic Council, 'Central Bank Digital Currency Tracker' (2023).

14. See Bank of England, 'HM Treasury and Bank of England consider plans for a digital pound' (7 February, 2023).

15. See Bank of England, 'The digital pound — speech by Jon Cunliffe' (7 February, 2023).

16. Bank of England and HM Treasury, 'The digital pound: a new form of money for households and businesses? Consultation paper' (February 2023), p 76.

More about this is said in the Bank of England's accompanying Technology Working Paper, in which it proposes the use of 'smart contracts' that provide 'API access to locking mechanisms with configurable conditions on the core ledger'. This locking mechanism would require:

- earmarking funds with set conditions on when the funds can be released;
- programming the earmarked funds to only release the payment when a linked event has completed conditions under the contract or programmed rules.[17]

The way the Bank of England has presented the programmability function of CBDC to the British public is as a means to check and transfer funds to our Digital Pound balance, purchase goods with a smartphone, pay for services, order commodities online, and allocate funds to pay our rent, standing orders and other regular payments.[18] Ease and convenience. So, nothing to worry about then! The Bank of England and the Treasury won't programme its digital currency with rules, but the commercial banks and information technology companies providing the Payment Interface through which we use it can, including contracted conditions of use which, if not met, activate a locking mechanism between us and the core ledger of Central Bank Digital Currency. But only, apparently, if we want it. What could possibly go wrong?

2. Other Programmes of the Great Reset

With such assurances from the Bank of England and HM Treasury, what are the worries and fears about Central Bank Digital Currency, and should we listen to them? These can be summed up with the argument that CBDC is not being put forward in isolation but as part of a revolutionary change not only in the technologies of what is being called the Fourth Industrial Revolution but also in the programmes implementing them. It is only by looking at these programmes, therefore, that we can grasp the economic, political, social and, as we've seen,

---

17. Bank of England, 'The digital pound: Technology Working Paper' (February 2023), p. 75.

18. See Bank of England, 'The digital pound: We are looking at the case for issuing a digital pound. This type of money is known as a central bank digital currency (CBDC). It would not replace cash' (last updated 1 June, 2023).

environmental contexts in which CBDC is being developed, will be implemented and, eventually, become operative within the next five years or so.

It's unlikely, to put it mildly, that the huge work of building the technology for the Digital Pound on which the Bank of England has embarked will be rejected by HM Treasury when it's completed. How, then, are they going to implement it against the expected resistance? The simple answer is, in conjunction with the technologies and programmes of the Global Biosecurity State and the regulations and restrictions that enforce them. Implemented as mere upgrades to the infrastructure of the nation state, these will fundamentally and perhaps irreversibly change the social contract between the citizen and the state, and with it the ability of the ruled to scrutinise, influence or hold their rulers to account. Largely unknown to the general public, these include but are not limited to the following.

- Digital Identity holding our biometric data and monitoring our compliance with the constantly updated requirements to be injected as many times and with whatever the state tells us made a condition of access to the rights of citizenship.[19] This will include our freedom of movement and, under future manufactured 'crises', our freedom of association and assembly, and perhaps, if the fundamentalists have their way, our right to education, work, medical treatment and liberty. In October 2019, the World Bank proposed acting as a central repository of data relating to the good practices of countries implementing a system of Digital Identity, facilitating the transfer of information to interested parties and incentivising compliance with preferential loans and grants.[20] As I have said, Digital Identity is the gateway to the enforcement of all the other programmes of the Great Reset. Indeed, in May 2021 the *Financial Times* reported:

> What CBDC research and experimentation appears to be showing is that it will be nigh on impossible to issue such currencies outside of a comprehensive national digital ID management system. Meaning: CBDCs

---

19. See Central Digital & Data Office, 'Consultation on draft legislation to support identity verification' (23 May, 2023).

20. See World Bank Group, 'Practitioner's Guide' (October 2019).

will likely be tied to personal accounts that include personal data, credit history and other forms of relevant information.[21]

- Universal Basic Income for the millions of workers, primarily from white-collar jobs, made redundant by the new technologies, markets and programmes of the Fourth Industrial Revolution and the Great Reset of Western capitalism it has enabled.[22] It's not impossible that reception of UBI will eventually be made conditional on accepting a Radio Frequency Identification (RFID) chip implanted under the skin that would not only allow us to receive and make payments without a credit card or smartphone, but also for the state to track our movements and monitor and limit those payments. One might soberly reflect that no-one is going to give us 'free money' unless they have absolute control over how we spend it.

- A system of Social Credit modelled on that currently employed in the People's Republic of China, where both citizens and businesses are given a credit rating based on their compliance not only with the laws but also with the behavioural norms of the state.[23] Among other means suggested by the International Monetary Fund in August 2020, this credit rating will be established through access to our personal online browsing, search and purchase history, and the compliance of our businesses with criteria of production, consumption, sustainability, employment rights, trade partners, etc.[24]

- Facial Recognition technology, which the police in the UK have been using for some time already to Stop and Search members of the public without

---

21. See Izabella Kaminska, 'Why CBDCs will likely be ID-based', *Financial Times* (4 May, 2021).

22. See Francis Hobson and Aaron Kulakiewicz, 'Potential merits of a universal basic income', *House of Commons Library* (13 June, 2022); World Economic Forum, 'Our network is preparing humanity for the Fourth Industrial Revolution' (2023); and 'The Great Reset' (2023).

23. Drew Donnelly, 'China Social Credit System Explained — What is it & How Does it Work', NH Global Partners (6 April, 2023).

24. See Arnoud W. A. Boot, Peter Hoffmann, Luc Laeven and Lev Ratnovski, 'Financial Intermediation and Technology: What's Old, What's New?', *IMF Working Papers* (7 August, 2020).

cause in order to build up a data base of the population, and which will be used in conjunction with Digital Identity to identify citizens not compliant with the norms and regulations of the biosecurity state.[25] As we have had demonstrated over the last three-and-a-half years, these are not being made by our elected national governments but rather by unelected and unaccountable international technocracies overseeing global finance, expenditure, consumption, energy, health, agriculture, animal husbandry, education and, as we are seeing in the Ukraine, war.

- Smart Cities, in which our freedom of movement, assembly, association, access, business, consumption, ownership, privacy, expression and thought will be monitored, analysed and controlled by the Internet of Things by which we are increasingly surrounded.[26] Since at least 2018, the Trilateral Commission has promoted the use of Artificial Intelligence technology to analyse, monitor and shape our behaviour.[27] This is currently being implemented in the UK by local authorities enforcing the restrictions of 15-Minute Cities, an invention of the World Economic Forum that violate our Freedom of Movement under Protocol No. 4, Article 2 of the European Convention on Human Rights.[28] As the Mayor of London's Ultra-Low Emission Zone is demonstrating, these restrictions on what initially are the number of times we are allowed to leave our designated limits in a car will be monitored by a panopticon of surveillance equipment, with punishments starting at fines and extending, undoubtedly, to electric cars being 'switched off' and other punitive measures already in use in China's system of Social Credit — which includes being refused the use of even public transport.

---

25. See Home Office, 'Automated Facial Recognition: ethical and legal use' (25 October, 2021).

26. See Lydia Harriss and Philippa Kearney, 'Research Briefing: Smart Cities', *UK Parliament* (22 September, 2021); and Mark Walport, 'The Internet of Things: making the most of the Second Digital Revolution', *Government Office for Science* (December 2014).

27. See Trilateral Commission, 'Task Force Report on Artificial Intelligence: Draft for Discussion' (25 March, 2018).

28. See Dan Luscher, 'The 15-Minute City: Putting people at the center of urban transformation', *The 15-Minjute City Project* (2023); European Court of Human Rights, 'Guide on Article 2 of Protocol No. 4 to the European Convention on Human Rights: Freedom of movement' (updated 31 August, 2022).

The environmental fundamentalists who justify such restrictions 'because it's in a car' are the same as the COVID fundamentalists who justified lockdown, masks and mandatory gene therapy, and are equally blind to where it will lead. Once you accept that human rights are contingent on what the state declares is the 'common good', you're on the road to fascism. And as I've already said, if we think this only applies to cars and is being implemented to 'save the planet', London Underground is implementing 'Smart Stations' using AI technology to monitor, record, analyse and learn from our every movement and action.[29] It is short and rapid step from stopping someone from leaving a jurisdiction in a car, bus or train to stopping them leaving — or entering — without other technologies, like Digital Identity and even more intrusive biotechnology.

As an example of which, the Internet of Bodies by which we are connected to this system of surveillance, measurement, regulation and control includes, so far, pharmaceutical products carrying a microchip registering when they are and are not ingested to ensure 'compliance'; a quantum dot dye delivered with gene therapy that stores information about the injected person's medical history and biosecurity status; a microprocessor storing encrypted payment data implanted under the skin of our hand to allow contactless payments; a smartphone app that tracks our individual carbon footprint in order to monitor and restrict what and how much we consume; and a microchip implanted in our brain to augment the reality of the conditions to which we are being restricted.[30]

You've probably heard these being dismissed as 'right-wing conspiracy theories' in the mouths of snorting Members of Parliament and the propagandists for compliance in our media. But the microchipped tablet was announced by Albert Bourla, the CEO of Pfizer, at the World Economic Forum in January 2018; the quantum dot dye vaccine by researchers funded by the Bill & Melinda Gates Foundation at the Massachusetts Institute of Technology in December 2019; the skin implants by Walletmore, a Polish-British startup company, in October 2021; the carbon footprint tracker by the President of the Alibaba Group at the World Economic Forum's annual meeting in May 2022; and the brain implant by the Vice-President of Research and Design for imec, the nanoelectronics and digital

---

29. See London Underground, 'Smart Station Proof of Concept' (2022).

30. See Maria Gardner, 'The Internet of Bodies Will Change Everything, for Better or Worse', *Rand Corporation* (29 October, 2020).

technology company, on the website of the World Economic Forum in August 2022.[31] Indeed, when it comes to the technologies of our enslavement, our conspiracy theories have fallen well short of the digital, virtual and augmented reality being prepared for us by the enemies of humanity.

- The Pandemic Prevention, Preparedness and Response Treaty, launched by the World Health Organization in December 2021 and adopted by the European Council in March 2022.[32] As I will discuss in greater detail in the next chapter, under this treaty the 194 member-states of the World Health Organization will be legally bound to implement restrictions on human rights and freedoms, such as mandatory face masks, lockdowns, compulsory gene therapy, censorship of speech and opinion, a system of Digital Identity and worse, on the judgement of an international health technocracy that is funded by and subject to lobbying by the most powerful nations and international companies in the world, and in particular by its largest private funder, the Bill & Melinda Gates Foundation. According to the terms of this treaty, nation states will in principle concede their sovereignty to decide which restrictions the elected executive and legislature will impose on their populations. Crucially, once written into a legally-binding treaty, the efficacy or logic of these biosecurity 'measures' will no longer be open even to what little debate we've had in this country. Instead, the WHO will effectively become a global form of the UK's Scientific Advisory Group for Emergencies, a politically appointed technocracy to which the governments of nation states must defer if they wish to retain their status in the Global Biosecurity State, and which serves to depict undemocratic and unaccountable forms of governance as technical responses to new crises.

---

31. See World Health Organization, 'Transforming Health in the Fourth Industrial Revolution', *YouTube* (25 January, 2018); Anne Trafton, 'Storing medical information below the skin's surface', *MIT News* (18 December, 2019); Francis Bignell, 'Walletmor Introduces a Payment Implant Chip To Allow For Cardless Payments', *The Fintech Times* (11 October, 2021); Tim Hinchliffe, '"Individual carbon footprint tracker, stay tuned": Alibaba president at WEF 2022', *The Sociable* (25 May, 2022); and Kathleen Philips, 'Augmented tech can change the way we live, but only with the right support and vision', *World Economic Forum* (16 August, 2022).

32. See Patrick Butchard and Bukky Balogun, 'What is the proposed WHO Pandemic Preparedness Treaty?', *House of Commons Library* (2 June, 2023).

- Sustainable Development Goals, which were adopted by the United Nations in 2015 under the rubric of Agenda 2030.[33] As I discussed in the previous chapter, behind their humanitarian objectives these allocate the flow of global capital, investment and other preferential treatment to governments and corporations according to their compliance with Environmental, Social and Governance criteria. Despite their UN branding, these are formulated and imposed by the wealthiest and most powerful international corporate asset managers like BlackRock, the Vanguard Group and State Street Global Advisor.[34] And far from saving the planet from exploitation by multinational corporations, Sustainable Development Goals are designed to increase the monopoly of wealthy Western economies and international companies able to meet their criteria over poorer countries, and in doing so to create the framework for purchasing their UN-assigned quota of emissions in carbon credits.[35] On the same justification, developing countries are loaded with debt by financial organisations like the World Bank and the International Monetary Fund in order to meet these goals, and those unable to meet repayments through increased taxation and spending cuts to their already impoverished populations will be invited to hand over their land and natural resources to their debtors.[36]

- And finally, Central Bank Digital Currency, which employs blockchain technology to log every transaction we ever make and is programmable, as we have seen, with restrictions and limits on expenditure contingent on, for example, our biosecurity status, carbon footprint and social compliance. Could it, for example, be used to switch off access to digital money for those who violate the limits of their 15-Minute City? Or of those who fail to meet the World Health Organization's definition of 'fully vaccinated'? Or who fail to

---

33. See United Nations, 'Transforming our world: the 2030 Agenda for Sustainable Development', Department of Economic and Social Affairs.

34. See Gibson Dunn, 'BlackRock, Vanguard and State Street Update Corporate Governance and ESG Policies and Priorities for 2022' (25 January, 2022).

35. See Jason Hickel, 'The World's Sustainable Development Goals Aren't Sustainable', *Foreign Policy* (30 September, 2020).

36. See Iain Davis and Whitney Webb, 'Sustainable Debt Slavery', *Unlimited Hangout* (13 September, 2022).

upgrade their car to an electric vehicle, neglect to recycle their rubbish, eat more than their allotted quota of meat and dairy products, or leave their heating on beyond the allotted times? Of those the state describes as a threat to the 'common good' for daring to criticise their government, or indeed the central banks? When our salaries and our savings are in CBDC, it will no longer be necessary to evoke Emergency Powers, as the Government of Justin Trudeau did in February 2022, to freeze the bank accounts of the non-compliant without a court order.[37]

In effect, CBDC will become a form of geo-fencing, but instead of receiving an electric shock in our ear for transgressing beyond the limits of our 15-minute grazing range, we will have our access to the necessities of life removed, including work, healthcare, energy or food from animals or crops that haven't been genetically modified.[38] The question I am trying to formulate is whether — given the contexts in which it will be implemented and the demonstrated willingness of the governments of the West to lockdown, spy on, control the movements of and punish their citizens for the 'common good' — CBDC is likely to be so programmed. It clearly can be. These contexts, I would suggest, make it more than likely that it will be, and, indeed, that this programming is the primary but undeclared purpose of Central Bank Digital Currency.

3. Towards Absolute Control

As I mentioned above, the Bank of England has said that it is working with the Bank for International Settlements, the central bank for its membership of 63 central banks that account for about 95 per cent of world GDP, and which include the Bank of England, the European Central Bank, the Bank of Japan, the People's Bank of China and the US Federal Reserve System. Its General Manager, Agustín Carstens, the primary advocate for the adoption of CBDC by its members, in

---

37. See Government of Canada, 'February 14, 2022 Declaration of Public Order Emergency' (14 February, 2022); Chrystia Freeland, 'Full text of Chrystia Freeland's remarks during Emergencies Act announcement', *Toronto Star* (14 February, 2022).

38. See Teltonika, 'Geofence Solution in the Event of a Pandemic' (2023).

December 2020 made this by now famous statement about the 'general use' of Central Bank Digital Currency.[39]

> We tend to establish equivalence with cash, and there is a huge difference there. With cash, we don't know who is using a $100 bill today. A key difference with CBDC is that central banks will have absolute control over the rules and regulations that will determine the use of that expression of central bank liability. And also, we will have the technology to enforce that. Those two issues are extremely important, and that makes a huge difference with respect to what cash is.[40]

What appears certain is that CBDC will allow Central Banks to act like commercial banks in providing loans to both private- and public-sector lenders. This is what happened following the second Global Financial Crisis in twelve years that started with the spike in interest rates in the repurchase agreement market in September 2019, three months before anyone had heard of COVID-19, and six months before lockdown was imposed across Western economies.[41] On the suggestion of BlackRock, the largest asset manager in the world with $10 trillion in assets under management, the US Federal Reserve injected hundreds of billions of dollars into the financial system, effectively providing zero-interest loans to JP Morgan, Goldman Sachs, Barclays, Deutsche Bank, the Bank of America and other favoured commercial banks.[42] By July 2020, the cumulative value of these loans was $11.23 trillion.

---

39. See Agustín Carstens, 'Digital currencies and the soul of money', Bank of International Settlements (18 January, 2022).

40. See Agustín Carstens, 'Bank for International Settlements head Augustin Carstens about CBDC and control', *YouTube* (1 January, 2021).

41. See Simon Elmer, 'Fascism and the Decay of Capitalism', *The Road to Fascism*, pp. 61-80; Emily Barrett and Jesse Hamilton, 'Why the U.S. Repo Market Blew Up and How to Fix It', *Bloomberg* (6 January, 2020).

42. See BlackRock Investment Institute, 'Dealing with the next downturn: From unconventional monetary policy to unprecedented policy coordination' (August 2019); Ellen Brown, 'Another Bank Bailout Under Cover of a Virus', *The Web of Debt Blog* (18 May, 2020); Board of Governors of the Federal Reserve System, 'Federal Reserve Actions to Support the Flow of Credit to Households and Businesses' (15 March, 2020).

As a result of this vast quantitative easing programme, which was adopted around the world on the justification of sustaining national economies under lockdown, by April 2022 the total assets of the US Federal Reserve (which had reached $8.9 trillion), the European Central Bank ($9.6 trillion), the Bank of Japan ($6.2 trillion) and the People's Bank of China ($6.3 trillion) had risen to $31 trillion, an extraordinary and unprecedented increase from $19 trillion in September 2019.[43] And although this has fallen to $26.8 trillion in September 2023, across the globe over $40.76 trillion in assets, nearly half the world's GDP, are now held by central banks.[44] With this increase in assets comes a corresponding increase in the liabilities over whose rules and regulations Agustín Carstens wants 'absolute control'. Liability, or what a bank owes to others, includes the total amount of currency in circulation, the reserves in commercial banks, mortgage-backed securities and equity capital, and with it the risks to the real and financial sectors of the economy.

We should remember that, when we think we are depositing our money into a bank, we are, under law, doing nothing of the sort. As explained by Richard Werner, the economist who invented the monetary policy of quantitative easing for the Bank of Japan in 1995, what we do when we think we deposit our money in a bank is make a loan to the bank, which borrows from the public.[45] And equally, when we think we take out a loan from a bank, in reality the bank purchases a security — which is to say, a promissory note — which is issued by us to the bank. But no money is transferred to our account. What we call a deposit is merely a record the bank makes of its debt to the public. And what we think we are receiving as money from a loan is merely the bank's record of what it owes us. Banks, despite their protestations to the contrary, are not intermediaries between depositors and lenders; they are magicians that magic money into existence with a sleight of hand. Having purchased our promissory note, they record what is an

---

43. See Edward Yardeni and Mali Quintana, 'Central Banks: Monthly Balance Sheets', *Yardeni Research, Inc.*

44. See 'Top 100 Largest Central Bank Rankings by Total Assets', *SWF Institute*; and Alexandra Dimitropoulou, 'Economy Rankings: Largest countries by GDP, 2022', *CEO World Magazine* (31 March, 2022).

45. See Richard Werner, *Princes of the Yen: Japan's Central Bankers and the Transformation of the Economy* (Routledge, 2003); and RT News, 'Prof. Werner brilliantly explains how the banking system and financial sector really work', *YouTube* (9 March, 2017).

accounts payable liability arising from the loan contract as a customer 'deposit'; but no money has been deposited. When banks lend, they create money out of nothing by inventing fictitious claims on themselves.

As long as bank credit — which is to say, the creation of money — is for investment and loans for new goods, services and technologies that add value to the economy, it creates stable economic growth without inflation, generating the sustainable income streams to repay the loans. However, when money is created to increase consumption, inflation rises, which is what is happening across the world as the vast sums of magic money printed to shore up the collapsing financial sector have entered into the real economy. Worse still, when money is created for financial transactions — which make up over 70 per cent of all lending in the UK — banks, rather than adding value to the economy, create new purchasing power over existing assets, whose prices are thereby pushed up: land prices, oil prices, housing prices, as we've seen over the past two decades, and as we're experiencing now, energy prices. This creates, on the one hand, greater and greater inequality and, on the other, credit bubbles as commercial banks increase the number and size of loans. Then the bubble bursts. One of the purposes of CBDC is to ensure that small, independent banks, with the power to make money, don't start lending money to small and medium-sized businesses to create new goods and services, thereby reducing inequality and increasing our independence from both the state for investment and the financial sector for credit.

When Central Bank Digital Currency has been implemented and doesn't 'exist alongside' cash — as the Bank of England assures us — but has instead replaced it — as seems far more likely — what we think of now as 'our' money will instead be, as Agustín Carstens very precisely phrased it, an 'expression' of Central Bank liability. What this means — what it could mean, what it appears likely to mean, what the wider contexts in which CBDC is being implemented overwhelmingly indicates that it does mean — is that if the Central Bank doesn't approve of how we are expressing its liability, it will have what Carstens boasted are the 'rules', the 'regulations' and the 'technology' to limit and control where, when and on what we can spend their money, up to an including the point of us having none to spend.

As the Bank of England and HM Treasury have specified, the private Payment Interface Provider — which is to say, the most powerful commercial banks and information technology companies — will have the technology to programme conditions into CBDC that will activate a locking mechanism when they are not met or violated. And since these private providers are operating under the Environmental, Social and corporate Governance criteria imposed by BlackRock, Morgan Stanley, JP Morgan and other corporate asset managers in furtherance of the UN's Sustainable Development Goals and the signed commitment of the governments of the West to Agenda 2030, they will be obliged — doubtless with a show of protest — to programme CBDC with the limits and requirements on expenditure and consumption that meet these goals and this agenda. The key point is, this will no longer be our money but instead an expression of Central Bank liability. The Bank of England is liable for how, when and on what we spend its digital currency, and it is the central banks and other stakeholders that compose the new global technocracy that will determine the rules and regulations by which we spend it.[46] Programmable CBDC is the technology.

Since its founding in 1694, the Bank of England has made it clear that money in the UK is a promissory note, with the terms written on the paper notes we call cash: 'I promise to pay the bearer on demand the sum of X pounds', signed by the Chief Cashier 'for the Governor and Company of the Bank of England'. When cash has been withdrawn as a form of currency and there is no longer anything for us to 'bear' in our wallets and one day, perhaps, even in our private bank accounts, that promise to pay will lie within the purview and liability of the central bank, and what we now call money will be reduced to the expression of its largesse. That, I believe, is what Agustín Carstens means by 'absolute control'.

Even for the overwhelming mass of the UK population that does exactly as it is told, including injecting experimental gene therapies into its own arms and those of its children, remaining within the boundaries of its 15-Minute Cities, consuming its allotted share of insects, and taking, without question or complaint, what it is given, CBDC will keep it poor and compliant. 'You'll own nothing. And you'll be happy', as the World Economic Forum has been telling us for many years now, or we will, ultimately, be deprived of the necessities of living. Central Bank Digital Currency is part of the infrastructure for a tokenised economy: currency not as a means of exchange but as reward for compliance. This is what Tom Mutton

---

46. See World Economic Forum, 'Measuring Stakeholder Capitalism: Towards Common Metrics and Consistent Reporting of Sustainable Value Creation' (2023).

intimated when he said that the Digital Pound 'can support wider public policy objectives' and prevent 'activity which is seen to be socially harmful'. Under these terms, CBDC will be an automated form of governance enforced outside of any legislative or juridical mediation. Comply or starve. This is a system of totalitarian control the like of which the world has never seen before, and it is being implemented now.

And once implemented, short of a revolutionary overthrow of the Global Biosecurity State it will be very, very difficult to reverse. Indeed, in the written evidence submitted to the UK Parliament in September 2022, the Digital Pound Foundation, whose board members have numerous links individually or through partner companies to the World Economic Forum, wrote: 'The introduction of new forms of digital money — whether public or private in form — is irreversible.'[47] I, for one, believe them. As does Richard Werner, who understands CBDC far better than I ever will, and who is unequivocal about its purpose. At a conference held by the Monetary Institute in Switzerland back in February 2018, he described the bid for Central Bank Digital Currency to achieve 'total control over all economic transactions' as 'the greatest concentration of central banking power in history', the aim of which is 'an Orwellian dystopia of total control over people and the end of any freedoms'.[48]

Was he right? Well, in Nigeria, the only large country to have implemented CBDC, the results have been disastrous. As Nick Corbishley, who has been following its implementation closely, has reported: out of a population of nearly 220 million people, only 905,000, 0.4 per cent, have downloaded a digital wallet, and a mere 282,600 accounts are active.[49] In response, the Government has issued repeatedly deferred deadlines for the withdrawal of cash from circulation.[50] As a result, some 80 per cent of the $7.2 billion previously held in private hands has been deposited with financial institutions, and a limit of around $225.00/per

---

47. See UK Parliament committees, 'Written evidence submitted by the Digital Pound Foundation' (September 2022).

48. See Monetary Institute, 'Richard Werner: Today's Source of Money Creation', *YouTube* (23 April, 2018).

49. See Nick Corbishley, 'This Was Another Big Week for Central Bank Digital Currency (CBDCs)', *Naked Capitalism* (10 February, 2023).

50. See 'Central Bank of Nigeria Delays Demonetization by 10 Days', *PYMNTS* (30 January, 2023).

week has been imposed on cash withdrawals for individuals, five times that for businesses, leaving the population with an acute shortage of money and businesses unable to trade.[51] Further reductions have been threatened. Unlike the Bank of England, the Central Bank of Nigeria has been open in its declarations that the motivation for these monetary restrictions is the drive towards a 'cashless economy'.[52]

4. The Masters of the World

I'll end with a question. The ten largest national economies in the world by Gross Domestic Product are the USA, China, Japan, Germany, the UK, India, France, Russia, Italy and Brazil.[53] Between them, these countries produce a Gross Domestic Product of $67 trillion, more than two-thirds of global GDP. As of October 2023, however, their collective debt is $81.5 trillion, a public debt to GDP ratio of 121 per cent. The odd one out in this list is Russia, with $428 billion of debt, about an eighth of that of Germany, the UK, India, France and Italy. In comparison, the USA has a national debt of over $33 trillion — 77 times that of Russia — giving it a public debt to GDP ratio of 92.5 per cent. This has risen from 63 per cent in 2007, the year when the last Global Financial Crisis began; from 55 per cent in 2001, the year the US created the 'Security State' under the cloak of the so-called 'War on Terror'; and from 31 per cent in 1981, the year Ronald Reagan was elected President and began to impose the monetary and fiscal policies of neoliberal capitalism not only on the USA but on the rest of the world too.[54] The US external debt to GDP ratio — that is, the debt owed by the US Government not to the US public but to other countries, which increases the risk of defaulting on repayments and decreases economic growth — is 89.54 per cent. In comparison, the external debt to GDP ratio of Russia is just 26.69 per cent, and of China just 17.88 per cent. In the UK, the ratio is 301.4 per cent, which is among

---

51. See Nick Corbishley, 'The Central Bank of Nigeria Just Gave a Whole New Meaning to the Term "Financial Repression"', *Naked Capitalism* (9 December, 2022); AFP in Lagos, 'Riots erupt in Nigerian cities as bank policy leads to scarcity of cash', *The Guardian* (15 February, 2023).

52. See Godwin I. Emefiele, Governor, Central Bank of Nigeria, 'Press Remarks on Issuance of New Naira Banknotes' (26 October, 2022).

53. See USDebtClock.org.

54. See Fiscal Data Treasury, 'What is the national debt?'.

the highest in the world. This is only one measure of the financial crisis Western capitalism is facing.

In June 2023, when US Government was facing defaulting on its repayments, an economic recession, the loss of up to 6 million jobs and raised interest rates, Congress, the legislature of the Federal Government of the United States of America, suspended the ceiling on its debt limit for issuing bonds until January 2025.[55] But with 58 per cent of the world's foreign currency held in US dollars, the debt to GDP ratio predicted to reach 118.4 per cent by 2025, and the US credit rating downgraded this August, will investors keep buying government bonds? In January, the US Treasury Secretary, Janet Yellen, called on Congress to raise the debt ceiling with an appeal not only to their patriotism but also to their faith. 'I respectfully urge Congress to act promptly to protect the full faith and credit of the United States.'[56] It is significant that in one sentence this brings together the meanings of the word 'credit', which derives from the Latin *credere*, meaning to trust, to believe, to have faith in.[57] But after 50 years and more of finance capitalism being the dominant faith in Western nations, complete with its dogma of 'Modern Monetary Theory' and the belief that fiat economies can simply print their way out of debt, nobody who isn't lying to themselves or others believes that creating money to defer repayments on interest rates and government bonds is infinitely sustainable; no-one has faith in an economy built not on the production of goods to meet human needs but on the buying, trading and selling of currencies, bonds, stocks, futures and other derivatives; and with debt outstripping GDP in every Western country, nobody trusts Western capitalism to dig itself out of a Global Financial Crisis that, when it finally breaks and crashes over us, will dwarf that of 2007-2008.

So, how have the leaders of the West responded to this crisis of faith? In January 2023, the ideologues and architects of stakeholder capitalism gathered at the World Economic Forum in Davos, Switzerland, where, on the justification of

---

55. See Tim Smith, 'U.S. Debt Ceiling: Definition, History, Pros, Cons, and Clashes', *Investopedia* (updated 28 September, 2023).

56. See U.S. Department of the Treasury, 'Secretary of the Treasury Janet L. Yellen Sends Letter to Congressional Leadership on the Debt Limit' (13 January, 2023).

57. See Giorgio Agamben, 'Capitalism as Religion', in *Creation and Anarchy: The Work of Art and the Religion of Capitalism*; translated by Adam Kotsko (Stanford University Press, 2019), pp. 66-78.

responding to numerous manufactured 'crises' whose causes and effects they took great pleasure in describing — all, of course, except the financial one — they elected themselves to form an openly technocratic, authoritarian, World Government.[58] I mentioned some of these in the previous chapter, but the threats of the powerful are always worth repeating, for we ignore them at our peril. Here are some of the things they said.

- Ursula von der Leyen, the President of the unelected European Commission and Agenda Contributor to the World Economic Forum who in October 2022 threatened the electorate of Italy that, if they didn't vote for the Commission's preferred candidate, it had the tools to cut off EU funding to Italy.[59] Declaring that we are facing the 'greatest industrial transformation of our times and maybe of any times', she predicted that 'those who develop and manufacture the technology that will be the foundation of tomorrow's economy will have the greatest competitive edge'.[60]

- Albert Bourla, the Chief Executive Officer of Pfizer, the largest pharmaceutical company in the world by revenue in 2022 and himself a long-standing Agenda Contributor to the World Economic Forum, announced that messenger RNA gene therapies sold and mandated as 'vaccines' for both COVID-19 and seasonal influenza combined will be sold to the governments of the world later this year.[61]

- Tony Blair, the former Prime Minister of the UK, unconvicted war criminal and another Agenda Contributor to the World Economic Forum who is one of those tipped to succeed the ageing Schwab as Director, said they should be 'helping' countries to develop a 'national digital infrastructure' for their healthcare systems, which they will need because of these gene therapies.[62]

---

58. See World Economic Forum, 'World Economic Forum Annual Meeting', (16-20 January, 2023).

59. See Wilhelmine Preussen, 'Von der Leyen's warning message to Italy irks election candidates', *Politico* (23 September, 2022).

60. See Sky News, 'European Commission President Ursula von der Leyen speaks at the World Economic Forum in Davos', *YouTube* (17 January, 2023).

61. See Bloomberg Television, 'Pfizer CEO on Vaccine Developments', *YouTube* (18 January, 2023).

62. See Larry Elliott, 'Mutiny erupts among WEF staff over role of "Mr. Davos"', *The Guardian* (18 January, 2023).

He added that this digital infrastructure would have 'an impact beyond any particular disease or pandemic'.[63]

- Satya Nadella, the CEO of Microsoft and another Agenda Contributor to the World Economic Forum, said Bill Gates' former company, which since 2007 has handed the private data of UK citizens to the US National Security Agency, is producing software that, through what he calls 'carbon accounting', allows banks to measure the carbon footprint of small businesses before granting them loans.[64]

- Jim Hagemann Snabe, the Chairman of Siemens AG, the largest industrial manufacturing company in Europe, and a Member of the Board of Trustees of the World Economic Forum, called not for a reduction in production or the bribery and price fixing for which the company has been fined $832 million since 2000, but for 'a billion people to stop eating meat'.[65]

- Patricia Poppe, the Chief Executive Officer of the Pacific Gas and Electricity Corporation that filed for bankruptcy in response to its liability for the California wildfires that, in 2017 and 2018, caused over $40 billion of damage, destroyed over 33,000 buildings and killed 124 people, said that, in order to transition to an electric grid, an automated system will be able to turn off supply to 'smart devices, wi-fi and electric vehicles'.[66] She added that those who had invested in electric cars should get its 'full value' by giving its power 'back to the grid'.[67]

- Bastien Girod, a Green Party Member of the Swiss National Council and corporate sustainability advisor to the South Pole Group, a Swiss carbon finance consultancy, said that governments should only buy from companies compliant with the Sustainable Development Goals of Agenda 2030, and that

---

63. See World Economic Forum, '100 Days to Outrace the Next Pandemic | Davos 2023', *YouTube* (21 January, 2023).

64. See Kadhim Shubber, 'A simple guide to the Prism controversy', *Wired* (10 June, 2013); World Economic Forum, 'A Conversation with Satya Nadella, CEO of Microsoft', *YouTube* (19 January, 2023).

65. See Good Jobs First, 'Violation Tracker Current Parent Company Summary: Siemens'; the recording of Snabe's speech at the WEF annual meeting has been removed by *YouTube*.

66. See Rebecca Falconer, 'PG&E bankruptcy judge sides with fire victims in liability challenge', *Axios* (28 November, 2019).

67. See World Economic Forum, 'Mastering New Energy Economics | Davos 2023', *YouTube* (17 January, 2023).

we should 'build environments' in which people not only cannot but do not want to use cars. He called this 'living in harmony with nature'.[68]

- Christopher Wray, the Director of the US Federal Bureau of Investigation that in 2022 was found to have searched the emails, texts and other electronic communications of 3.4 million US citizens without warrants, boasted that the 'collaboration between the private sector and the Government, and especially the FBI' had made 'significant strides' in the new technologies, particularly in Artificial Intelligence, in which he saw 'great opportunities but great dangers' in what he called 'the wrong hands'.[69] By this he meant both Russia and China, which he called 'the bad guys'.[70]

Finally, at the World Government Summit held in Dubai in February of this year, Klaus Schwab, the Founder and Executive Chairman of the World Economic Forum which for decades has worked to replace the sovereignty of the nation state and governance of the people by our democratically elected representatives with the rule of an unelected technocracy in a global political economy he calls stakeholder capitalism, declared that those who master the new technologies of the Fourth Industrial Revolution will be 'the masters of the world'.[71]

So, the question we should be asking ourselves is: what do we think this new master-race founding another thousand-year World Government will do with Central Bank Digital Currency?

---

68. See Nativa Economics, 'Open forum: In Harmony with Nature, WEF23 Davos', *YouTube* (17 January, 2023).

69. See Chris Strohm, 'FBI Searched Data of Millions of Americans Without Warrants', *Bloomberg* (29 April, 2022).

70. See 'World Economic Forum Discussion on Technology and National Security', *C-Span* (19 January, 2023).

71. See Harris Gleckman, 'How the United Nations is quietly being turned into a public-private partnership', *Open Democracy* (2 July, 2019); World Economic Forum, 'Measuring Stakeholder Capitalism: Towards Common Metrics and Consistent Reporting of Sustainable Value Creation'; and World Government Summit, 'The State of the World', *YouTube* (15 February, 2023).

4. The World Health Organization's Pandemic Treaty

The World Health Organization is the One Ring to Rule them All, and its written goal, inscribed in fiery letters along both sides of its gold band, is the Pandemic Prevention, Preparedness and Response Treaty. Fashioned by the Dark Lord of the Twenty-first Century, the United States of America, in its own iteration of Mount Doom, it only appears to yield US sovereignty to an external organisation. In reality and practice, the Treaty will give Washington increased power over the G20 nations — the subordinated holders of the other 'rings' — and through them the rest of the Western World: not only its people but also its animals, its eco-systems, its resources. This, and not the health of the globe, is its dark purpose.

1. The Civil War

The World Health Organization, which since January 2020 has received $817 million in grants from the Bill & Melinda Gates Foundation, is a corporate-funded and lobbied agency of the United Nations without legal jurisdiction over the populations of its 194 member-states — to which it acts, at least in principle, in an advisory role.[1] But that's going to change soon.

On 3 March 2022, as lockdown regulations were revoked across Europe and NATO declared its proxy war on Russia, the European Council adopted a decision to authorise the opening of negotiations for an international Treaty on Pandemic Prevention, Preparedness and Response.[2] Under the terms of this Treaty, the member-states of the World Health Organization will be legally bound to implement restrictions on human rights and freedoms — such as further

---

1. See Bill and Melinda Gates Foundation, 'Committed Grants: World Health Organization'; Katheryn N. Russ, Phillip Baker, Manho Kang and David McCoy, 'Corporate Lobbying on US Positions Toward the World Health Organization: Evidence of Intensification and Cross-Industry Coordination', *Science Digest* (19 May, 2022).

2. See European Council, 'An international agreement on pandemic prevention and preparedness' (last reviewed 6 June, 2023); World Health Organization, 'World Health Assembly agrees to launch process to develop historic global accord on pandemic prevention, preparedness and response' (1 December, 2021).

lockdowns, mandatory face masking, compulsory gene therapy, a system of Digital Identity and programmes of surveillance and censorship — all on the judgement of the WHO.

The basis of this agreement is Article 19 of the Constitution of the World Health Organization, which states that the General Assembly of the WHO can adopt agreements that, if passed by a two-thirds majority, are binding on all member states. Under these agreements, nation states, including the UK and the 193 other members of the WHO, will in principle concede their sovereignty to decide which restrictions the elected executive and legislature of those nations will impose on their populations.

Crucially, once written into a legally-binding treaty, the efficacy or logic of these so-called 'measures' — none of which have been used before January 2020 as responses to viral pandemics, all of which have been shown to be ineffective and many times more dangerous than the virus itself — will no longer be open to debate.[3] Instead, the World Health Organization will effectively become a global form of the UK's Scientific Advisory Group for Emergencies; that is to say, a transnational technocracy to which the governments of nation states can defer when they choose to, and which serves to depict undemocratic forms of governance as technical responses to new crises.[4]

Like the World Economic Forum with which it entered into partnership on 11 March 2020 — the same day the World Health Organization declared the 'pandemic' — this unelected and unaccountable international technocracy is the new paradigm of governance to have emerged from under the cloak of the manufactured coronavirus 'crisis', and its globalist intentions become more apparent every day.[5] Behind the facade of democracy represented by our national governments, there is the rule of an increasingly authoritarian international technocracy, of which the United Nations and the European Commission are the

---

3. See Simon Elmer, 'Lockdown: Collateral Damage in the War on COVID-19' (2 June, 2020); collected in *Virtue and Terror*, pp. 97-145.

4. See Simon Elmer, 'Betrayal of the Clerks: UK Intellectuals in the Service of the Biosecurity State', *Architects for Social Housing* (12 November, 2020).

5. See World Economic Forum, 'World Economic Forum launches COVID-19 Action Platform to fight coronavirus' (11 March, 2020); and World Health Organization, 'WHO Director-General's opening remarks at the media briefing on COVID-19' (11 March, 2020).

models inherited from the past, and the World Health Organization and the World Economic Forum are those of the present.

The UK Government and Parliament is ready to sign up to the World Health Organization's resolution on Pandemic Prevention, Preparedness and Response, for which more than 70 member-states, including the European Union and the UK, have advocated a strong and legally-binding international Treaty.[6] It appears that, when it serves to expand and increase its power over the national population, the UK Government that was elected to an 80-seat majority on the back of the Brexit referendum is more than willing to cede UK sovereignty to global and technocratic forms of governance intent on reducing us to a neo-feudal form of capitalism.

In practice, however, rather than relieving nation states of their sovereignty, this Treaty will allow national governments to justify and excuse the devastating consequences of lockdown restrictions, masking mandates, gene therapies and other biosecurity programmes as the technical decisions of an international health technocracy to which it is obligated by international law. When it is adopted, therefore, the Pandemic Prevention, Preparedness and Response Treaty will depoliticise and remove from either parliamentary or juridical contestation our governance by the Global Biosecurity State.

Behind its woke principles of equity, inclusivity and a paternal state, 'No one is safe until everyone is safe' — the slogan that first entered public discourse in February 2021 and was quickly adopted by the G7, the United Nations, the World Health Organization, the European Union, GAVI and an ever-increasing number of Western governments, including the UK, Germany, France, Spain, Portugal, the Netherlands, Norway, Greece, Serbia, the Ukraine and the USA — is as perfect an expression of the totalitarian aspirations of the Global Biosecurity State as *'Ein Volk, ein Reich, ein Führer'* was of the Third Reich.[7]

The adoption of this Treaty by every Western government, without a referendum, parliamentary vote, public debate or mention in the media, demonstrates that the facade of democracy these governments struggled to

---

6. See Patrick Butchard and Bukky Balogun, 'What is the proposed WHO Pandemic Preparedness Treaty?', *How of Commons Library* (2 June, 2023); and Luke Taylor, 'World Health Organization to begin negotiating international pandemic treaty', *British Medical Journal* (2 December, 2021).

7. See Robert Hart, '"Nobody Is Safe Until Everyone Is Safe": World Leaders Call For Global Pandemic Preparedness Treaty', *Forbes* (30 March, 2021).

maintain over two years of lockdown and 'vaccine' mandates has now been torn down, and we are now, in effect, at war. And like every war waged by the West since 1945, it was started by the USA. What makes this one different and new is that it is being waged not only against nations not yet brought within the West's axis of forced compliance — Russia, China, Iran, etc. — but primarily against the civilian populations of the West itself. It is, therefore, as the text of the Treaty makes clear, a civil war, waged by governments and the apparatuses of the state against their own people — against us.

The weapons of this war — for which the West's proxy-war in the Ukraine is the continuation and justification — aren't tanks and long-range missiles but Digital Identity, Central Bank Digital Currency and Gene Therapy. Its alliances are Agenda 2030 and the Pandemic Prevention, Preparedness and Response Treaty. Its campaigns are lockdowns and 15-Minute Cities. It's battle-cries are 'sustainability', 'diversity', 'inclusivity', 'equity' and 'biosecurity'. And its peace terms, as we shall see, are the complete surrender of the rights and freedoms of the populations of the West to the programmes of our enslavement. You don't believe me? Then read on.

2. Obligations of the Treaty

Under the World Health Organization's Pandemic Prevention, Preparedness and Response Treaty, the first draft of which was published on 1 February, 2023, 194 member-states will allocate 5 per cent of their health budgets and an as-yet-unspecified percentage of their Gross Domestic Product to implementing its Articles.[8] This will, potentially, give the WHO control over a bigger budget than that of the US Department of Defence, and to similar ends. The terms of the Treaty are so outrageous — even in this age of outrage — that I can do no better than quote key passages from the draft of the Articles to which Parties to the Treaty will be legally bound, and which are the fullest realisation so far of that incorporation of the judicial institution into the apparatuses of biopower I discussed in the preface to this book. Extracts are indented, *italics* of words and phrases to which I refer in my subsequent commentary, are mine.

---

8. See World Health Organization, 'Zero draft of the WHO CA+ for the consideration of the Intergovernmental Negotiating Body at its fourth meeting' (1 February, 2023).

Article 4. Human Rights

2.   **The right to health** — The enjoyment of the highest attainable standard of health, defined as *a state of complete physical, mental and social well-being*, is one of the *fundamental rights* of every human being without distinction of age, race, religion, *political belief, economic or social condition*.

3.   **Sovereignty** — States have, in accordance with the Charter of the United Nations and the principles of international law, the sovereign right to determine and manage their approach to public health, notably pandemic prevention, preparedness, response and recovery of health systems, pursuant to their own policies and legislation, *provided that activities within their jurisdiction or control do not cause damage to their peoples and other countries*.

Article 5. Scope

The WHO CA+ [convention, agreement or other international instrument on pandemic prevention, preparedness and response] applies to pandemic prevention, preparedness, response and health systems recovery at *national, regional and international* levels.

Article 7. Access to technology

3.   During *inter-pandemic times*, all Parties shall:

(a) coordinate, collaborate, facilitate and incentivize manufacturers of *pandemic- related products* to transfer *relevant technology* and know-how to capable manufacturers . . . including through product development partnerships.

(c) encourage entities, including manufacturers within their respective jurisdictions, that conduct research and development of pre-pandemic and pandemic-related products, in particular those that receive *significant public funding* for that purpose.

73

Article 8. Regulatory strengthening

2.   Each Party shall build and strengthen its *regulatory* capacities and performance for timely approval of pandemic-related products and, in the event of a pandemic, *accelerate the process of approving and licensing* pandemic-related products for *emergency use.*

Article 9. Increasing research and development

5.   The Parties shall establish, no later than XX (*sic),* with reference to existing models, a global compensation mechanism for *injuries resulting from pandemic vaccines.*

Article 10. WHO Pathogen Access and Benefit-Sharing System

Fair and equitable benefit-sharing

(h) Such options shall include, but not be limited to: (i) real-time access by WHO to *20% of the production of* safe, efficacious and effective *pandemic-related products*, including diagnostics, vaccines (*sic*), personal protective equipment and therapeutics, to enable equitable distribution, in particular to developing countries, according to public health risk and need and national plans that identify priority populations. The pandemic-related products shall be provided to WHO on the following basis: *10% as a donation and 10% at affordable prices* to WHO; (ii) commitments by the countries where manufacturing facilities are located that they will *facilitate the shipment to WHO* of these pandemic-related products by the manufacturers within their jurisdiction, according to schedules to be agreed between WHO and manufacturers.

Article 11. Strengthening and sustaining preparedness

4.   Each Party shall, in accordance with international law, adopt *policies and strategies*, supported by implementation plans, across the *public and private*

sectors and relevant agencies . . . and strengthen and reinforce public health functions for:

(c) *surveillance;*

(h) creating and maintaining up-to-date, universal *platforms and technologies* for forecasting and timely *information sharing*, through appropriate capacities, including building *digital health and data science capacities*.

Article 14. Protection of human rights

2.   Towards this end, each Party shall:

(a) *incorporate into its laws and policies* human rights protections during public health emergencies, including, but not limited to, requirements that any limitations on human rights are aligned with international law, including ensuring that: (i) any restrictions are necessary to achieve the public health goal and the least restrictive necessary to protect the health of people.

Article 15. Global coordination, collaboration and cooperation

1.   The Parties recognize the need to coordinate, collaborate and cooperate . . . with competent *international* and regional *intergovernmental* organizations.

2.   Recognizing the *central role of WHO* as the directing and coordinating authority on international health work . . . *the WHO Director-General shall*, in accordance with terms set out herein, *declare pandemics*.

Article 17. Strengthening pandemic and public health literacy

1.   The Parties commit to increase science, public health and pandemic literacy in the population . . . and tackle *false, misleading misinformation and disinformation*. In that regard, each Party is encouraged to:

(b) conduct *regular social listening and analysis* to identify the prevalence and *profiles of misinformation*, which contribute to *design communications and messaging strategies for the public to counteract misinformation, disinformation and false news*, thereby strengthening *public trust*.

2.   The Parties will contribute to research and inform policies on factors that *hinder adherence to public health and social measures*, confidence and *uptake of vaccines*, use of appropriate therapeutics and *trust in science and government institutions*.

Article 18. One Health

3.   The Parties will identify and integrate into relevant pandemic prevention and preparedness plans interventions . . . including but not limited to *climate change, land use change.*

6.   The Parties commit to strengthen multisectoral, coordinated, interoperable and integrated *One Health surveillance systems*.

Article 19. Sustainable and predictable financing

1.   The Parties

(c) commit to . . . *allocating in its annual budgets not lower than 5% of its current health expenditure* to pandemic prevention, preparedness, response and health systems recovery;

(d) commit to *allocate*, in accordance with its respective capacities, XX% (*sic*) *of its gross domestic product* for international cooperation and assistance on pandemic prevention, preparedness, response and health systems recovery, *particularly through developing countries.*

2.   The Parties shall ensure, through . . . financing of global, regional and national systems, strengthening pandemic prevention, preparedness, response and recovery of health systems . . . *particularly in developing countries.*

3.   The Parties shall promote . . . funding for the development and strengthening of pandemic prevention, preparedness, response and health system recovery programmes of *developing country Parties.*

5.   The Parties represented in relevant regional and international intergovernmental organizations and financial and development institutions shall encourage these entities to provide *financial assistance for developing country Parties* to support them in meeting their *obligations* under the WHO C+ [Treaty].

Article 21. The Governing Body for the WHO CA+

2.   The Governing Body shall be composed of:

(a) the Conference of the Parties (COP) , which shall be the supreme organ of the Governing Body, composed of the Parties and constituting *the sole decision-making organ*; and

(b) the Officers of the Parties, which shall be the administrative organ of the Governing Body.

4.   The Officers of the Parties . . . shall:

(b) *endeavour to make decisions by consensus*; however, if efforts to reach consensus are *deemed by the Presidents to be unavailing*, decisions may be taken by *voting by the President and Vice-Presidents.*

Article 22. Oversight mechanisms for the WHO CA+

1.   The Governing Body, at its first meeting, shall consider and approve cooperative procedures and institutional mechanisms to *promote compliance*

with the provisions of the WHO C+ [Treaty] and also *address cases of non-compliance*.

Article 25. Reservations

1.   *No reservations or exceptions* may be made to this WHO CA+ [Treaty]

2.   A reservation *incompatible with the object and purpose* of the WHO CA+ *shall not be permitted*.

Even expressed in this euphemistic language of veiled threats and financial inducements, what this draft shows is that the Pandemic Prevention, Preparedness and Response Treaty is a convention, agreement and international instrument designed to bring about the following:

1.   The annual expropriation of billions and perhaps trillions of dollars of public funds from the coffers of signatory nations into the budget and administrative control of the World Health Organization;

2.   With these public funds, the privatisation of global health care through outsourced contracts with the growing number of companies providing designated 'pandemics products' — from personal protection equipment and RT-PCR tests to gene therapies and surveillance technology — over a fifth of which the World Health Organization will have rights of distribution;

3.   With these products, the monitoring and censorship of any opinion, data, evidence, arguments or knowledge that contradicts the pronouncements, judgements and decisions of the World Health Organization;

4.   With this enforced consensus, the imposition and legal enforcement of the illegal regulations, programmes and technologies of global biosecurity on the populations of member nations, from lockdowns, mandatory masking and gene therapy to systems of Digital Identity and Social Credit, 15-Minute Cities and Central Bank Digital Currencies;

The Pandemic Prevention, Preparedness and Response Treaty, therefore, is a declaration of war — a civil war — waged by the governments of the signatory nations, employing the apparatuses of the state, against their civilian populations, the sovereignty of the elected legislatures of those nations, and the institutions for their democratic oversight and accountability. In place of which, the World Health Organization, through this Treaty, will exert the authority of the biosecurity arm of an unelected, technocratic, unaccountable, authoritarian and totalitarian World Government that subordinates the authority of the nation state to the interests of international corporations. The Treaty, in other words, is an instrument of stakeholder capitalism.

3. The Principles of Biopower

So, how is all this being implemented on the justification of protecting our health? To answer this question, we need to understand the legally-enforceable principles that are being written into the World Health Organization's Pandemic Prevention, Preparedness and Response Treaty.

The first of these principles is the 'One Health approach', which the WHO doesn't define in its draft of definitions, but recognises that 'all lives have equal value'.[9] This extends the Treaty's remit from the prevention of pandemics to the duty to 'optimize the health of people, animals and ecosystems'.[10] In order to 'better address any One Health-related issue' arising from this drive to optimization, the World Health Organization has formed a 'quadpartite' with the Food and Agriculture Organization of the United Nations, the World Organisation for Animal Health and the United Nations Environment Programme — three more unelected technocracies. As a consequence of this principle, the Treaty recognizes health as 'a precondition for, and an outcome and indicator of, the social, economic and environmental dimensions of sustainable development and the implementation of the 2030 Agenda for Sustainable Development'.[11]

Of particular concern to the WHO, and the justification for the Treaty's extraordinary claim to 5 per cent of the health budget and an undisclosed

---

9. World Health Organization, 'Zero draft of the WHO CA+ for the consideration of the Intergovernmental Negotiating Body at its fourth meeting' (1 February, 2023), pp. 9 and 4.

10. *Ibid*, p. 6.

11. *Ibid*, p. 6.

percentage of the GDP of signatory nations, as well as the right of distribution over 20 per cent of all 'pandemic products', is that pandemics hamper the ability of 'developing' nations to implement the United Nations' 'Sustainable Development Goals'.

This is what the WHO understands by 'inclusiveness' and 'equity' — two of its 'guiding principles and rights': that developing nations will be loaded with debt from the budgets of wealthier signatory nations and organisations like the World Bank and the International Monetary Fund, in order to implement Sustainable Development Goals that are designed to allocate the flow of global capital to governments according to their compliance with Environmental, Social and Governance criteria.[12] The WHO says nothing about the fact that the coronavirus, which was manufactured into a crisis by these wealthier nations in collaboration with the WHO, left barely a trace on the overall mortality of the developing nations it is being used to justify the imposition on them of this model of debt.

As I have previously shown, behind their UN branding ESG criteria are formulated by US corporate asset managers like BlackRock, Goldman Sachs and JP Morgan, the same companies elected to 'coordinate' the €314.84 billions of investment in the Ukraine so far.[13] The Sustainable Development Goals written into the WHO Treaty, and of which 'health' is now a 'precondition and indicator', will further increase the monopoly of wealthy nations and international companies able to meet Environmental, Social and Governance criteria over poorer countries and smaller companies.

And those countries unable to fulfil these criteria, implement these goals or meet the repayments on their loans from doing both — particularly in the resource-rich 'developing nations' with which the Treaty is so concerned in Article 19 — will be 'invited' (just as the Ukraine has been 'invited') to hand over their assets to their creditors.[14] This is what the Pandemic Treaty means by 'Universal

---

12. *Ibid*, p. 11.

13. See Gibson Dunn, 'BlackRock, Vanguard and State Street Update Corporate Governance and ESG Policies and Priorities for 2022' (25 January, 2022); Goldman Sachs, 'Unpacking what ESG Investing Really Means'; and Ben Norton, 'Ukraine's Zelelnsky Sends Love Letter to US Corporations, Promising "Big Business" for Wall Street', *Scheerpost* (27 January, 2023);.

14. Jake Kallio and Ben Norton, 'West prepares to plunder post-war Ukraine with neoliberal shock therapy: privatization, deregulation, slashing worker protections', *Geopolitical Economy* (28 July, 2022).

Health Coverage', which the WHO defines as a 'fundamental aspect of achieving the Sustainable Development Goals through promoting health and well-being for all'.[15]

It is also why the Treaty defines the 'Central role of WHO' as 'the directing and coordinating authority on global health, and the leader of multilateral cooperation in global health governance'.[16] To this end, under Article 4, 'The right to health' — which it defines as a by-definition never-attainable 'state of complete physical, mental and social well-being' — is now made 'fundamental' to human beings, 'without distinction of age, race, religion, political belief, economic or social condition'.[17]

What this means — or, rather, what it can be interpreted to mean — is that our now fundamental right to a utopian 'complete well-being' — legally upheld through, for example, lockdown restrictions, mandatory masking or gene therapy — will overrule the qualified rights to our political or religious beliefs, or the effect their enforcement will have on our economic or social condition. In other words, we can be forced to live in a totalitarian surveillance state, be imprisoned in our 15-Minute Cities, be isolated from our families and each other, be reduced to poverty and deprived of our freedom of movement, association, thought or expression — but at least we'll be what the World Health Organization defines as 'healthy'.

And if we disagree with that definition, under Article 17, we'll be prohibited from expressing such 'misinformation' and 'disinformation' through the new technologies and programmes developed to enforce compliance. No matter how long it takes under lockdown, no matter how many masks we must wear, no matter how many courses of experimental gene therapies we have to be injected with, we will learn, eventually, 'to trust in science and government institutions'.

This is the founding principle of biopower, in which the former citizen's right to health-care and medical treatment is turned, through changes to both legislation and the norms of thought and behaviour, into our legally enforced obligations to meet and comply with the regulations, programmes and technologies of the Global Biosecurity State. It's over this new biopolitical

---

15. *Ibid*, p. 12.

16. *Ibid*, p. 12.

17. *Ibid*, p. 10.

paradigm of global governance that the World Health Organization will preside on behalf of its corporate and government funders. The Pandemic Treaty, therefore, will make the State of Emergency under which we lived for two years during lockdown the paradigm of our future governance — under which, on the justification of upholding our 'right to health', our lives will effectively be taken into the protective custody of this 'global health government'.

The World Health Organization has made it clear that any signatory who fails to meet the obligations of the Treaty will be subject to what it calls 'compliance mechanisms' decided by member states.[18] This means, in effect, by the United States of America, which despite President Donald Trump suspending funding in 2020, remains the WHO's largest single source of funding, having invested $1.178 billion in its programmes between then and May 2023.[19] So the Treaty will also act as an instrument for sanctions on Russia, China, Iran and other states not compliant with the 'rules-based international order' unilaterally imposed by the USA and collectively enforced by its economic, political, security and military allies.

As we saw in the threat made by the US Vice-President, Kamala Harris, at the Munich Security Conference this February, any signatory failing to implement the WHO's legally-binding recommendations could, for example, be accused of 'crimes against humanity' justifying intervention by a WHO coalition — which is to say, once again, the US military — enforcing the 'right to health' of the citizens of the non-compliant nation.[20] Under Article 4, any signatory nation whose 'approach to public health' is deemed by the WHO to 'cause damage to their peoples and other countries' will be subject to such compliance mechanisms. And as we saw over the two years of lockdown, *anything* not compliant with government regulations — including, and perhaps above all, our thought and expression — can be deemed a threat to others.

---

18. See World Health Organization, 'Pandemic prevention, preparedness and response accord' (24 February, 2023).

19. See Pien Huang, 'Trump And WHO: How Much Does The U.S. Give? What's The Impact Of A Halt In Funding?', *NPR* (15 April, 2020); 'The U.S. Government and the World Health Organization', *KFF* (22 May, 2023).

20. See Kamala Harris, 'Remarks by Vice President Harris at the Munich Security Conference', The White House (18 February, 2023).

Where once we cried 'Hear come the peace-keepers!' as the might and terror of the US military-industrial complex descended on any nation unfortunate enough to be deemed worthy of 'liberation', in the future we will cry 'Here comes the health-protectors!' as hazmat-suited US-Marines invade and take over the governance, economy and resources of yet another dangerous country, closely followed, when all opposition has been crushed, by US asset managers.

Since one of the purposes of the Treaty is to define what constitutes a 'pandemic' — which, as we've had demonstrated, can be manufactured by national governments and their media and declared by the World Health Organization — a pandemic justifying the enforcement of biosecurity restrictions can be declared in any country the US chooses at almost any time. With such financial inducements and geo-political motives to do so, why wouldn't the WHO, as it says in Article 15(2), 'declare pandemics' where and when it is told to by its masters? This is the intended purpose and ultimate goal of the Pandemic Prevention, Preparedness and Response Treaty.

But there is hope, if from an unlikely source of freedom. In a 'Joint statement of the Russian Federation and the People's Republic of China on the deepening of relations of comprehensive partnership and strategic interaction entering a new era', which was released on 21 March, 2023, the governments of Vladimir Putin and Xi Jinping stated in what appears to be — without naming it — a veiled response to the WHO's Pandemic Treaty:

> The Parties will continue to develop cooperation in the field of ensuring the sanitary and epidemiological well-being of the population in order to counter the threats of epidemics, and will jointly oppose attempts at the platforms of international organizations to adopt legally binding mechanisms that limit the sovereignty of countries in the field of prevention and control of infectious diseases, prevention and response to biological threats.[21]

In the next chapter, I'll look at what this and statements like it tell us about the New World Order emerging from the crisis in Western capitalism.

---

21. Quoted in Riley Waggaman, 'Putin & Xi's Moscow agreements', *Off-Guardian* (28 March, 2023).

5. War on Russia and the New World Order

'It is in the ranks of the Party, and above all the Inner Party, that the true war enthusiasm is found. World-conquest is believed in most firmly by those who know it to be impossible.'

— George Orwell, *Nineteen Eighty-Four*, 1949

1. Western Oligarchy

One of the obstacles to understanding the managed and apparently deliberate destruction of the small and medium-sized businesses that in the UK have decreased in number by half a million since 2020, and the removal of our national sovereignty on the justification of saving us from, by turns, a health crisis, an environmental crisis, an energy crisis or a cost-of-living crisis, is the question of how anyone can benefit from doing so.[1] It's always difficult to look into the future and predict what is going to happen, but we can look back on and try to learn from the recent past. If we want to know where this immiseration and disenfranchisement of the British people is leading and who will benefit, we could do worse than look at what happened to Russia in the 1990s.

When Mikhail Gorbachev became General Secretary of the Communist Party of the Soviet Union in March 1985, he immediately began his programme of *perestroika* ('restructuring') the economic and political policy of the USSR. Five years later, in September 1990, under the policy reform called *glasnost* ('openness'), the Soviet Parliament granted Gorbachev, now the newly elected President of the USSR, emergency powers of privatisation. These included the authority to transform state-owned enterprises into joint-stock companies with shares offered on stock exchanges. After Gorbachev's resignation and the formal dissolution of the USSR in December 1991, the first Russian President, Boris Yeltsin, initiated a programme of privatisation that sought to compress twenty years of Western neoliberalism into a few years in a country whose population had

---

1. See Department for Business, Energy and Industrial Strategy, 'Business population estimates for the UK and regions 2022: statistical release' (6 October, 2022).

no experience of how finance capitalism works. Two years later, more than 85 per cent of Russian small businesses and more than 82,000 Russian state-owned companies, about one-third of the total in existence, had been privatised.[2]

One of the first initiatives was Voucher Privatisation, which between 1992 and 1994 distributed 144 million vouchers that could be converted into stock shares in more than 100,000 state-owned companies among 98 per cent of the Russian population, in principle giving each citizen a share of the national wealth. However, the Russian worker, impoverished and increasingly unemployed by the rapid dismantling of the Soviet economy, had little understanding of shareholder capitalism, and these vouchers were almost entirely bought up for a few rubles by Russian bureaucrats, who had a clearer idea of the state of the Russian economy, by state-owned company directors, who had a better grasp of the value of Russian resources, and by the mafia, who after years of trading Western commodities on the Soviet black market had a better idea of the future value of these shares. By the end of June 1994, ownership of 70 per cent of Russia's large and medium-sized companies and about 90 per cent of its small businesses had been transferred into private hands.

In 1995, with the Government facing a fiscal deficit and in return for funding his re-election campaign, Yeltsin initiated the Loans for Shares scheme, through which state industrial assets in petroleum, gas, coal, iron and steel were auctioned for loans by commercial banks. Since these loans were never returned, largely because they were used to pay off the interest on existing Government debt, and because the auctions were rigged by political insiders, the state assets were effectively sold for a fraction of their value.[3] Yukos Oil, for example, worth around $5 billion, was sold for $310 million; Sibneft, the third-largest producer of oil in Russia and worth $3 billion, was sold for $100 million; and Norilsk Nickel, which produced a quarter of the world's nickel, sold for $170 million, half as much as a competing bid.

This scheme created a new class of oligarchs (from the Ancient Greek *oligarkhía*, 'the rule of the few'), industrialists and bankers who now controlled not just the Russian economy but also its Government. Conscious, however, that

---

2. See 'Privatization of Russian Industry', *Facts and Details* (last updated May 2016).

3. See Alessandra Stanley, 'Russian Banking Scandal Poses Threat to Future of Privatization', *New York Times* (28 January, 1996); Marshall I. Goldman, 'Putin and the Oligarchs', *Foreign Affairs* (1 November 2004).

future governments might reverse Yeltsin's carpet-sale of the nation's wealth, the oligarchs, instead of investing in these industries, immediately set about stripping their assets to increase their equity. The vast wealth they accumulated from doing so was invested abroad, largely in Swiss banks, but also into UK property through the largest money-laundering service in the world, the City of London.[4]

This flight of capital out of the country left the Government unable to collect taxes, leading to it defaulting on debt repayments and ultimately to the Russian financial crisis of 1998. When foreign investors began to pull out of the market, selling Russian currency and assets, the Central Bank of Russia, which had only been founded in July 1990, had to spend its foreign reserves to defend Russia's currency, expending approximately $27 billion of its US dollar reserves. This led to the most cataclysmic peacetime economic collapse of an industrial country in history. By 1999, the gross domestic product of Russia had fallen by more than 40 per cent, and the increase in retail prices by 2,520 per cent in 1992 had wiped out what personal savings the Russian people had accumulated. A decline in meat consumption was mirrored by a huge increase in crime, corruption and mortality rates, the latter of which reached the highest in history of an industrial country not at war. Unemployment in a country where it had previously been unknown reached 13 per cent. Inflation peaked at 85.7 per cent. Government debt reached 135 per cent of GDP, and Russia, consequently, became the largest borrower from the International Monetary Fund, with loans amounting to $20 billion in the 1990s. Little of this served its ostensible purpose, however. A quarter of this sum, some $4.8 billion, was stolen upon its arrival in Russia on the eve of the financial crisis, and disappeared into an anonymous account registered in the offshore tax jurisdiction of Jersey.[5]

If all this sounds familiar, Yeltsin's reforms were based on the Washington Consensus, ten principles of economic neoliberalisation first implemented in Augusto Pinochet's Chile and by the Argentinian Junta in the 1970s, and imposed by the International Monetary Fund, the World Bank and the US Treasury as a

---

4. See Transparency International, *At Your Service: Investigating how UK businesses and institutions help corrupt individuals and regimes launder their money and reputations*; edited by Steve Goodrich (24 October 2019).

5. See David Hoffman, 'Audit Shows Russia Misled IMF on Loan', *The Washington Post* (1 July,1999).

condition of receiving loans.[6] These include redirecting public spending from funding state services to investment in pro-growth services like education and healthcare; eliminating restrictions on import trade and foreign investment; abolishing regulations on safety, health and polluting the environment that impede the market; and above all privatising state industries. As a result of these reforms, on October 1998 the Government of Russia, despite being the largest exporter of natural gas and oil reserves in the world, had to appeal for international humanitarian aid.[7] It was a long way but only a short time since the Soviet Union had been one of two world superpowers, and a lesson in how quickly the wealth and national assets of a country can be stripped when its population is exposed naked to the predations of finance capitalism.[8]

Although it has 'recovered' to the extent that today — particularly following the rise in energy prices consequent upon the West's sanctions — Russia is in the top ten largest economies in the world by nominal GDP, per capita it drops to 53rd.[9] A decade ago, the gap between rich and poor in Russia was the largest of any country in the world, with 35 per cent of the wealth of a country of 144 million people owned by just 110 billionaires, with much of that wealth stored in offshore financial jurisdictions.[10] In 2021, the 500 richest Russians, each with a net worth of more than £100 million and making up just 0.001 per cent of the total population, still controlled 40 per cent of the country's entire household wealth — more than the poorest 99.8 per cent, 114.6 million people, combined.[11] This is what finance capitalism does to a nation and a people without the political and institutional means to protect themselves.

---

6. See Guillermo Rozenwurcel, 'Reasons for the success or failure of structural reforms: Argentina and Chile's contrasting experiences revisited', *Documento de Trabajo no. 28* (November 2007).

7. See Michael R. Gordon, 'Facing Severe Shortage of Food, Russia Seeks Foreign Relief Aid', *The New York Times* (10 October, 1998).

8. See Janine R. Wedel, 'The Harvard Boys Do Russia', *The Nation* (14 May, 1998).

9. See 'Russia enters the top ten economies in the world for GDP at current prices', *Nova Mews* (31 December, 2022).

10. See Ron Synovitz, 'Russia Has Highest Level of Health Inequality', *Radio Free Europe* (10 October, 2013).

11. See 'Russia's Super Rich Wealthier Than Poorest 99.8% — Report', *The Moscow Times* (10 June, 2021).

Today, across the neoliberal democracies of the West, national governments in thrall to the new forms of global governance formed on the justification of addressing multiple manufactured 'crises' are implementing equivalent programmes of managed economic collapse devised by the same international institutions of global macro-economic management. Instead of Perestroika, Glasnost, Voucher Privatisation and Loans for Shares, these programmes of economic and political 'reform' are called Agenda 2030, Sustainable Development Goals, Universal Basic Income and Central Bank Digital Currency. And although these are being implemented not on the collapse of a centralised command economy like that of the Soviet Union but in neoliberal economies facing the second Global Financial Crisis in two decades, the aim of these programmes is the same: impoverishment of national populations, bankruptcy of independent businesses, expropriation of national land and resources, instalment of puppet governments to present a facade of democracy to technocratic rule, and an economic and political power-grab by a financial ruling class.[12]

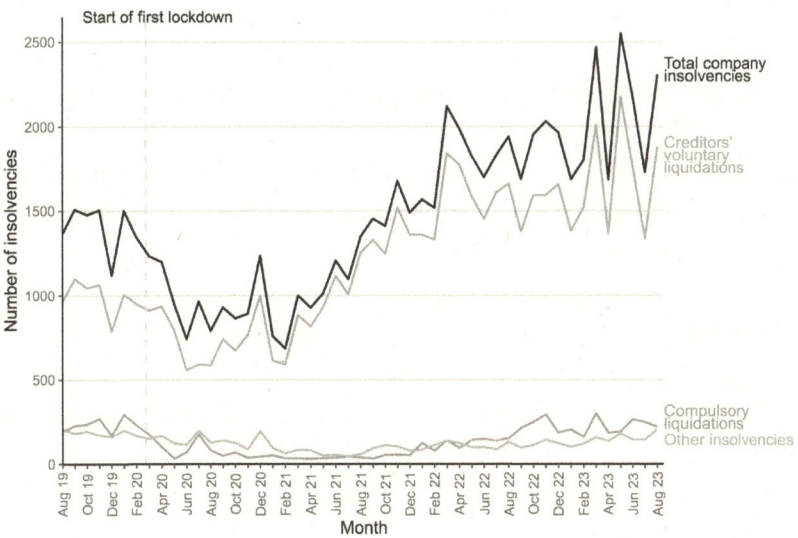

Source: The Insolvency Service

---

12. See Simon Elmer, 'Fascism and the Decay of Capitalism', *The Road to Fascism*, pp. 61-80.

The removal of our rights, driving down of our standard of living, reduction in our food and energy consumption, spiralling inflation and the economic sanctions and programmes enforcing these, are all designed to transfer our national and personal assets into the hands of this global elite. Just as happened in Russia in the 1990s, the Bank of England has increased its quantitative easing programme to bail out the UK economy, spending £19.3 billion in October 2022 buying up Government bonds to prop up the failing pound, with the commitment to spend £65 billion if necessary.[13] With the number of company insolvencies in May 2023 nearly double what they were four years earlier and on the rise, small businesses driven into bankruptcy by two years of government-enforced lockdown and rocketing energy prices have had their market share bought up by corporate monopolies.[14] The annual rate of inflation reached 11.1 per cent in October 2022, a 41-year high, before falling to 6.7 percent in August 2023; and in September 2023 the Bank of England has set interest rates at 5.25 per cent, the fourteenth successive increase since December 2021, and the highest rate since December 2007.[15] And the duties and authority of the UK state continue to be outsourced by our Government to international companies, who are being empowered by new legislation to set the limits of our previously inalienable rights and freedoms. Finally, our new globalist Prime Minister, Rishi Sunak, has not been elected by UK voters or even by his own parliamentary party, but appointed by the international financiers, bankers and technocrats who, just as they do in Russia and the Ukraine, now dictate not only our economic policies but also our politics.[16]

Let me clarify what I mean and don't mean by this comparison. I am not saying that post-Soviet Russia is a mirror of the UK in 2023. The differences between the historical circumstances and the economies of the two countries are

13. See Sarah Taaffe-Maguire, 'Bank of England ceases bond-buying after spending £19.3bn', *Sky News* (14 October, 2022).

14. See Insolvency Service, 'Official Statistics: Commentary — Monthly Insolvency Statistics May 2023' (16 June, 2023).

15. See Brigid Francis-Devine, Daniel Harari, Matthew Keep, Paul Bolton, Wendy Wilson and Cassie Barton, 'Rising cost of living in the UK', *House of Commons Library* (22 September, 2023); and Bank of England, 'Official Bank Rate history'.

16. See Jack Mendel, 'Ex Fed official says Bank of England "contributed to the Truss govt's demise"', *City A.M.* (28 October, 2022); and Adam Forrest, 'Ex-Bank of England boss in scathing attack on Truss as he claims she turned UK into "Argentina on the Channel"', *Independent* (19 September, 2023).

too great. What I'm arguing is that the managed destruction of the Russian economy after the dissolution of the Soviet Union is an image of where we are heading and why we are being driven to such an end. The Russian and Ukrainian oligarchs weren't only motivated by the wealth they could take out of their countries and into offshore tax jurisdictions managed by financial advisers in the City of London; they were, and are, interested in the political power that wealth gave them. And just as they chose Vladimir Putin to be the successor to the shambling Boris Yeltsin, so too our oligarchs have chosen Rishi Sunak as the successor to the shambling Boris Johnson.

The UK hasn't been a democratic state since at least March 2020, when the country was placed in a *de facto* State of Emergency and thousands of regulations stripping us of our rights and freedoms were made by ministerial decree without oversight or approval by our elected representatives in Parliament.[17] But in the wake of those restrictions having largely been lifted in March 2022 — while still being imposed by private and public companies, including airlines and the National Health Service, as a condition of access, service or employment — Sunak's unilateral decision to impose the programmes of biosecurity and Agenda 2030 outside of any democratic process is the brazen admission that we are now ruled by international technocracies of global governance run by corporate CEOs, international bankers and government-appointed technocrats. And although today we call them 'philanthropists', 'entrepreneurs' and 'global investors', the actions of these unelected globalists are every bit as criminal as those of the Russian and Ukrainian oligarchy in the 1990s, except that they're acting on a far greater stage and with far more damaging consequences for their by turns outraged or applauding but always deceived audience.

The economic and cultural sanctions placed on Russia and the immense financial and military investment in the Ukraine by this World Government since March 2022 are instrumental to the financial war these Western globalists are waging against Russia's oligarchs; but contrary to the rhetoric of our politicians and actors, they are doing so not to defend the human rights of Ukrainians and a puppet government installed by the US in 2014 for precisely this reason, but rather

---

17. See Simon Elmer, 'The State of Emergency as a Paradigm of Government' (12 May, 2020); collected in *Virtue and Terror*, pp. 55-96; and Hansard Society, 'Coronavirus Statutory Instruments Dashboard, 2020-2022' (4 March 2022).

to emulate, replace and surpass that oligarchy in wealth, political influence and above all control over the immense natural resources of Russia and, more immediately, of the Ukraine.

The announcement by President Volodymyr Zelenskyy that, following the €100 billion in military, financial and humanitarian aid the West handed over to his Government in 2022, the US asset-managers BlackRock, JP Morgan and Goldman Sachs will 'coordinate' its investment in the Ukraine and its vast natural resources — not only in grain, oil and gas but also in minerals and the lithium that is the primary component in electric batteries — should demonstrate to all but the most fervent blue-and-yellow-flag-waving zealots what interest the West has in this geopolitical, military and energy crisis, whose manufacture I will examine in the rest of this chapter.[18]

But in preparation for the neoliberalisation of the Ukraine, Zelenskyy has already banned opposition political parties, worker's unions and independent media platforms, passed laws to privatise state-owned businesses, banks and assets, promised to cut the upper rate of tax and deregulate businesses, and issued hit lists on journalists critical of his Government's policies.[19] If we want an image of where we are being led by this globalist coup — which is being implemented on the spurious justifications of protecting our health from a deadly new virus, defending Europe from 'Mad Vlad' Putin, and saving the planet from man-made global warming — the economic inequality, financial corruption and political disenfranchisement of the Russian people and, closer in time, the puppet Government of the Ukraine and its dance-contestant President, is a good place to look. This is an image of our future.

18. See Kiel Institute for the World Economy, 'Ukraine Support Tracker: A Database of Military, Financial and Humanitarian Aid to Ukraine'; Ben Norton, 'Ukraine's Zelelnsky Sends Love Letter to US Corporations, Promising "Big Business" for Wall Street', *Scheerpost* (27 January, 2023); Geeta Mohan, 'Are Ukraine's vast natural resources a real reason behind Russia's invasion?', *Business Today* (25 February, 2022).

19. See Jake Kallio and Ben Norton, 'West prepares to plunder post-war Ukraine with neoliberal shock therapy: privatization, deregulation, slashing worker protections', *Geopolitical Economy* (28 July, 2022); Abdul Rahman, 'Opposition political parties banned in Ukraine and "unified information policy" imposed', *Peoples Dispatch* (21 March, 2022); Vanessa Beeley, 'Assassinated for telling the truth about Ukraine', *The Wall Will Fall* (17 April, 2022).

2. The International Criminal Court

On 17 March, 2023, the International Criminal Court (ICC) issued a warrant for the arrest of Vladimir Putin, the President of the Russian Federation, for the illegal deportation and transferal of children from occupied regions in the Ukraine into the Russian Federation, which it judged to be a war crime.[20] 123 states are party to the judgement of the International Criminal Court, including Brazil and South Africa but not including India, China or Russia itself. The USA also doesn't recognise the authority of the ICC. Indeed, in 2018, the US threatened to arrest ICC judges if they pursued an investigation of US military personnel for war crimes committed in Afghanistan; and in 2020 the US imposed sanctions against two judges for investigating human rights violations by the US military.[21] So why has the ICC — apparently at the bidding of the US, and certainly to its benefit — issued a warrant for the arrest of Vladimir Putin? The answer lies in how this warrant will be deployed by the US and its military allies in the geopolitical struggle against Russia.

First, the West, through what is in effect its kangaroo court, has put pressure on parties bound to enact the ICC warrant to arrest Putin if he visits their countries, effectively trying to prohibit him from diplomatic relations with the rest of the world.[22]

Second, the USA is forcing NATO states to choose between alliance with the West — which means, first and foremost, allegiance to the US dollar as the dominant reserve currency of the world — and the BRICS nations (Brazil, Russia, India, China and South Africa), three of which are not parties to the International Criminal Court. As an example of which, in June the South African Minister for Foreign Affairs invited Putin to attend the BRICS summit there in August, effectively aligning South Africa with this growing economic alliance of nations and its threat to Western hegemony.[23]

---

20. See International Criminal Court, 'Situation in Ukraine: ICC judges issue arrest warrants against Vladimir Vladimirovich Putin and Maria Alekseyevna Lvova-Belova' (17 March, 2023).

21. See Human Rights Watch, 'US Sanctions on the International Criminal Court' (14 December, 2020).

22. See International Criminal Court, 'The States Parties to the Rome Statute'.

23. See 'South Africa Invites Putin to Summit Despite ICC Arrest Warrant', teleSUR English (26 June, 2023).

And third, by including the Russian President on a list of wanted criminals, the International Criminal Court has laid the legal ground for a declaration of war against Vladimir Putin himself.[24] The same legal trick was used in 1815 when, in response to his escape from enforced exile on the Mediterranean Island of Elba, the Congress of Vienna declared war not on France but on Napoleon Bonaparte personally, declaring the former Emperor of the French a 'criminal' for violating the terms of his banishment.[25] More recently, in 2003, the USA and its European allies declared war not on the Iraqi people but on the government of President Saddam Hussein, thereby justifying their illegal and genocidal invasion of Iraq and the theft of its oil reserves as a desire for 'regime change'.[26]

As it did with the equally manufactured war on Iraq, HM Governments like to declare war in March, as it gives military campaigns in the Northern Hemisphere the maximum time before winter returns. If I were a betting man, I'd have a flutter on the most servile Parliament in UK history declaring war on Russia next March. The UK brazenly sells arms to Saudi Arabia, Israel and other criminal states, so if all we were going to do was sell some armour-piercing rounds containing depleted uranium to the Ukraine, there was no need for the absurd pomp and circumstance that attended President Zelenskyy's visit in February 2023.[27] When the UK state dusts off the stained-glass windows and gets its monarch out of moth-balls, you know it means murder. And just like we were in 2003, the UK will be at the rear of a long coalition led by the US, endorsed by the UN, financed by the arms dealers and energy companies and paid for by us, the tax-payers.

But whenever we do go to war, I suspect it will be declared against Putin himself, as a criminal wanted by the International Criminal Court, in pursuance of whose arrest the West will justify its illegal war on Russia and theft of its oil and mineral resources. In this respect, the ICC warrant is the ratification and legal form of the unilateral judgement of the USA — which was imperiously announced by US Vice-President Kamala Harris at the Munich Security Conference in February

---

24. See International Criminal Court, '31 Cases'.

25. See Napoleon Series, 'Declaration of the Powers against Napoleon' (13 March, 1815).

26. See George W. Bush, 'President Bush Announces Start of Iraq War', *YouTube* (13 March, 2013).

27. See 'What are depleted uranium munitions the UK is sending to Ukraine?', *Al Jazeera* (23 March, 2023); 'Ukraine war: President Volodymyr Zelensky visits the UK', *BBC News* (8 February, 2023).

— that Russia has committed 'crimes against humanity', and that Putin will be held personally accountable.[28]

As a measure of the influence the West has over the so-called International Criminal Court it funds and why so many non-Western nations refuse to recognise it as independent and impartial, the ICC, which was founded in 1998, has issued no equivalent warrants for the arrest of the Prime Minister of Saudi Arabia, Mohammed bin Salman and before him the King of Saudi Arabia, for crimes against their own people and war crimes against the people of Yemen; for the arrest of the Prime Minister of Israel, Benjamin Netanyahu, for the genocidal treatment of the Palestinian people; for the arrest of the Presidents of the Ukraine, Volodmyr Zelenskyy and before him Petro Poroshenko, for the ethnic cleansing of the Donbass; or for the arrest of living Presidents of the USA, Bill Clinton, George W. Bush, Barack Obama and Joe Biden, for war crimes committed by US forces in Kosovo, Afghanistan, Iraq, Libya, Syria and every other country they have invaded since the end of the Second World War.[29]

When NATO — which is the military form of US hegemony in Europe — declares war on Russia, I believe it will do so not on the grounds of the military defence of the Ukraine but on a legal basis. In doing so, the ensuing conflict will be placed outside the political realm, and therefore not open to debate in our legislatures. Like the equally manufactured 'war' on COVID, this will be a war for biosecurity. And like all wars of biosecurity, it will be waged not against the Russian people but for them; not to defeat them but to save them; not for our benefit but for theirs. And like the police who, under coronavirus-justified regulations, beat the non-compliant with weighted truncheons, sprayed their eyes with tear-gas and shot them with rubber bullets in order to 'protect public health', we'll make those *Ruskis* free — or they'll die trying!

The more recent example of a war waged against a head of state is the so-called 'decapitation strikes' launched by the US military in 2011 against the

---

28. See Kamala Harris, 'Remarks by Vice President Harris at the Munich Security Conference', The White House (18 February, 2023).

29. See Amnesty International reports 'Saudi Arabia 2022', 'Yemen 2022', 'Afghanistan 2022', 'Libya 2022', 'Israel's apartheid against Palestinians: a cruel system of domination and a crime against humanity' (1 February, 2022); 'Iraq: 20 years since the US-led coalition invaded Iraq, impunity reigns supreme' (20 March, 2023); and Terry Boardman, 'Ukrainian policy in the Donbass: Is it fair to call it genocide?', *UK Column* (25 February, 2023).

President of Libya, Muammar Gaddafi, who two years before had initiated the Gold Dinar as an alternative currency for Africa.[30] The Dinar was intended to divert Africa's oil revenues towards state-controlled funds rather than through US banks; and just as Gaddafi was assassinated by US-backed rebels for this threat to the dollar, so the criminal cartel we call the US Department of Defence will attempt to do the same against Vladimir Putin. Doubtless the gloating crime bosses in the US military who took pleasure in circulating photographs of the dead and mutilated bodies of Muammar Gaddafi and Saddam Hussein one day hope to add the body of Vladimir Putin to their pin-up board of assassinated Presidents.

There is a problem with their plan, however, which is, of course, that Russia is not Libya or Iraq or the other small countries the US invades with impunity as the rest of the West sits on its hands in the International Criminal Court, the European Court of Human Rights and the United Nations. Russia has the second strongest military in the world and the largest nuclear arsenal; and it has reaffirmed — very publicly — its alliance with China, which has the third strongest military in the world.[31] Moreover, the Deputy Chairman of Russia's Security Council, Dimitry Medvedev, has made it very clear that any attempt by a foreign power to enact the ICC warrant and arrest Putin — or to invade the Crimea — will be taken as a declaration of war, and that Russia would respond with all its military capabilities, including nuclear missiles.[32]

However, beyond the military balance of power between NATO and the Moscow-Beijing alliance, there is the balance of foreign debt to GDP, with that of the USA, as I discussed in an earlier chapter, at 89.54 per cent, compared to Russia's 26.69 per cent and China's 17.88 percent. At their meeting in Moscow in March 2023, Xi Jinping, the President of the People's Republic of China since 2013, said to Vladimir Putin, the President of the Russian Federation since 2012: 'Change is coming that hasn't happened in a hundred years, and we are driving

30. See Drago Bosnic, 'Dangers of Pentagon's "decapitation strike" against Russia', *Brics Information Portal* (28 December, 2022); and 'Gold Dinar: the Real Reason Behind Gaddafi's Murder', *Millenium State* (3 May, 2019).

31. See Global Fire Power, '2023 Military Strength Ranking'; International Campaign to Abolish Nuclear Weapons, 'Which countries have nuclear weapons?', Graham Allison, 'Xi and Putin Have the Most Consequential Undeclared Alliance in the World', *Foreign Policy* (23 March, 2023).

32. See Vladimir Isacchenkov, 'Russia's security chief blasts West, dangles nuclear threats', *AP News* (23 March, 2023); and 'Russia Warns Ukraine Over Crimea "A Threat To State Existence"', *TeleSUR English* (26 June, 2023).

this change together.'[33] Both these men have long experience of leading their countries and, in Putin's case, years in his country's security services. They have consistently run rings around the senile automatons, bankrupt game-show hosts, recovering alcoholics, born-again fundamentalists, former bankers, ex-hacks and World Economic Forum puppets struggling to formulate the foreign policy of the West as they pump more and more magic money into their failing economies.

Every 'global crisis' that we face — geopolitical, environmental, health, energy, cultural — has been manufactured in response to this unavoidable fact: the largest economy, military and political power in the world is $33 trillion in debt, and has no way to repay it. We should never forget that only one nation has ever used nuclear weapons in an act of war, that it used them against a defeated enemy, that it used them against a civilian population, and that it did so twice. And as it is demonstrating in the Ukraine, the USA is not above starting World War Three in order to wipe out its debt.

US hegemony — which has lasted less than 80 years — is nearing the end of its bloody and genocidal history, and a New World Order is on the point of forming.[34] However, the more its economic monopoly over the globe wanes, the more the US flexes its oversized military muscle. The challenge facing the rest of the world is to survive it's downfall. Like all school bullies who don't realise the playground has turned against them until they're surrounded and without a friend to turn to, it isn't going to be pretty. Either China will become the new hegemon as the lead partner in a Beijing-Moscow axis, or the US will take us all down with it — and a king whose crown is threatened is a dangerous thing! As Richard III told his doomed army in 1485 at the Battle of Bosworth Field:

> *Our strong arms be our conscience, swords our law.*
> *March on! Join bravely. Let us to it pell-mell —*
> *If not to Heaven, then hand in hand to hell!* [35]

---

33. See Alex Blair, 'Xi Jinping predicts "change not seen in 100 years" as he departs Russia after Vladimir Putin meeting', *News.com* (22 March, 2023).

34. See Ray Dal, 'Principles for Dealing with the Changing World Order', *YouTube* (2 March, 2022).

35. William Shakespeare, *King Richard III*; edited by Antony Hammond (The Arden Shakespeare, 1981), p. 325.

3. Washington's Puppet

In my book, *The Road to Fascism*, I argued that, although fascism has returned to the political economy, laws and ideology of the West — most explicitly in our governance by unelected international technocracies, the suspension of our previously inalienable human rights under a more-or-less permanent state of emergency, and our indoctrination into behaviours of compliance, censorship and violence by the orthodoxies of woke — the figure of the leader, with which historical fascism is so closely associated in the form of the Italian *Duce*, German *Führer* and Spanish *Caudillo*, has not.[36] But watching the rise of the newly-butch, paramilitary figure into which Volodmyr Zelenskyy — the former dance-show contestant and soap-opera comedian — has transformed, I'm not now so sure.[37]

It's a rigorously suppressed fact that Zelenskyy is the second US puppet (the first was the oligarch, Petro Poroshenko) to occupy the office of President since the US-engineered coup overthrew the democratically-elected government of the Ukraine in 2014, and that the war we're constantly told began when Russian forces moved into the Donbas region of Eastern Ukraine in February 2022 in actuality started eight years earlier, when the majority Russian-speaking population formed itself into a people's militia and rose up against the intervention of the USA in their country.[38]

Zelenskyy was elected as President in May 2019 on a promise to end the resulting civil war in the Donbas, and until the Russian intervention he appeared on the media platforms of the West in the role of a diminutive, clean-shaven, suited-and-booted office boy, trying to work out the dramatic arc of his new character. This was no longer as the star of the television show, *Servant of the People (Слуга народу)*, in which he had played the gun-toting President of the Ukraine since 2015, but as the actual President of a country for which the USA had very definite plans. To his obvious confusion, his new status as a 'Reality TV' star didn't preclude him from, for example, being humiliated by Donald Trump on

---

36. See Simon Elmer, 'The Psychological Structure of Fascism', Chapter 5 of *The Road to Fascism*, pp. 81-100.

37. See 'Zelensky Winning "Dancing with the Stars"', *YouTube* (28 February, 2022).

38. See Seumas Milne, 'It's not Russia that's pushed Ukraine to the brink of war', *The Guardian* (30 April, 2014).

US television as the whipping boy for the poorest and most corrupt nation in Europe that was ripe for salvation from its Russian oppressor.[39]

Then all that changed last year. A few months in the gym, a new designer beard, imitation army fatigues embroidered with a golden trident, a fashion shoot with his model wife for *Paris Vogue*, and the former naked exponent of cock jokes on Ukrainian music-television famous for wearing high heels and bondage gear and playing a piano with his penis became the new *Führer* before whom the leaders of Western capitalism have been only too ready to abase themselves.[40] Despite presiding over a neo-Nazi Government whose ethnic cleansing of its own population had been reported by Western media for eight long years, that has banned the music of Tchaikovsky and Prokofiev and pulped 72 tonnes of Russian-language books, including Tolstoy and Dostoievsky, and turned them into toilet paper, Zelenskyy is now fêted in the West as a hero of democracy.[41]

Indeed, the UK Prime Minister, Rishi Sunak, the French President, Emmanuel Macron and the US President, Joe Biden, appear to be competing for the role of most adoring fan as they pose in photo after photo of them hugging Zelenskyy, holding hands with Zelenskyy, kissing Zelenskyy, gazing adoringly into the eyes of Zelenskyy, awarding Zelenskyy with honours and medals, before handing over more weapons and tax payers' money to be laundered through their proxy war with Russia.[42]

---

39. See CBS News, 'Trump meets with Ukrainian president amid whistleblower controversy', *YouTube* (25 September, 2019).

40. See Eve Edwards, 'Where to buy Zelensky's Sweatshirt as Ukrainian Trident Jumper goes Viral', *HITC* (22 December, 2022); Rachel Donadio, 'Portrait of Bravery: Ukraine's First Lady, Olena Zelenska', *British Vogue* (26 July, 2022); 'President Zelensky and Ukrainian people singing and dancing naked in supermarkets', *YouTube* (10 March, 2022); 'Ukraine President Zelensky in High Heels singing', *YouTube* (2 March, 2021); 'Volodymyr Zelenskyy 2016 Playing Piano with Penis', *YouTube* (1 March, 2022).

41. See Marc Bennetts, 'Ukraine's National Militia: "We're not neo-Nazis, we just want to make our country better"', *The Guardian* (13 March, 2018); Catherine Philp, 'On the front line of Ukraine's cultural de-Russification', *The Times* (26 June, 2023); Hannes Stein, 'Zelensky As Churchill, An Iconic "V" For Victory Sign By Other Means', *World Crunch* (22 December, 2022).

42. See BBC News, 'Ukraine: Rishi Sunak meets Volodymyr Zelensky in Kyiv' (19 November, 2022); *The Independent*, 'Macron presents Legion of Honour medal to Zelensky during Paris visit', *YouTube* (9 February, 2023); *Guardian News*, 'Biden and Zelenskiy hug after visiting Kyiv church to pay tribute to fallen soldiers', *YouTube* (20 February, 2023).

I'll leave it to the plentiful students of LGBTQIA+ theory to untangle the tortuous erotics of masculine desire between contemporary Western leaders when spending the lives of working-class Ukrainian soldiers as recklessly as their tax-payers' money; but like Mussolini and Hitler before him, Zelenskyy now always appears in mock khaki fatigues, as if just returned from the Russian front. Unlike his fascist predecessors, however, Zelenskyy has never been a soldier or even completed military service, having earned his living since the age of seventeen as a professional comedian. But like Mussolini and Hitler — who were chosen by, respectively, Italian landowners and German industrialists to defeat the threat of the workers' movement to European capital — Zelenskyy's elevation from preening dance-show contestant to butch President is serving the financial interests of Western capitalists.

It's an inconvenient fact for those who continue to describe fascism as a form of socialism that Western capitalists supported and funded fascist movements in the 1920s and 1930s in order to counter the threat of a politically-organised working class, and that without their financial and political support neither Mussolini nor Hitler would have formed governments.[43] Even before Hitler became Chancellor in 1933, nearly 27 per cent of the German aristocracy had joined the Nazi Party; and between 1928 and 1942, 270 princes from the various old royal families became Nazis.[44] I think it's safe to say that they had a better appreciation of the putative 'socialist' credentials of the Nazi Party than post-war ideologues of Western capitalism. More importantly, the monopolies that funded the Third Reich were not state-owned but bore the names of Germany's most powerful capitalists: Thyssen (which controlled more than 75 per cent of Germany's iron ore reserves), Krupp (the largest company in Europe) and Siemens-Schuckert (Germany's largest industrial conglomerate).[45] Indeed, Fritz Thyssen was one of the nineteen industrialists, financiers and landowners who, in November 1932,

---

43. See, *inter alia*, Peter Hitchens, 'End this crude smear against conservatives — Hitler's Nazis were in fact left-wing racists', *The Mail on Sunday* (11 March, 2023).

44. See Mark Felton Productions, 'Hitler and the Hohenzollerns — The Kaiser's Family & the Nazis', *YouTube* (27 March, 2023).

45. See Dwight Jon Zimmerman, 'The Faustian Bargain: Industrialist Fritz Thyssen and the Nazis', *Defense Media Network* (15 August 2017); Global Security, '1933-1945: Krupp under the Nazis'; Katja Hoyer, 'Nazi Billionaires: The Dark History of Germany's Wealthiest Dynasties', *The Spectator* (23 April, 2022).

petitioned the Reich President to appoint Hitler as Chancellor and, the following year, financed the successful election campaign of the NSDAP with over 2 million Reichsmark, without which it's doubtful they would have come to power.[46]

As I argued in my book, the story that fascism is a form of socialism is a product of post-war US imperialism, which sought both to erase the history of capitalism's pre-war support for fascism and to denigrate the moral status communism emerged with after the war as both the military defeaters of fascism and the leaders of resistance groups across Europe.[47] Despite the revelatory character attributed to it by defenders of neoliberalism today, the 'horseshoe' depiction of fascism and communism meeting at the extremes of the political spectrum isn't a theory: it's a pictogram to convince US citizens why, for example, they should hand over $886 billion of their tax dollars to the US Defense Department this year.[48] And it doesn't stop there.

As of July 2023, the West has handed over an astonishing €314.84 billion to the Ukraine's US puppet Government while inviting Zelenskyy to perform to the legislatures of Western nations — something for which, unlike leading a country, he is far more qualified and even adept, according to his starry-eyed fans.[49] Personally, I see nothing convincing or charismatic about a small man speaking with the faked gravelly voice Zelenskyy uses when begging for more money from Western nations. But I appear to be in the minority. The spectacle of Zelenskyy, in designer fatigues, demanding more weapons from the UK in the semi-religious setting of Westminster Hall this February didn't stop a crowd of breathless MPs from making themselves ridiculous by snapping his now quasi-sacred presence on their smartphones and then posting the photograph on their Twitter accounts with some variation on the statement that the puppet-President of the Ukraine —

---

46. See Wikipedia, 'Industrielleneingabe'.

47. See Simon Elmer, 'Fascism, Neoliberalism and the Left', Chapter 7 of *The Road to Fascism*, pp. 123-151.

48. See William Hartung, 'Biden's new whopping $886B defense budget request', *Responsible Statecraft* (9 March, 2023).

49. See Kiel Institute for the World Economy, 'Ukraine Support Tracker: A Database of Military, Financial and Humanitarian Aid to Ukraine' (as of 31 July, 2023); and CNN World, 'Watch Zelensky's historic speech to Congress' (22 December, 2022).

as our Chancellor of the Exchequer, Jeremy Hunt, wrote — is 'the bravest man I have ever met'.[50]

But how did this bravest man rise from MTV star to President of the Ukraine? In March 2018, four years after the US-led coup, Servant of the People, a political party named after Zelenskyy's soap opera, was registered with the Ukrainian Ministry of Justice by its then leader, Ivan Bakanov, an entrepreneur in the field of hydro-electricity.[51] A year later, on a promise to stop the civil war in the Donbass, the show's star was elected President of the Ukraine. Upon assuming office, he appointed Bakanov, who is Zelenskyy's childhood friend, First Deputy Chief of the Security Service, which is the main directorate against corruption and organised crime in the Ukraine. Three months later, Bakanov became Head of the Security Service with unlimited and uncontrolled powers, which he didn't hesitate to use for the benefit of his inner circle, including Zelenskyy.

I'll come back to Mr. Bakanov later, but how did such a farce materialise? It's hard for reality to keep up with the fantasies of US foreign policy, but I can imagine Geoffrey Pyatt, the US ambassador to the Ukraine in 2016, watching Zelenskyy's television show late one night and putting in a call to Victoria Nuland, the US Secretary of State for European Affairs who famously picked the post-coup Ukraine Cabinet in 2014.[52] 'Hey, Vickie, I think we found our next President of the Ukraine!' Since it elected Ronald Reagan to the office in 1981, Washington has preferred B-movie actors, recovering alcoholics, game-show hosts and senile senators to play their Presidents, so it makes perfect sense that the hawks in Washington thought someone who has played one so successfully on Ukrainian television would make the perfect puppet for US foreign policy. That is, of course, if the US didn't itself create the television show — which charts the rise of Zelenskyy's character from primary school teacher to President on an anti-corruption platform — in order to promote Zelenskyy from actor to the same position in what we continue to call, increasingly unconvincingly, 'real life'.

50. See *Daily Mail*, 'Ukraine's Zelensky addresses UK in Westminster Hall', *YouTube* (8 February, 2023); and @Jeremy_Hunt, 'The bravest man I have ever met. Slava Ukraini!', *Twitter* (8 February, 2023).

51. See 'Volodmyr Zelensky on Dancing with the Stars Ukraine', *YouTube* (7 March, 2022); *Wikipedia*, 'Servant of the People'.

52. See '"Fuck the EU!" Victoria Nuland & Geoffrey Pyatt secret phone talk', *YouTube* (20 February, 2015).

But there's a more serious side to this elevation of a professional actor to the puppet *Führer* of NATO. Just as Western capitalism found that, once the socialists and communists had been defeated in Italy and Germany there was no one left to control Mussolini and Hitler, so Zelenskyy's call for NATO to launch 'pre-emptive' nuclear strikes on Russia — furiously denied by back-peddling 'Fact checkers' — has pushed the world closer to World War Three than at any time since the Cuban Missile Crisis of 1962.[53] Of course, as a puppet President, Zelenskyy only speaks when someone's hand is up his trousers, so these motions towards World War Three are mouthed on the command of Washington hawks intent on Russia's oil and gas reserves. In preparation for which, the dehumanisation of the Russian people and banning of Russian culture by the neo-Nazi Government of the Ukraine — which for nearly a decade now has waged a genocidal war on the 8.3 million ethnic Russians within its own borders — is presumably preparing Western audiences for the ethnic cleansing of Russians 'post-conquest'.

I was recently listening to the famous recording of Ludwig van Beethoven's *Piano Concerto No. 5 in E-flat* (Op. 73) by the great Russian pianist, Emil Gilels, which was made in London in the Spring of 1957; and it suddenly struck me that this would never have happened in today's climate of censorship, no-platforming and virtue-signalling. On the grounds not only that Beethoven was a German — and therefore as responsible for the Second World War as Tchaikovsky apparently is for the current war in the Ukraine — but that the UK was in a Cold War with the Soviet Union — although not as heated as the one we are in today with Russia — this recording would instead have been voluntarily and proudly cancelled by the Philharmonia Orchestra, just as the Cardiff Philharmonic Orchestra cancelled a performance of Tchaikovsky's music last year.[54] Thankfully, even under the threat of nuclear annihilation that has returned today, in the 1950s we still remembered that such censorship is a characteristic of totalitarian regimes — something we have forgotten with the return of fascism to the West. For myself, I dissociate myself from this contemptible behaviour towards the Russian people and their

---

53. See Brendan Cole, Fact Check: Did President Zelensky Call on NATO to Start Nuclear War?', *Newsweek* (7 October, 2022).

54. See Matthew Weaver, 'Cardiff Philharmonic removes Tchaikovsky performance over Ukraine conflict', *The Guardian* (9 March, 2022).

thankfully still-intact national culture, and condemn the geopolitical aggression of the West it is being used to justify.[55]

Fantasies of conquest aside, the fact that Washington's performing puppet has the unrestrained admiration, here in the lapdog Kingdom of Great Britain and Northern Ireland, not only of the Conservatives but of Labourites, the Greens, the Left, the Woke, and of every other idiot across the West — all of whom have collaborated willingly, fervently and unquestioningly with this attempt to dehumanise Russia and its people — shows just how little we have learned from history, how low we have sunk as a nation, and how ripe we are for the return of fascism.[56]

4. The Fall of Volodmyr Zelenskyy

But things have now changed. When Vladimir Putin and Xi Jinping signed the fourteen agreements between the Russian Federation and the People's Republic of China in March, the Zelenskky puppet fell silent as its master's hand was removed from its strings.[57] The braying mouths of Western politicians closed in the face of this threat to their hegemony.[58] Even the constant references to 'Russian aggression' have begun to falter.[59] Now, for the first time in over a year-and-a-half, it's possible that Zelenskyy and his wife will be arrested and executed by the People's Militia of the Donetsk People's Republic and — like Mussolini and his mistress in 1945 — hung by their heels and put on display for their former victims to mock. That might be unlikely — especially since Zelenskky spends so little time in the Ukraine, let alone near the frontline — but we can still dream. In

---

55. For examples of a national culture that hasn't been erased by US imperialism and replaced by US consumerism, see Beloe Zlato, 'Russian folk Ансамбль "Белое злато" — За тихой рекой', *YouTube* (11 November, 2013); and 'Katyusha Хор Пятницкого MSK-US', *YouTube* (19 December, 2014).

56. See Seumas Milne, 'The demonisation of Russia risks paving the way for war', *The Guardian* (4 March, 2015).

57. See Rilet Waggaman, 'Putin and Xi's Moscow agreements', *Off Guardian* (28 March, 2023).

58. See Rob Merrick, '"Unprecedented" sanctions can still reverse Putin's invasion of Ukraine, UK minister insists', *The Independent* (24 February, 2022).

59. See 'G20 declaration adopted with no mention of Russian aggression in Ukraine', *The Daily Star* (9 September, 2023).

the remainder of this chapter, I'm going to show why Washington's puppet deserves such a fate.

Since Russian forces moved into the Donbass region, my newsfeed — I imagine like yours — has been inundated with advertisements for Ukrainian women.[60] Apparently, they are beautiful, warm, have traditional values, prefer older men, and — most alluring of all — they value the wealth of would-be husbands over their looks. This information is related over footage of women in various stages of undress, pouting their lips and kneading their breasts, as a narrator invites us to 'take what is yours'.[61] Perhaps not coincidentally, this was the Twitter hashtag of the fabled Ukrainian 'counteroffensive' that sputtered and died in the Spring of 2023. But there's a less than metaphorical connection between these online brothels selling Ukraine's women to the highest bidder and what Volodmyr Zelenskyy is doing to their country. Under the cover of this proxy war, Ukraine has been turned into a brothel for the West. Zelenskyy is the pimp pulling tricks off the street; Nuland is the Madame running the whores; US asset managers are their favoured clients; Von der Leyen is the headline act; Macron is the men's room attendant; Sunak is the coat-check boy; Trudeau's the head fluffer. The analogies are endless. This isn't a war, it's a gang bang, a snuff movie of drone strikes for Twitter; and it's the people of the Ukraine that are being raped and murdered.

With the eyes of UK journalists focused on important issues like pronouns, they missed or have since forgotten the fact that the war in the Ukraine began in 2014, not 2022, and it was started by the USA, seeking to annex both Georgia and the Ukraine into the North Atlantic Treaty Alliance and impose the same practices of neoliberalisation it imposed in Chile and Argentina in the 1970s.[62] One might ask how the US would respond if Russia — or, more comparably, China — staged a political coup deposing the democratically-elected President of Mexico, set up a puppet government in his place, severed Mexico's trade relations with the US, and sought to draw it into an economic and military alliance with itself — and did so with the whole of South America already in its pocket under a 'South

60. See 'UkraineSingles.com', *YouTube*.

61. See Maia Rakovic, 'This Unnerving 2-Minute YouTube Ad Encourages American Men To "Take" Ukrainian Women', TrillMag (27 June, 2022).

62. See John J. Mearsheimer, 'Why the Ukraine Crisis Is the West's Fault', *Foreign Affairs* (September/October 2014).

Atlantic Treaty Organisation'. The impossibility of the USA permitting even the first stage in such geopolitical aggression to take place suggests that, in advancing to the last of these stages in the Ukraine, Washington was deliberately trying to provoke Putin into a response — which it got when Russia occupied and then annexed the Crimean Peninsula in March 2014.

Zelenskyy, like all politicians, is a liar; but he is also a thief who has embezzled the Ukrainian people, handing over the grain, oil, gas, mineral and lithium resources of his country in shady deals with predatory US asset managers BlackRock, JP Morgan and Goldman Sachs.[63] Without democratic mandate from the Ukrainian electorate and under cover of the war with Russia, Zelenskyy has implemented something like the Washington Consensus, the ten principles of neoliberalisation enforced by the US Treasury, the World Bank and the International Monetary Fund as a condition of receiving loans and investment.[64] These include removing import tariffs, cutting corporate taxes, revoking employment laws, deregulating industries, privatising state-owned companies, assets and banks, and, of course, cutting Ukraine's economic ties with Russia, formerly its largest trading partner.[65]

As I said in my preface, Zelenskyy has also overseen the transformation of the Ukraine by US technology information companies into the world's first fully digitalised state, including its education, health and civil services, with a Central Bank Digital Currency due to be made into law in 2024, and a military and judiciary run by Artificial Intelligence, which will include producing pre-trial and pre-sentencing reports assessing the risk of a defendant reoffending.[66]

---

63. See Geeta Mohan, 'Are Ukraine's vast natural resources a real reason behind Russia's invasion?', *Business Today* (25 February, 2022); Ben Norton, 'Ukraine's Zelelnsky Sends Love Letter to US Corporations, Promising "Big Business" for Wall Street', *Scheerpost* (27 January, 2023).

64. See Tejvan Pettinger, 'Washington Consensus — definition and meaning', *Economics help* (25 April, 2017).

65. See Jake Kallio and Ben Norton, 'West prepares to plunder post-war Ukraine with neoliberal shock therapy: privatization, deregulation, slashing worker protections', *Geopolitical Economy* (28 July, 2022).

66. See 'Ukraine lays out plan to be "most digital" country', *Kyiv Post* (5 July, 2022); and Nimrah Khatoon, 'Ukraine to Become the World's First 100% Cashless Country by 2025, Says National Bank Official', *BNN* (7 September, 2023).

In order to pre-empt any opposition to these policies and the technologies they are implementing, Zelenskyy has banned eleven opposition political parties and all independent media platforms in the Ukraine, made laws prohibiting around 73 per cent of workers from forming unions or engaging in collective bargaining, and issued hit lists against journalists and academics denounced as 'enemies of Ukraine' for criticising his Government.[67]

In this, at least, the Zelenskyy puppet has learned its lesson. It was the refusal of President Viktor Yanukovych, the democratically-elected President of the Ukraine, to implement the IMF's demands to cut wages, slash spending and end gas subsidies in preparation for the assimilation of the Ukraine into the European Union, and instead to sign a new trade deal with Russia, that led to him being toppled in the US-engineered coup in 2014. As Washington's puppet, Zelenskyy has presented no such barrier to US imperialism — if we can use that word to describe Western capitalism's rape and pillage of the Ukraine and its people under the cover of war and its propaganda. Those in the West calling for the restoration of Ukraine's sovereignty from the Russian invasion couldn't be more wrong: the entire country is being sold — lock, stock and 40,000 barrels of oil per day — to US asset managers.

To this end, Zelenskyy has obediently and repeatedly refused diplomatic moves by China to broker peace between Russia and the Ukraine, and instead sent tens of thousands of Ukrainian soldiers to their deaths in the war against Russia that has also killed unknown thousands of Ukrainian civilians.[68] Nobody knows what the actual casualty figures are since February 2022, which the UN estimates at around 10,000 civilians killed and 18,000 wounded, and the US estimates at 70,000 military personnel killed and between 100,000 and 120,000 wounded.[69] But the cannon-fodder for Western capital must be running low, as this January Zelenskyy dropped the age of at which Ukrainian nationals must

---

67. See Abdul Rahman, 'Opposition political parties banned in Ukraine and 'unified information policy' imposed', *Peoples Dispatch* (21 March, 2022); and Yana Dianova, 'Assassinated for telling the truth about Ukraine', *The Wall Will Fall* (17 April, 2022).

68. See Ministry of Foreign Affairs of the People's Republic of China, 'China's Position on the Political Settlement of the Ukraine Crisis' (24 February, 2023).

69. See Office of the United Nations High Commissioner for Human Rights, 'Ukraine: civilian casualty update 24 September 2023' (25 September, 2023); and Andrew Roth, 'Battlefield deaths in Ukraine have risen sharply this year, say US officials', *The Guardian* (18 August, 2023).

register for the military to 16 for men and 18 for women.[70] Indeed, it was unsurprising to see what were, in effect, the 4,000 Ukrainian draft-dodgers who paid the average weekly wage in Ukraine for a seat in Wembley Stadium to watch representatives of their nation play England in the European Cup qualifiers this March.[71] And who can blame them, even if we might question the sincerity of their rather too loudly protested patriotism?

By continuing the proxy war with Russia, Zelenskyy has perpetuated the cover under which the €314.84 billion of Western 'aid' can be laundered into anonymous accounts in offshore jurisdictions.[72] In October 2021, the Pandora Papers revealed that Ivan Bakanov — I said I'd get back to him — the Head of the Security Service, his chief Aide, Serhiy Shefir, and Zelenskyy himself, together own a network of offshore companies in the British Virgin Islands, Cyprus and Belize that, among their investments, include London property[73]. Indeed, in October 2019, even before the billions of dollars in 'aid' was sent to Ukraine, Transparency International estimated that £100 billion of dirty money enters the UK every year, with Ukraine surpassed only by Russia as the greatest source of high-end corruption and money laundering in which UK financial services are involved.[74] So, financially speaking, the proxy war is only extending what the City of London has been doing since the last Global Financial Crisis sent Ukrainian and Russian billionaires scurrying for tax havens in which to hide their booty, and looking for hedge-fund managers who wouldn't ask questions about where and how they got it.

Of course, the purpose of such offshore financial jurisdictions is not only to hide the money but also who owns it, so nobody knows how much Zelenskyy has made from this vast programme of embezzlement, which has been very much

---

70. See Daria Zubkova, 'Cabinet Introduces Military Registration from Age of 16', *UkraNews* (4 January, 2023).

71. See Jack Rosser, 'United We don't care about the England result, we just want 90 minutes where we can forget about the war says Ukraine fan', *The Sun* 25 March, 2023).

72. See Nick Fenton and Andrew Lohsen, 'Corruption and Private sector Investment in Ukraine's Reconstruction', *CSIS* (8 November, 2022).

73. See Elena Loginova, 'Pandora Papers Reveal Offshore Holdings of Ukrainian President and his Inner Circle', *OCCRP* (3 October, 2021).

74. See Transparency International, *At Your Service: Investigating how UK businesses and institutions help corrupt individuals and regimes launder their money and reputations*; edited by Steve Goodrich (24 October 2019).

modelled on that employed in Russia after the dissolution of the Soviet Union. But one estimate of the net worth of this former TV comedian has put his personal fortune at $596 million.[75] However, the page reporting this figure cited no source for this estimate, so the only indicator of its possible accuracy is that, as soon as it was published, the corporate-funded fact checkers employed to do so immediately denounced it as 'false', as they have every other 'conspiracy theory' that has turned out to be true.[76]

According to a more reliable source, Seymour Hersh, the internationally-respected journalist who broke the story about the sabotage of Russia's Nord Stream gas pipeline by covert US operatives, Zelenskyy and his Cabinet have embezzled at least $400 million from the 'aid' package of the USA.[77] Reportedly, Ukrainian Government Ministers are competing to set up shell companies in order to export weapons and ammunition supplied by ever-generous Western governments to private arms dealers around the world. Many of these companies are registered in Poland and the Czech Republic, others in the Persian Gulf and Israel, and suspected others in the Cayman Islands and Panama. According to Hersh's source, Zelenskyy has been criticised by his own Ministers for taking more than his fair share of the kickbacks from this money-laundering scheme.

My own view is that, given Zelenskyy is handing over an entire country to the oligarchs of Western capitalism, either this figure is far short of his actual compensation or he needs a new agent. I have little doubt that the UK's 'world-beating' financial advisors could cut him a better deal. But beyond the personal profit accrued with the blood and soil of his countrymen by this thief, liar and war criminal, if you're looking for the simplest reason why the UK Government, Parliament, media and their financiers in the City of London are all so committed to the war in the Ukraine, this is it.

Finally, and not least in the list of crimes Washington's puppet has committed or enabled, since 2014 the policies and actions of the Governments of the Ukraine

---

75. See The General Consensus, 'This, ladies and gentleman, is what corruption looks like', *Facebook* (19 July, 2022).

76. See Andy Nguyen, 'There's no evidence that Ukraine's president has a net worth of $596 million', *PolitiFact* (21 July, 2022); Brea Jones, 'Social Media Posts Make Unsupported Claims About Zelensky's Income, Net Worth', *FactCheck.org* (21 July, 2022).

77. See Seymour Hersh, 'Trading with the Enemy', *Substack* (12 April, 2023), and 'How America took out the Nord Stream Pipeline', *Peoples Dispatch* (10 February, 2023).

against the people of the Donbas — where thousands of ethnic Russians, including an estimated 3,400 civilians, have been killed by ultranationalist armed forces like the Azov Regiment, the Aidar Volunteer Battalion and Right-Sector paramilitaries, and Russian language and culture is banned from public consumption and official use as effectively as that of the European Jews was under the Third Reich — meet the United Nations' definition of genocide.[78]

For all these crimes, Volodmyr Zelenskyy should be at the top of the International Criminal Court's list of criminals wanted for war crimes and theft. But, personally, I hope the People's Militia get him first. But where to hang this puppet from his severed strings?

After their execution, the bodies of Mussolini and his fellow fascists were strung up in Piazzale Loreto in Milan. The partisans that captured them chose this site because, the previous year, fifteen Milanese civilians had been shot by the Gestapo in retaliation for partisan attacks on a German military convoy. Forty years later, the Monument to the Liberators of Donetsk, built in the Lenin Komsomol Park in the capital of the Donbass, commemorated the liberation of the Ukraine from the German occupation during World War Two. Beginning with the massacre at Babi Yar outside Kyiv in September 1941, the Germans, with the willing help of their Ukrainian collaborators, managed to kill, in a little over two years, 5 million Ukrainian nationals, including 1.5 million Jews, as well as executing and starving hundreds of thousands of Soviet prisoners of war.[79] The 14th Waffen Grenadier Division of the SS raised from Ukrainian volunteers during this occupation is still celebrated in street marches through Kyiv today; and the wolf's hook and black sun on the emblem of the Neo-Nazi Azov Regiment of the Ukrainian National Guard are both taken from SS insignia, as are the death's head and other emblems of Nazism worn by Ukraine's armed forces and openly

78. See Terry Boardman, 'Ukrainian policy in the Donbass: Is it fair to call it genocide?', *UK Column* (25 February, 2023); United Nations High Commissioner for Human Rights, 'Conflict-related civilian casualties in Ukraine' (27 January, 2022); 'Profile: Who are Ukraine's far-right Azov regiment?', *Al Jazeera* (1 March, 2022); Amnesty International, 'Ukraine: Abuses and war crimes by the Aidar Volunteer Battalion in the north Luhansk region' (8 September, 2014); United Nations Office on Genocide Prevention and the Responsibility to Protect, 'Definitions'.

79. See Jadwiga Rogoża, 'Ukraine's disputes over the 80th anniversary of the Babi Yar massacre', *Centre for Eastern Studies* (22 October, 2021).

displayed across the country.[80] It's a well-known maxim that the first casualty of war is truth; and part of the truth this proxy war has sought to kill is that Zelenskyy, his political allies, the Ukrainian military and elements of Ukrainian society glorify the country's past collaboration with the Nazis and still have links with Neo-Nazi organisations today.[81]

In September of this year, Zelenskky invited a former member of the Waffen SS Grenadier Division, Yaroslav Hunka, to join him on a visit to the Canadian Parliament where he was introduced by the Speaker of the House, Anthony Rota, as a 'Ukrainian hero' who had fought for 'Canadian independence against the Russians' during World War Two, and given a standing ovation by the entire House of Commons.[82] I don't know if Canadian MPs are a little hazy on their history, but that means he was fighting against the Red Army in which 7 million Ukrainians served and that ultimately defeated the Third Reich. When it subsequently emerged that Hunka was an actual Nazi, Prime Minister Justin Trudeau apologised and Rota resigned, both saying they had made a 'mistake'. But there was no mistake. Trudeau, the Speaker and the entire Canadian Parliament invited a known Nazi into their House and applauded him. His name is Volodmyr Zelenskyy. In abject obedience to the US, anti-Russian hatred has reached such a pitch in the West that anyone who opposes them, now or sixty years ago, is welcomed as a hero and ally, even if they are Nazis. And why wouldn't they be, when the West itself is so clearly on the road to fascism — is, indeed, entering its gates as I write? It's hard to imagine how the West can sink any lower in moral turpitude, but I have no doubt whatsoever that we will, that we are, and that in the future there will be no more apologies, no more admissions of mistakes. Subsequently, in a gesture worthy of Orwell's Ministry of Truth, the

---

80. See Cnaan Liphshiz, 'Hundreds in Ukraine attend marches celebrating Nazi SS soldiers', *The Times of Israel* (4 May, 2021); Shaun Walker, 'Azov fighters are Ukraine's greatest weapon and may be its greatest threat', *The Guardian* (10 September, 2014); Cnaan Liphshiz, 'Staircase in Ukraine mall decorated with giant swastika', *The Times of Israel* (18 February, 2019).

81. See Shira Silkoff, 'Kyiv to name street for Ukrainian Nazi collaborator after public vote', *Jerusalem Post* (13 April, 2023); Alexander Rubinstein and Max Blumenthal, 'How Ukraine's Jewish president Zelensky made peace with neo-Nazi paramilitaries on front lines of war with Russia', *The Grayzone* (4 March, 2022).

82. See Holly Evans, 'Canadian Parliament accidentally honours Nazi — with Zelensky and Trudeau applauding', *Independent* (26 September, 2023).

House leader moved to strike the recognition of Hunka from Hansard, the official record of proceedings in Canada's House of Commons available to the public.[83]

As they were in 1943, the liberators of the Ukraine are the lesser of two evils, but I can't think of a more fitting end to the Zelenskyy puppet and his collaborators than to be strung by their heels from the monument to the defeat of fascism eighty years ago — unless, of course, it is to be strung from a newly-erected monument to the liberation of the whole of Europe from contemporary Western fascism and its puppet dictator.

Am I joking? I'm certainly not laughing. I find nothing funny about Zelenskyy, although the obsequiousness with which he is treated by the UK Parliament and media would be laughable if it wasn't so utterly contemptible. And I, for one — and I know I'm not alone, although most still daren't say it — would rejoice to see such justice served by those on whom he has inflicted such suffering. It's unlikely, perhaps, given the brazenness with which even greater criminals than Zelenskyy walk free in the glare of the media and the indifferent eye of the law today, and there are hundreds if not thousands more who should share his scaffold. But as I said, we can dream. The task facing those of us opposed to the return of fascism as the political economy of the West is to turn this dream of liberation and justice into reality.

---

83. See Aaron D'Andrea, 'Liberals try to strike Hunka recognition from official record. What that means', *Global News* (27 September, 2023).

6. Trans Rights and the Order of Speech

'There is a new word in Newspeak', said Syme, 'I don't know whether you know it: duckspeak, to quack like a duck. It is one of those interesting words that have two contradictory meanings. Applied to an opponent, it is abuse; applied to someone you agree with, it is praise.'

— George Orwell, *Nineteen Eighty-four*, 1949

I didn't go to London Pride this year.[1] In truth, I haven't been for years, since the early 2000s, not only because of the festival's increasing commercialisation as a platform for corporate advertising in search of the so-called 'pink pound', but because of its more recent embrace of the Metropolitan Police Force and the London Mayor, who have used it to promote themselves as 'LGBTQIA+ friendly' while overseeing the increase in their power over us, whether that's in new Stop and Search powers against protesters or the Ultra-Low Emission Zone that has enclosed all London in its tax and surveillance regime.[2] Now, though, I am not merely disappointed — if no longer surprised — by the failure of the increasingly apolitical gay community to resist or even question this appropriation and co-option of Pride, or concerned about how a festival of resistance and solidarity in which I was proud to participate back in the 1990s has become the enforced orthodoxy of the UK biosecurity state to which every politician, institution and public figure must pay homage and exhibit dogmatic obedience.[3] Today, in 2023, I am directly opposed to Pride's recent, politically dubious and morally

---

1. See Pride in London, 'Pride in London 2023', 2023.

2. See Metropolitan Police Service, 'LGBT+ community liaison officers', 2023; Conor Clark, 'Sadiq Khan: "The Trans community should not be stigmatised, demonised or weaponised"', *Gay Times* (2023); Liberty, 'Public Order Act: New Protest Stop & Search Powers', 2023; Colin Fernandez, 'Sadiq Khan slammed over "nonsense data" behind ULEZ scheme which council chief says didn't take into account his region's older population', *Daily Mail* (14 February, 2023).

3. See Nina Lloyd, 'Inclusive workplaces unlock growth, Starmer tells LGBT+ business leaders', *Independent* (29 June, 2023); RIBA Architecture, 'RIBA celebrates Pride Month 2023' (31 May, 2023); Danielle Stacey, 'Prince William shows support for LGBTQ+ community ahead of London Pride', *Hello!* (30 June, 2023).

indefensible embrace of the violence, abuse and misogyny of what has come to be known as 'trans-rights'.[4] In this chapter I'm going to discuss why.

I've been meaning to write this text for some time, maybe years, since the orthodoxies of trans first crept into our culture comparatively recently. It was only in January 2017 that *National Geographic*, then the most-read magazine in the world, put a 9-year old boy on its cover with the quote: 'The best thing about being a girl is now I don't have to pretend to be a boy' (the boy later recanted).[5] I've discussed the authoritarianism of woke in my book, *The Road to Fascism*, and why it is now the official ideology of the West; and I've made reference to the link between the transhuman programmes of the Global Biosecurity State — which has emerged from the coronavirus 'crisis' as the new paradigm of governance in the West — and the practices of trans identity, which include the use of puberty blockers on children and the promise of 'transitioning' from one sex to another through hormone therapy and surgical mutilation.[6] But as these practices and the ideology driving them have become more institutionalised, particularly in our schools, I have known that I would have to write a text devoted solely to this topic.

I have found it unusually difficult, however, to put my thoughts on this issue in order. Partly, this is because of my horror and fears at the thought of children being subjected to the predations of a medical industry that has just shown itself, under the guise of a vaccination programme, willing to inject experimental gene therapies into a demographic that is statistically immune to the disease their parents were told it would protect them from.[7] Partly it is because of the absurdity and tedium of having to argue rationally and calmly against the irrationality and hysteria of these orthodoxies, which fly in the face of everything we know about human biology — and, indeed, what we call intellectual and moral debate.

But there is another reason, too. Since I am talking not only about an ideology, a political practice and an industry but also about people, it's hard to discuss the former without speaking of my relation to the latter. In the past I have

---

4. See Charlotte Manning, 'Pride in London unveils 2023 campaign "Never March Alone" in support of trans community', *Attitude* (26 May, 2023).

5. See 'Gender Revolution', special issue of *National Geographic* (January 2017).

6. See Simon Elmer, 'The Ideology of Woke', *The Road to Fascism*, pp. 109-121.

7. See Simon Elmer, 'The UK "Vaccination" Programme. Part 2. Virtue and Terror. 2. Suffer Little Children' (22 September, 2021); collected in *The New Normal*, pp. 223-235.

known and, as a Londoner, still on occasion meet transvestites, drag queens and, occasionally, a man or women who is undergoing or has undergone some sort and degree of medical 'transition' that, they hope, will make or has made them happier, more content with themselves, more at ease in the world — nothing more, perhaps, than what we all want. I once counted several of them as my friends, and although I am repelled by the new breed of violent young men who think wearing a dress gives them the right to threaten and attack women and then denounce anyone who disagrees with their dogma as 'Nazis', I am very aware that anything I say about the enforced orthodoxies of this ideology will undoubtedly be interpreted as an attack on those who, under the doctrinaire catch-all of 'trans', have had all the distinctions between their practices, behaviours, beliefs and identities reduced to the descriptively inaccurate, sociologically reductive, politically totalising, biologically meaningless and medically fraudulent term 'transgender'. How this has been done, why and to what ends is what I want to address in this chapter.

1. The Castrated Self

On 23 March this year a protest was organised by students at Purdue University in the State of Indiana, USA.[8] Unusually, it took the form not only of chants and banners at the protest but, later in the day, of a block party and drag show organised by oSTEM (Out in Science, Technology, Engineering and Mathematics, Inc.), an LGBTQ+ organisation with over 100 professional and student chapters in the USA and UK. The occasion for these actions was the visit of the conservative political commentator, Michael Knowles, who during his talk to a sold-out crowd of 400 students called for the 'eradication of the ideology of transgenderism', and discussed how parents could protect their children from educational institutions enforcing its orthodoxies. Purdue is a prestigious research university specialising in science, engineering and aviation, and whose alumni include twenty-five astronauts, Nobel Prize-winning physicists and chemists, Pulitzer Prize winning journalists and senior politicians in the US and other countries. Of its more than 50,000 undergraduate and postgraduate students, 85 per cent are categorised as

---

8. See Noe Padilla, '"Crisis of Identity": Michael Knowles speaks to a packed room at Purdue University', *Journal & Courier* (24 March, 2023).

'affluent' — and they need to be. This year, Purdue charged an annual tuition fee of $9,992 for in-state students and $28,794 for out-of-state students. As Mr. Knowles gave his lecture, in the hallway outside students stood chanting 'Fuck off Nazis' over and over for the duration of his talk.[9] Many of them wore medical masks. Along the corridor, young women marched like drill sergeants between their lines. One wore the pale-blue, pink and white trans flag emblazoned with a black assault rifle and the words 'DEFEND YOURSELF', which means far more in the US, where 327 people are shot every day, than it does in the UK.[10] The home-made banners said a lot about this ideology. 'Eradicate transphobia'. 'Unite to fight anti-trans bigotry'. 'For the good of society conservativism must be eradicated'. 'Intellectual discourse requires intellect'. 'Shut the fuck up'. These are not the terms of a debate, in a university or anywhere else. These are authoritarian instructions issued from a platform of growing cultural and political hegemony that has come to be known as 'woke', and these wealthy students from the US middle classes are its future politicians, civil servants, lawyers, doctors, scientists, professors, teachers, curators, journalists, company directors and institutional administrators.

The policing and manipulation of human sexuality has always been used by authoritarian and particularly totalitarian states to control the behaviour of its citizens. But across the West today, not only the adolescent, puritanical, censorial and increasingly legislated sexual orthodoxies of woke but now also the gender orthodoxies of trans are being indoctrinated into children by our education and entertainment industries, normalised to the British public in our media and cultural industries, and written into our laws and policies by our government, parliament and local authorities. And the goal is the same: to control the behaviour of UK citizens. To this end, the UK biosecurity state has programmes and technologies undreamed of by the totalitarianisms of the Twentieth Century, whether that's repressing desire in obedience to the orthodoxies of biosecurity (for example, the effective ban on sex between people from separate households under lockdown restrictions) or — as demonstrated by the students of Purdue University — releasing the pent-up libido of the compliant in exaggerated anger and hatred

---

9. See 'Far-left student protestors chant "f*ck off nazis" in reaction to Michael Knowles speaking event at Purdue University', *The Post Millenial* (24 March, 2023).

10. See Brady United, 'The Facts That Make Us Act', 2019.

directed against those who fail to obey.[11] Indeed, the contempt for and violence against women we associate with the machismo of historical fascism, and which has returned today in the guise and on the justification of defending so-called 'trans-rights', demonstrates how easy it is for the ideologues of woke to direct the emotions and behaviour of its acolytes.

If we look to historical parallels, it took just twelve years for the Third Reich to make soldiers from the Hitler Youth, the membership of which was compulsory for all German children between 10 and 18 years of age, and less than that for the Nazi Party to turn them into paramilitary Brownshirts (*Sturmabteilung*) whose membership had risen to 3 million by the time they formed a government in 1933. In the wake of a similar financial crisis to that which gave rise to fascism, woke started to receive governmental, institutional and financial backing after the Occupy Movement of 2011-12, which drew attention to the inequality produced by the global financial system — pronouns being easier to police than challenges to finance capitalism. But we should remember the trajectory of the Hitler Youth when judging the import and seriousness of the growing number of activists calling on transvestites to arm themselves and — as they openly declare — 'Kill the TERFS' (an acronym for 'Trans-Exclusionary Radical Feminists').[12] Just as the National Socialists propagated such attitudes towards Bolsheviks and Jews, trans has fashioned a paranoid and absolutist ideology that reduces any questioning of its dogma to a threat to the existence of its acolytes. We've seen this repeatedly stated by trans activists claiming that anything less than vocal agreement ('silence is violence') and obedient compliance with their dictates ('respect existence or expect resistance') is a murderous attack on their lives ('protect trans kids'). As Pastor Martin Niemöller might have said: 'First they came for the TERFS . . . '[13]

Given which, is it any wonder that the pathetic young men lining the corridors of the Purdue University union shouting 'fuck off Nazis', their every utterance policed by 'butch' girls of indeterminate gender, are so ready to pull on a dress and cut off their genitals in a desperate attempt to gain access to the phallic order

---

11. See Georgia Simcox, 'Six-in-ten Britons have gone without sex during lockdown — and from today it will be illegal to romp at home with someone from another household', *Daily Mail* (1 June, 2020).

12. See TERF Is A Slur, 'Documenting the abuse, harassment and misogyny of transgender identity politics'.

13. See Holocaust Memorial Day Trust, 'First they came — by Pastor Martin Niemöller', 2023.

they've so easily surrendered to trans tyranny? The phallic order, as we have had demonstrated over the past three-and-a-half years, determines who has the right to speak. The phallus, in psychoanalytic theory, is not the penis but the sign of this right. When Prime Minister Jacinda Ardern, for example, proclaimed that her Government was the 'single source of truth' and that New Zealanders should trust no other, she was laying claim to the phallus.[14] When radical feminists claim that 'all men are rapists', or a transgender exponent of critical race theory claims that 'all white people are racist', they are making the same claim to the phallus.[15] And, once again, it's to the same ends as the Nazis who declared that all Jews were bankers, or all Bolsheviks were degenerate. The stereotypes are different, but their ideological function in identifying an imaginary threat (coronavirus, rape, racism, transphobia) and silencing its representatives (conspiracy theorists, men, white people, TERFS) is the same. Trans, like every absolutist ideology, refuses to debate with what it classifies and dismisses as 'transphobes'. Indeed, this refusal is one of the principles of this ideology, which its acolytes are proud to declare.

As examples of which, in 2021 Richard Dawkins, one of Britain's most eminent evolutionary biologists, author of *The Selfish Gene*, one of the most influential science books of all time, the former Professor for Public Understanding of Science at the University of Oxford, an outspoken atheist, vocal critic of pseudo sciences and defender of free speech, declared that, while race is a spectrum, 'sex is pretty damn binary'.[16] In response, the American Humanist Association that in 1996 had awarded Dawkins the Humanist of the Year award stripped him of the title, and he was vilified in the press as 'anti-trans' and 'right wing'.[17] Then earlier this year, when the LGBTQ+ online newspaper, *Pink News*, claimed that science in fact 'debunks' what they call 'anti-trans myths', they began their learned rebuttal by asserting that those who 'deny trans rights' — by which they mean the right to control what we can say — also 'deny the fact that humans drive global

14. See Rebel News, 'New Zealand Prime Minister sounds like Ministry of Truth leader', *YouTube* (16 July, 2021).

15. See Suzanne Harrington, 'Not all men? Yes, actually, all men are part of the problem', *Irish Examiner* (24 March, 2021); Helena Horton, 'Transgender model who said "all white people are racist" appointed as Labour adviser', *The Telegraph* (27 February, 2018).

16. See Richard Dawkins, 'Race Is A Spectrum: Sex is Pretty Damn Binary', *Areo Magazine* (5 January, 2022).

17. See Heron Greenesmith, 'Atheist Richard Dawkins swings to anti-trans right in grasp at broader intellectual relevance', *Religion Dispatches* (30 November, 2021).

climate change and spread misinformation about the COVID-19 vaccine'.[18] The rest of the article, of course, contained no 'science' but simply repeated the founding principle of this new order of speech — which, as the author rightly points out, encompasses not just the orthodoxies of trans but also those of the experimental gene therapies and environmental fundamentalism — that disagreeing with its dogma is harmful, dangerous and 'rooted in harmful beliefs'.[19] Like the acolytes of critical race theory who proudly declare they're 'no longer talking to white people about race', the ideologues of trans don't 'do' debate.[20]

Contrary to what its ideologues and fanatics assert, disagreeing with someone's beliefs does not endanger their existence. Like the majority of the population of the UK, I do not believe that someone can change their biological sex through medical 'transition'; nor do I believe they should be permitted simply to declare their gender and then be regarded as such under UK law. But that doesn't mean that I don't extend the courtesy of addressing a transvestite man, for example, with a female pronoun and by his female name when he's in drag; but that is conditional upon him not accusing me of wanting to kill him and his fellow transvestites for not obediently repeating the mantra that 'transwomen are women'. And I won't be made to do so by the threat of arrest for 'hate speech' for not according someone's personal fantasy the value of biological reality. There are many people in this country with whom I disagree on any number of beliefs without hating them or endangering their existence. Many, indeed, despite our difference of opinion, I continue to debate with, because the agreement to disagree with someone without attacking them physically or threatening them with arrest is how a mature society arrives at coexistence of its population. That is how inclusivity works. By contrast, accusing someone who disagrees with your beliefs of endangering your existence and then threatening to arrest them is how a spoilt child behaves and an authoritarian and dictatorial society controls its population.

The flip side to this absolutism is that obedience to the orthodoxies of trans requires a symbolic and sometimes an actual act of emasculation, and with it a

---

18. See Maggie Baska, 'Three common anti-trans myths easily debunked by science', *Pink News* (31 March, 2022).

19. See Simon Elmer, 'The UK "Vaccination" Programme. Part 1: Adverse Drug Reactions and Deaths' (15 September, 2021); collected in *The New Normal*, pp. 161-205.

20. See Reni Eddo-Lodge, 'Why I'm no longer talking to white people about race', *The Guardian* (30 May, 2017).

willing yielding of speech, which is replaced by repetition of its dogma. Castration, whether through medical procedure or symbolic transition into the masquerade of femininity, is the cutting out of the tongue, the organ of speech, but also the severing of the Western male's historic domination of the phallic order for no other reason than his sex. However, this is not to the benefit of women or a feminist discourse of gender. The castrated self, who has voluntarily torn out not only the organs of 'their' sexual identity — penis, vagina, breasts — but also their tongues, is the ideal because sexless subject of the Global Biosecurity State. They speak in dogma (Orwell's 'duckspeak') because their tongue-less mouths are now the organs of the state, empty instruments for the sounding of its propaganda.[21] The penis — whether that which has been surgically removed from the male body or that which has been moulded from the flesh of an arm or leg and grafted onto the female body as its functionless but symbolic representation — has become the phallus of the state. In this respect they resemble those actors and celebrities who sold their mouths and reputations to promote the lies of the government about the justification for social distancing, masking and lockdown or the safety and efficacy of the gene therapies injected into the public as vaccines.[22]

Trans, however, contrary to its ubiquitous slogan, isn't a demand for new human rights apparently unique to this castrated self. Trans is an imposed order of speech determining who can and cannot speak, what can and cannot be said, what must be repeated without question and what must be silenced — if necessary by physical violence. Like fascism, trans is not content merely with censoring the speech of those outside its symbolic order — and which it has identified and categorised with the prefix 'cis' — but demands, in addition, that those so designated speak only its dogma. This starts with the new division of humankind not into the old and now rejected biological difference between male and female but into the new ideological differentiation between 'cisgender' and 'transgender'. And like the Nazi distinction between Aryan and Jew, or the Zionist distinction between Jew and Arab, this is not a difference between equals but a new hierarchy between the chosen people and those whose identities the acolytes

---

21. See George Orwell, *Nineteen Eighty-Four*; Everyman's Library, with an introduction by Julian Symonds (Alfred A. Knopf, 1992), p. 57.

22. See *The Telegraph*, 'Celebrities share "lockdown" coronavirus moments for a new charity song in aid of Telegraph Appeal', *YouTube* (9 April, 2020); NBC News, 'Elton John, Michael Caine in Comic Vaccine Ad', *YouTube* (10 February, 2021).

of trans describe with such derogatory terms as 'toxic' (masculinity or femininity), 'unreconstructed' (male or female).

This language explicitly suggests that the signifiers of our sexual difference require purging, surgically removing, and the bodies and identities to which they belonged reconstructing — more, that humans are born into a defective male or female identity that requires correcting by the chemical, surgical and ideological intervention of the biosecurity state. In this respect, trans shares the Puritan's notion of original sin, which it seeks to redress through a biomedical model of the human being the trans consumer is invited to assemble from a choice of identities — agender, androgyne, butch, femme, genderfluid, intersex, non-binary, pangender, queer, transsexual, and a hundred other brands.[23]

Perhaps because it has been prefabricated for its consumers, the ideology of trans, while denouncing anyone who questions it as a 'Nazi', is open and even proud about using the methods of historical fascism to threaten and silence its opponents. As an example of which, during her recent trip to New Zealand to speak on the threat to women's rights presented by the ideology of trans, the British woman and founder of Standing for Women, Kellie-Jay Keen, was nearly lynched by a crowd of male and female trans-activists.[24] In response to which, Tess Hall, a New Zealand writer and herself a trans-activist, published footage of herself burning a book by the writer, J. K. Rowling, whose defence of women's rights and the biological difference between the sexes have made her a unique target for the vitriol and hatred of the trans movement.[25] And the parallels with historical fascism don't stop there.

Whether fluttering on their flagpoles above the Houses of Parliament, the Foreign Office, the Department for Education, the Department for Communities and Local Government, the Greater London Authority and — most incongruously of all — MI6, or hung the length and breadth of London's Regent Street that so recently held the Union Jack, or printed on the vehicles used by the Metropolitan

---

23. See Steven Edginton and Robert Mendick, 'Exclusive: Welcome to woke Whitehall, where more than 100 genders are recognised', *The Telegraph* (27 May, 2022).

24. See Meghan Murphy, 'Kellie-Jay Keen is attacked and mobbed by trans activists in New Zealand', *Feminist Current* (25. March, 2023).

25. See Steve Watson, 'Video: Trans "Activist" Literally Burns Harry Potter Book', *Summit News* (28 March, 2023); Abby Gardner, 'A Complete Breakdown of the J. K. Rowling Transgender-Comments Controversy', *Glamour* (25 April, 2023).

Police Service, Essex Police and the Oxfordshire Fire and Rescue Service, or displayed on walls in the Victoria and Albert Museum and the British Library, or hung from the porticos of University College London and Brunel University, or sprayed across the new link bridge of the Princess Royal University Hospital in Farnborough, or hung by a transvestite minister across the windows of the prayer room of a children's hospital in Edinburgh, or hoisted above the Town Halls of Brighton and Hove, Barking and Dagenham, Bristol and Liverpool, or painted over pedestrian crossings in the London Boroughs of Sutton and Camden, or minted on the Royal Mint's new 50-pence piece, or printed on the cricket stumps used in this summer's Ashes series: not since the Nazi swastika has a symbol and flag branded so many aspects of society or been so widely imposed.[26] But that was in the Third Reich and its occupied territories, which even at its height ruled over just

---

26. See UK Parliament, 'Parliament fly LGBT rainbow flag for the first time' (3 June, 2016); Foreign, Commonwealth & Development Office, 'Transgender Pride Flag' (20 November, 2017); Department for Education, 'Proud to be flying the Armed Forces Day flag and Pride flag alongside the Union Jack today', *Twitter* (27 June, 2015); Ministry of Housing, Communities & Local Government, 'Rainbow flag flown with pride' (28 June, 2013); Mayor of London, 'Celebrating Transgender Awareness Week' (20 November, 2018); Sean Rayment, 'MI6 flies transgender flag for first time as boss speaks of his pride in staff', *The Mirror* (3 April, 2021); Sam Damshenas, 'Regent Street hangs Intersex-Inclusive flags to mark 50 years of Pride in the UK', *Gay Times* (2023); Tom Slater, 'The policing of "non-crimes" and the dark side of rainbow cars', *The Spectator* (23 August, 2021); Kurt Zindulka, 'UK police force poses with progress pride flag, vows to "monitor" hate speech responses', *Breitbart* (7 June, 2022); Oliver Price, 'Fury after fire brigades spend £17,000 of taxpayers' money on decorating engines in LGBT rainbow colours', *Daily Mail* (3 September, 2022); Daniel Quasar, 'Progress Pride flag', V&A (2021); British Library, 'Wishing all a happy and hopeful Pride Month', *Twitter* (1 June, 2023); UCL News, 'Transgender pride flag flies at UCL', (15 November, 2018); Brunel University London, 'Brunel celebrates Pride Month 2022' (2022); King College Hospital, 'New link-bridge at the PRUH incorporates Intersex-Inclusive Pride flag design' (2 June, 2023); Martin Robinson and Iwan Stone, 'Hospital facing backlash after chaplain puts up LGBT flags in prayer room for gravely ill children — leaving one practising Christian mother "shaking with anger"', *Daily Mail* (29 June, 2023); Daniel Green, 'Trans Day of Visibility: Flag flown from Brighton town halls', *The Argus* (1 April, 2023); Barking & Dagenham, 'Rainbow flag flies over town hall to mark LGBT+ History Month' (1 February, 2022); Bristol Pride, 'Flag Raising, Stonewall Remembered' (28 June, 2019); Richie Wright, 'Liverpool town hall rainbow flag', *Wikipedia* (30 May, 2012); Sutton Council, 'New crossing will celebrate Sutton's transgender community' (15 May, 2021); Camden Council, 'Camden unveils crossing to celebrate Transgender Awareness Week' (9 November, 2021); The Royal Mint, 'Celebrate with Pride — Introducing the Pride UK 50p Coin' (2022); Andrew Prentice, 'Why a small but very important change was made to the stumps at Headingley for the third Ashes Test', *Daily Mail* (7 July, 2023).

280 million people in Europe; whereas the LGBTQIA+ Intersex-Inclusive Progress Pride flag — which every year adds another letter, incorporates another colour, assimilates another movement, swallows another identity, creates another community of victims — is the adopted symbol of the New World Order in the West and the 900 million people on whose speech it has imposed its orthodoxies.[27]

As the last three-and-a-half years have shown, the international technocracies from whom our elected governments take their orders like to trial their programmes on smaller countries before implementing them in the Anglosphere. And just as coronavirus-justified restrictions in New Zealand, Australia and Canada were testing grounds for the USA, so too the more extreme applications of trans laws have been tested in Scotland, Wales and Ireland before they are implemented in the UK. The Gender Recognition Reform (Scotland) Bill was passed by the Scottish Parliament on 22 December, 2022, empowering a child as young as 16 and a man or woman of any age to attain a Gender Recognition Certificate that would allow them to change the sex on their birth certificate without a diagnosis of gender dysphoria.[28] Although subsequently vetoed by the Secretary of State for Scotland on the grounds that it was incompatible with the Equality Act 2010, the Scottish Government has promised to challenge this decision through a judicial review.

Similarly, although the UK Government has no power over the Government of Ireland, the latter's National Council for Curriculum and Assessment is currently consulting on the draft for their updated Senior Cycle Social, Personal and Health Education (SPHE) programme.[29] It is indicative of the biopolitical dimension of this programme that it includes the social and personal development of students aged 15-18 with education in 'mental health and well-being'; but among the reasons for updating the curriculum the Council includes the need to 'address gender equality' and 'gender-based violence'.[30] If we imagined that this refers to the

---

27. See 'German-occupied Europe', *Wikipedia*; Elizabeth Yuko, 'The Meaning Behind 32 LGBTQ Pride Flags', *Reader's Digest* (22 June, 2023).

28. See David Torrance and Douglas Pyper, 'The Secretary of State's veto and the Gender Recognition Reform (Scotland) Bill', *House of Commons Library* (26 April, 2023).

29. See NCAA, 'Draft Senior Cycle Social, Personal and Health Education (SPHE) Specification' (2023).

30. NCAA, 'Information note: Draft Senior Cycle SPHE Curriculum' (July 2023), p. 1.

equality between women and men, the draft clarifies that, in the 60 hours of classroom learning allocated to this programme, teachers will adopt an approach that is 'inclusive of all genders', and ensure that learning outcomes are taught in a way that 'LGBTQ+ identities' are 'fully integrated and reflected in teaching and learning'. And in case we aren't sure what this entails, SPHE, the draft states:

> Affirms diversity as an aspect of human life and human sexuality, enabling all students to feel valued and included in the teaching and learning in their classrooms. This involves using inclusive and affirming language.[31]

Inclusivity, according to this by now familiar distortion of the term, means strict adherence to the ideological orthodoxies of trans. As confirmation of which, students, as part of their assessment, will have to demonstrate what the draft calls 'a change or confirmation of beliefs/attitudes/assumptions/values'.[32]

It's not difficult to believe that an equivalent programme of indoctrination into this order of speech will be imported into the UK sooner rather than later. Indeed, it already has been in the forms of Personal, Social, health and Economic Education (PSHE), which under the Children and Social Work Act 2017 became statutory in September 2020, and Relationship and Sexual Education (RSE), which is compulsory in primary schools.[33] But apart from observing that these beliefs, attitudes, assumptions and values were, until recently, held by a tiny, marginal and culturally extreme minority of the UK or, indeed, the Irish population, we should also ask when our schools became institutions of indoctrination into this or any other ideology. Admittedly, all education contains an ideology implicit in its understanding of the world, cultural assumptions, historical justifications and pedagogical methods; but imposing a new order of speech represents a radical departure from the principles of a liberal arts education that have been

---

31. NCAA, 'Draft Senior Cycle Social, Personal and Health Education (SPHE) Specification' (2023), p. 10.

32. NCAA, 'Draft Senior Cycle Social, Personal and Health Education (SPHE) Specification' (2023), p. 16.

33. See Department for Education, 'Changes to personal, social, health and economic (PSHE) and relationships and sex education (RSE): New curriculum introduction in September 2020' (25 June, 2019); and Dr. Anna Z. Loutfi, *Reclaim Education: The Case Against PSHE* (Bad Law Project, 2023).

progressively erased by forty years of neoliberalism. As this example demonstrates, this is being replaced by a model of education that has more in common with those employed in totalitarian regimes of the past and present.

I want to conclude these remarks with a passage I quote a lot, from the inaugural lecture delivered at the Collège de France in 1977 by the French semiologist and critic, Roland Barthes, a homosexual man (long before the nomenclature of 'gay' was universally adopted) who — I like to think — would be appalled by and opposed to the fascism of trans ideology:

> Language is legislation, speech is its code. We do not see the power which is in speech because we forget that all speech is a classification, and that all classifications are oppressive. [The Russian linguist Roman] Jakobson has shown that a speech-system is defined less by what it permits us to say than by what it compels us to say. To speak, and, with even greater reason, to utter a discourse is not, as is too often repeated, to communicate; it is to subjugate. Language — the performance of a language system — is neither reactionary nor progressive; it is quite simply fascist; for fascism does not prevent speech, it compels speech.[34]

2. A New Lysenkoism

The characteristics of trans qualify it as a form of Lysenkoism.[35] This is named after the Stalinist biologist, Trofim Lysenko, who rejected the genetic theory of hereditary formulated by the German-Czech biologist, Gregor Mendel. In place of which, Lysenko argued not only that characteristics of organisms that were acquired from their environment over their lifetime can be inherited by their offspring, but also that in doing so one species can transform into another. Lysenkoism — which at the time was called 'Michurinism', after the Russian plant breeder, or 'agrobiology' or 'Soviet Darwinism' — was adopted as the official doctrine of the USSR in 1948. After which, Soviet scientists were forced to denounce criticisms of Lysenkoism as 'bourgeois' or 'fascist'; genetics, in which

---

34. Roland Barthes, 'Lecture in Inauguration of the Chair of Literary Semiology, College de France, 7 January, 1977'; translated by Richard Howard, *October*, Vol. 8, no. 162 (Spring 1979).

35. See Michael D. Gordin, 'Lysenkoism', *Encyclopedia of the History of Science* (Carnegie Mellon University, 2023).

the Soviet Union led the world at the time, was dismissed as a 'pseudo-science'; and some 3,000 Soviet biologists were fired from their posts, imprisoned or in some cases executed by the state. At the height of his power over Soviet biology, when he denied the existence of genes, Lysenko claimed that wheat raised in the appropriate environment could produce seeds of rye. This was an absurdity unmatched in biology, perhaps, until today's assertion that a man who undergoes surgical 'transition' can become a woman not only in law but in fact. Applied with disastrous results to agricultural policy after the Soviet famine of 1932-33 that had been caused by the collectivisation of farming, Lysenko's theories in practice reduced crop yields in the USSR; and, when applied in China, contributed to the Great Famine that between 1959 and 1961 killed tens of millions of Chinese. In this respect, Lysenkoism has parallels with the imposition of so-called 'organic' agricultural policies in Sri Lanka in 2021, which like Lysenko meant banning pesticides and fertilizers, and which in a year reduced rice production by more than 50 per cent.[36] Largely regarded now as a pseudo-science, 'Lysenkoism' has come to be used as a term for any deliberate distortion of scientific facts or theories for politically or ideologically expedient ends.

A more recent example of Lysenkoism is the once popular and now discredited notion of the 'gay gene', which itself was a product of the increasing biomedicalisation of what is socially or psychologically or otherwise determined, and which shared with the ideology of trans an essentialist understanding of identity.[37] By this I mean the increasingly dominant idea that we are born with an essential self — whether 'gay' or 'female' — but that normalising social and sexual conventions have repressed this true identity as 'straight' or 'male'. We hear this expressed in the endlessly repeated injunction in popular culture and advertising alike to 'be who you are', 'become the real you'. The authentic self is the dream of the commodity. However, I don't subscribe, either intellectually or morally, to these perceptions of gender or sexuality or indeed of identity, all of which are products of the relatively recent and deeply regressive ideology of identity politics. Whether deployed in advertising campaigns, by government 'nudge' units or by city mayors appealing to targeted demographics, such essentialism is always an

36. See Krishan Francis and Elaine Kurtenbach, 'Explainer: Why Sri Lanka's economy collapsed and what's next', *AP News* (11 July, 2022).

37. See Kate O'Riordan, 'The life of the gay gene: from hypothetical genetic marker to social reality', *The Journal of Sex Research*, Vol. 49, issue 4 (2012), pp. 362-368.

attempt to control others by categorising the multiplicity of identities we assume throughout our lives into some preferably biologically-authorised, state-legislated 'I' whose religious, racial, sexual and now gender 'characteristics' are protected under the Equality Act 2010.[38] I don't believe — and I oppose the assertion — that a pubescent girl uncomfortable at growing breasts, or a teenage girl who doesn't conform to the behavioural codes of femininity, should be told that they are boys; just as I don't believe and oppose the assertion that a pubescent boy who likes to wear his sister's dresses, or a young man finding it hard to enter adulthood in an economy and society in which the roles particular to men have so rapidly diminished, are therefore girls or women.

Contrary to the fundamentalist belief on which transgenderism has constructed its orthodoxies, one cannot be 'born into the wrong body', because there is no I separate from the body. This notion of a dualism between mind and body originated in ancient philosophies and religions, but has long been refuted by post-Cartesian philosophy and is incompatible with modern psychiatry and neuroscience. The division — whose terms the advertising for so-called medical 'transition' promises to unite — is not between the body of the transvestite and their 'true' self, but between the perception of the transgender-identifying individual and everything we know about reality.

It beggars belief that such an explicitly ideological pseudo-science has been embraced by the UK state and its institutions, and with rare exceptions has not been challenged by the scientific community.[39] But unfortunately — and disgracefully — UK biologists and geneticists have been as threatened into compliance and funded into promoting the orthodoxies of trans as UK epidemiologists and virologists were on the equally fraudulent 'consensus' over a threat to public health that never existed and the largely medieval responses to a pandemic that never materialised. If we think that Lysenkoism is a phenomenon of the past, in the last few years alone the equally manufactured scientific 'consensus' on the threat of SARS-CoV-2, on the effectiveness of social distancing and so-called lockdown, on the justification for mandatory masking and experimental gene therapies, on the imminence of environmental catastrophe

---

38. See UK Public General Acts, 'Equality Act 2010' (8 April, 2010).

39. See Debbie Hayton, 'How Richard Dawkins fell victim to the transgender thought police', *The Spectator* (21 April, 2021).

and on the sustainability of so-called 'green' sources of energy, have all demonstrated that the deliberate distortion of science for political ends is alive and well and thriving in the West.[40]

And just as the ideas of Trofim Lysenko could only have gained a scientific 'consensus' in a totalitarian regime, so too the orthodoxies of trans are the products of a new digital totalitarianism. In a decade which is facing previously unimagined programmes and technologies of identification, surveillance and control — the foremost of which is a system of Digital Identity that will be verifiable by biometric data — the division and categorisation of the populations of the West into, as of 2023, an absurd 107 genders is inseparable from the trans-human ideology that has made us, in such a short period of time, accept and even embrace the new orthodoxies of speech and belief being enforced by the Global Biosecurity State.[41]

As a biopolitical strategy, indoctrinating young children into trans ideology, which now includes exposing them to transvestite male strippers, will drive parents to take them out of schools in such numbers that it will be used to justify legislation taking children into the care of the state.[42] In this respect, trans is the ideology of biopolitics, creating consensus for changes to law that are already being made, and whose aim is to place the human being under the authority of the state from the moment it is born — and one day, perhaps, even earlier.

We have already taken the first step in that direction with the Domestic Abuse Act 2021, which was made into law in April 2021, when the UK was still under lockdown restrictions, and in the same month the UK Health Security Agency was formed from Public Health England, the NHS Test and Trace programme and the

---

40. See Simon Elmer, 'Lies, Damned Lies and Statistics: Manufacturing the Crisis'; collected in *The New Normal*, pp. 73-101; Simon Elmer, 'Lockdown: Collateral Damage in the War on COVID-19' (2 June, 2020); collected in *Virtue and Terror*, pp. 97-145; Simon Elmer, 'The Science and Law of Refusing to Wear Masks: Texts and Arguments in Support of Civil Disobedience', *Architects for Social Housing* (11 June, 2020); Simon Elmer, 'Bowling for Pfizer: Who's Behind the BioNTech Vaccine?' (9 December, 2020); collected in *The New Normal*, pp. 33-52.

41. See Sexual Diversity, 'How Many Genders Are There? Gender Identity List', *Education and LGBT Publications* (7 December, 2022).

42. See Kathryn Knight, 'They say it's harmless fun, but some parents think it's inappropriate indoctrination. . . . So why are our councils spending taxpayers' cash on getting drag queens to read stories to children?', *Daily Mail* (5 August, 2022).

Joint Biosecurity Centre.[43] In response to this legislation, in December 2022, the Crown Prosecution Service expanded the definition of 'abuse' by partners and family towards 'trans and non-binary' persons to include 'withholding money for transitioning' and 'refusing to use their preferred name or pronoun'.[44] In effect, this means that, once a child has been convinced by trans ideology that he or she was 'born in the wrong body', the UK state now has the legal right and duty to force that child's family not only to recognise this psychological disorder as a biological fact but to pay for their child's surgical mutilation — or face criminal charges. Before this guidance was published, in May 2022 the CPS hired a 'diversity and inclusion' officer who, in addition to being a male transvestite, has publicly used the derogatory terminology of 'TERF' to insult women who challenge his definition of their sex.[45] It's a measure of how officially sanctioned the ideology of trans now is that such a man is now shaping the enforcement of UK law.

Beyond censoring dissent and criminalising non-compliance, however, the ultimate goal of trans ideology is eugenics — that is, the medical sterilisation of those members of a population that are ideologically susceptible or legally subject to its orthodoxies. Under changes to legislation and policy, that may one day include the entire population, and not just of the UK. Indeed, the justification and promotion of the surgical mutilation of children by the medical industry on the spurious grounds of upholding their 'trans rights' is the realisation of boasts by World Economic Forum founder, Klaus Schwab, that the Fourth Industrial Revolution will lead to 'a fusion of our physical, our digital and our biological identities'.[46] The WEF has already issued instructions on how US corporations should incorporate 'transgender women' into their workplace, and have identified LGBT+ inclusion as the secret to the post-pandemic success of 15-Minute Cities.[47]

---

43. See UK Public General Acts, 'Domestic Abuse Act 2021' (29 April, 2021).

44. See Crown Prosecution Service, 'Domestic Abuse' (5 December, 2022).

45. See Connor Boyd, 'Fury as CPS hires transgender activist in new £31,000 working from home diversity job who has backed using the derogatory term "womxn" instead of "woman"', *Daily Mail* (2 June, 2022).

46. See Chicago Council on Global Affairs, 'World Economic Forum founder Klaus Schwab on the Fourth Industrial Revolution', *YouTube* (13 May, 2019).

47. See World Economic Forum, 'Great Reset: Why LGBT+ inclusion is the secret to cities' post-pandemic success' (3 June, 2020); and 'Trans-inclusive workplaces: 5 considerations for companies' (2 November, 2022).

The government legislation criminalising dissent and compelling compliance with this new ideology, the parallel corporate development of the technologies for the surveillance and enforcement of its laws, and the institutional promotion and implementation of its orthodoxies, all demonstrate that the universal adoption of trans is not coincidental to the Great Reset of Western civilisation but, rather, the post-human ideology driving this revolution into the new totalitarianism of the Global Biosecurity State.

This point was made most explicitly by Yuval Harari, the Israeli transhumanist, ideologue of the Fourth Industrial Revolution, personal advisor to Klaus Schwab, and author of the best-selling trilogy *Sapiens: A Brief History of Humankind* (2014), *Homo Deus: A Brief History of Tomorrow* (2016) and *21 Lessons for the 21st Century* (2018) — the first of which has been turned into both a graphic novel and a child's book in order to better disseminate and popularise his ideas. In an interview given in 2017, Harari laid out his vision of this transhuman future with all the cruelty and inhumanity of a latter-day Joseph Goebbels. I quoted this passage in *The Road to Fascism* in the context of the planned immiseration of the global population by the Great Reset; but it takes on new meanings when read in the light of the technologies of biopower by which those made redundant by stakeholder capitalism will be controlled:

In the industrial revolution of the Nineteenth Century, what humanity learned to produce was stuff like textiles and shoes and weapons and vehicles, and this was enough for [the] very few countries that underwent the revolution fast enough to subjugate everybody else.

What we are talking about now is like a second industrial revolution, but the product this time will not be textiles or machines or vehicles or even weapons; the product this time will be humans themselves. We are basically learning to produce bodies and minds. Bodies and minds are going to be the two main products of the next wave. And if there is a gap between those that know how to produce bodies and minds and those who do not, then this [gap will be] far greater than anything we have seen before in history.

This time, if you're not part of the revolution fast enough, then you'll probably become extinct. Once you know how to produce bodies and minds, cheap labour in Africa or South Asia or wherever counts for nothing. I think that the biggest question in the economics and politics of the coming decades will be what to do with all these useless people. I don't think we have an economic model for that.

My best guess — which is just a guess — is that food will not be a problem. With that kind of technology, you will be able to produce food for everybody. The problem is more boredom — what to do with them, and how will they find some sense of meaning in life when they are basically meaningless, worthless.[48]

Harari's projected solution to this problem was a combination of 'drugs and computer games'. Six years later, however, the drugs being prescribed for our children by so-called 'trans-therapists' are more than recreational; the computers in the digital camp of Global Digital Health Certification, the surveillance infrastructure for 15-Minute Smart Cities and Central Bank Digital Currency will do more than distract us from our 'meaningless' lives; and the World Economic Forum's final solution to the problem of 'useless people' is to do much more than alleviate our boredom.

Trans is not a cult, as some critics have dismissed it as, thereby unwittingly or otherwise diminishing its origins, reach and goals.[49] Trans is the official ideology of the Global Biosecurity State. And although it is both explicitly and violently misogynist and implicitly and increasingly homophobic — most violently and unsurprisingly demonstrated by transvestite heterosexual men demanding lesbians have sex with them or be shamed as 'transphobic', 'far right' and 'TERFS' — its orthodoxies have been welcomed into mainstream culture through the conduit of LGB activism.[50] This has largely succeeded because of the Left's embrace of the latter under its obligations to the orthodoxies of 'political correctness', which have been extended, without question or debate or apparent thought, to imposing the new order of speech that is the first orthodoxy of trans ideology.

---

48. The recording of Yuval Harari's comments has been removed from *YouTube*, but has been downloaded and may be viewed in Simon Elmer, 'Fascism and the Decay of Capitalism (The Road to Fascism: For a Critique of the Global Biosecurity State)', *Architects for Social Housing* (24 April, 2022).

49. See Claudia Aoraha, 'Woman, 36, attacked at NYC Pride for brandishing a "stop female erasure" sign is a "deprogrammer" who believes the transgender movement is a CULT for kids', *Daily Mail* (26 June, 2023).

50. See Caroline Lowbridge, 'The lesbians who feel pressured to have sex and relationships with trans women', *BBC News* (26 October, 2021).

Lysenkoism was the ideological product of the subjection of Soviet science to the politically opportunist and crude application of the orthodoxies of Marxist-Leninism following the final defeat of the Bolshevik Revolution in 1929. Similarly, transgenderism is the most recent product of Western capitalism's counter-revolution against the brief and too-easily defeated social revolutions of the 1960s and 70s. In this fight back, which is nearing its final victory, the socialist critique of capitalism has been replaced by the self-obsession, victimhood and internal division of identity politics; the critique of European colonialism has been recuperated into the racism of critical race theory; the post-structuralist critique of discourse has been transformed into woke's policing of speech and thought; and feminism's critique of patriarchy has undergone a full reversal into the state-sanctioned misogyny of trans.

Despite its uncritical embrace by the Pride festival in cities across the West, trans is to the gay liberation movement of the 1970s what the Left of today is to socialism: a state-legislated, corporate-financed, institutionally-imposed programme designed to appropriate the language of human rights, civil liberties and popular protest from movements of social, sexual and political emancipation. Indeed, my own opinion is that the Left has so universally embraced woke because it has the same goal — to police opposition to capitalism. But to what end? This is what I'll try to address in the rest of this chapter.

3. The Misogyny of Trans

Let's begin with a question few have the courage to pose and fewer still dare to answer honestly. Why is it always male transvestites who demand access to women's toilets, men who want to compete in women's sports, and male rapists who want to go to women's prisons? Why do female transvestites never want to go into men's toilets, men's prisons or compete in men's sports? The answer — which numerous feminists have given before me — is that most violence against women is committed by men, however they're dressed. Men go into women's toilets because the transgression of the prohibition against doing so turns them on, not necessarily sexually. Men compete against women in sports and athletics because their unfair physical advantages give them a better chance of beating the women against whom they're competing, and they enjoy, perhaps, enacting this revenge against the women that have rejected them — sexually, maybe, or as a member of their sex. Men who have been found guilty of raping women choose women's prisons in which to serve their sentence because if gives them the chance to rape more women, and to avoid the threat of themselves being raped in a men's prison. In other words, they are sexual predators and cheats: nothing to be proud of, and certainly not in street festivals and state celebrations lasting now an entire month.

It's part of their attempt to intimidate women that the transvestite men who go into women's toilets photograph themselves doing so and then share the image online, much as kids often do the same when committing petty crimes or, as happened recently in London, threatening young women on the street.[51] Perhaps there are transvestite women who photograph themselves in men's toilets, but I doubt they'd do it when men are present, certainly not when alone. Though I don't object to it myself, especially when the queues to women's toilets are always so much longer, I know from experience that some men do not like women in men's toilets. But I haven't heard of a single woman competing in men's sports, or a woman criminal asking to be sent to a man's jail. If the overwhelming reason for doing so was because that man or woman felt he or she was a woman or man and needed to 'be himself/herself', then female transvestites would do so regardless. They don't, of course, because that's not the reason. Men compete in women's sports because they win, and male rapists asked to be sent to a woman's prison so they can intimidate, exert power over and rape more women.

To take three of the most public examples of men claiming to be women, Eddie Izzard (who now calls himself Suzy Izzard), William Thomas (who calls himself Lia Thomas) and Adam Graham (who called himself Isla Bryson after he was arrested), all have penises, the last of whom used his to rape two women, while Adam Graham exposed his penis, erect, to women swimmers in the locker room they are forced by law to share with him.[52] They are transvestite men who,

51. See, for example, Tyler Porter, *Twitter* (10 September, 2019); Nicky (She/Her), *Twitter* (12 July, 2023); and Joe Smith, 'Tik Tok clown Mizzy's mum is "sick of his stupid pranks" and wants him to get a job', *The Mirror* (3 June, 2023).

52. See Jean Hatchet, 'Eddie Izzard uses the ladies loo in Sheffield', *The Critic* (30 September, 2022); Alyssa Guzman and Stephen M. Lepore, 'Trans swimmer Lia Thomas "dropped her pants" and exposed her "male genitalia" in a women's locker room after a meet, claims University of Kentucky athlete Riley Gaines', *Daily Mail* (9 February, 2023); Danya Bazaraa, 'Trans double rapist

quite evidently, enjoy exerting power over women, whether that's by invading women-only places, unfairly beating them in women-only competitions, or using their greater physical strength to sexually assault them. In that sense, all three are representative of the aggressive and sometimes violent men pushing trans ideology.

For the same reason, all three are completely unrepresentative of the mostly straight transvestites, gay drag queens and transsexuals I have known, whom I would imagine — my clubbing days being long past, alas, I can no longer ask them — dislike being associated with the explicitly misogynist and implicitly homophobic orthodoxies of this new Lysenkoism, or its embrace and enforcement as the official ideology of Western capitalism. I'm risking presenting anecdote for evidence, but all the male transvestites I knew were heterosexual men who had a far greater love and respect for women than your average 'bloke'. None used the language of misogyny, although that couldn't be said of all the drag queens, as there is a strain of misogyny, or more accurately gynophobia, that runs through elements of gay culture as much as it does through straight culture.

But then, there are many reasons why men dress up in 'women's' clothing — even when few women wear such clothing anymore — private, public, sexual, sensual, social, professional, even political, and I've yet to meet a 'tranny' — as my friends called themselves — who wanted to blend in, or who wanted to be thought of as 'normal'. Some, of course, cross-dress for none of these reasons, but out of an often-undefined desire or drive to do so; but in all the conversations I had with them about transvestism, none ever said they wanted their kink to become an orthodoxy, or for their difference to be promoted to children as the norm, or for it to be written into legislation and policy that they were 'women'. There was always a very clear dividing line between when they were called by their female names and pronoun and when by their male.

That isn't the case for those men who clearly, publicly and so far with impunity enjoy threatening and physically attacking women for standing up for their rights and those of their children, and then in their defence declare themselves to be 'transwomen'. I've only ever met one of these, a young man who dressed in standard anarchist garb but with the addition of smudged red lipstick

---

Isla Bryson who attacked two women while living as a man is jailed in male prison for eight years: Judge tells sex predator "you are NOT the victim"', *Daily Mail* (28 February, 2023).

— more like Robert Smith than a transvestite — and who accused me of 'misgendering' him when I called him 'mate'. He was a coward and a bully, later being arrested and fined for assaulting a 61-year-old woman and feminist during a protest at Speakers' Corner in 2017.[53]

The widely repeated defence of such violence on the grounds that, if male transvestites are forced to use men's toilets it will place them in physical danger and they should therefore be allowed into women's toilets, is a flawed one. First, the men who enter men's toilets dressed in women's clothes do so out of personal choice; while the women and girls who enter women's or gender-neutral toilets to find a man, possibly dressed in women's clothing and photographing himself before posting it on his Twitter page to 'piss off TERFS', have made no such choice. There are many ways in which we can choose not to conform with social norms, and some of them may place us in physical danger; but we have to take individual responsibility for those choices rather than claiming the unique right to inflict those choices on others without their agreement or consent. Second, whatever danger a male transvestite may place himself in by entering a men's toilet dressed in women's clothing, the danger is at least between him and other men. There is a reason men were once not permitted into women's toilets, and that is because men present a physical threat to women in a way that they don't to other men to the same degree. And third, as for the argument that transvestite men do not attack women or girls in toilets, doubtless most don't; but some undoubtedly do, and by entering what were until recently female-only spaces, they risk intimidating the majority of women who do not agree with the recent conversion of our legislatures and courts to the Lysenkoism of trans, and are justifiably concerned about a man sharing a public toilet with themselves or their daughters.[54]

It would do a huge amount for the public perception of transvestites the ideology of trans has done so much to damage if some of the 'old-school' trannies who knew exactly who and what they were publicly organised themselves to

---

53. See Bridie Pearson-Jones, 'Transgender model who punched feminist and smashed her £120 camera in violent brawl at Hyde Park Speakers' Corner protest walks free from court', *Daily Mail* (13 April, 2018).

54. See, for example, Jack Newman, 'Transgender woman, 18, sexually assaulted girl, 10, in Morrisons' female toilets — just weeks after using mobile to peep on another girl in Asda loos', *Daily Mail* (15 March, 2019).

protect these women from the violent and misogynist new breed that have appropriated their kinks and practices for their trans human ideology. For a movement that claims that failure to comply with its dogma and dictates is an act of violence and even murder against its adherents, the authoritarianism, absolutism and violence of its ideologues have done more to endanger the safety of transvestites than any conservative or 'Nazi' — as they like to call anyone who disagrees with them. That now includes an increasing number of lesbians, gays and bisexuals that are becoming aware not only that violent men attacking women are doing nothing but harm for their community, but that the ideology of trans is itself homophobic ('genital preferences are transphobic'), and its adherents are just as likely to turn on them as it has so-called 'gender-critical' feminists.[55]

As Deacon Joy Everingham, a married father of two children and the first transvestite man to be ordained by the Methodist Church, famously said in 2019: 'If gender is on a spectrum, then homosexuality doesn't really exist, because it can only exist on a binary. . . . Sexuality is redundant.'[56] Again, it isn't the existence of transvestites that is under threat but rather those of us who maintain the equivalence between biology and sex and decline to occupy our allotted place on the transgender spectrum of make-up, dress-up and reconstructed identity. But in response, we might ask Mr. Everingham why, if gender is a spectrum, he — like other male transvestites who dress in women's clothes without their wife's knowledge — went from 'man' to 'woman', rather than trying out one of the other genders on his rainbow flag of biology.[57] Or why, out of all the different shades on this gender spectrum, he chose an image of a female clergyman apparently based on *The Vicar of Dibley*.[58] The answer to both questions, of course, is that the identity Joy Everingham has assumed is not biologically determined but a composite of his personal psychology and the cultural norms available to him.

---

55. See The Student Brexit Group, 'The University of Liverpool are telling their students that "genital preferences are transphobic", *Twitter* (2 March, 2020).

56. See Radical Faeries Men, 'Homophobic trans chaplain claims homosexuality doesn't exist', *YouTube* (18 November, 2020).

57. See Stoyan Zaimov, 'Father of Two Who "Hid Identity for 40 Years" Becomes UK Methodist Church's First Transgender Minister', *The Christian Post* (20 November, 2017).

58. See 'The Vicar of Dibley: TV Series, 1994-2020', IMDb; in which Dawn French played the character of a female minister in a conservative small town's church.

Trans is another and currently popular identity in the fragmentation of our culture into competing tribes.

And yet, even after the relentless promotion of this ideology in recent years by the UK state, in our educational, cultural and religious institutions, and by the media and business sector, the 2021 Census for England and Wales reported that, out of a population of 59,642,000, just 48,000 men identified as a 'trans woman', 0.1 per cent of respondents and 1 in 1,250 of the total male population.[59] In contrast, 30.4 million people in England and Wales identified themselves on the same census as 'women and girls', 51 per cent of the population. It is this majority that are having their toilets and changing rooms invaded, their sports competitions stolen, and their safety put at risk by the 0.08 per cent of men who are under the illusion that they are women.

To put this in context, ten years earlier, in the 2001 Census, 390,000 people in England and Wales identified 'Jedi' as their religion, 0.8 per cent of the respondents.[60] That's 50 per cent more than the 262,000 people who responded 'no' to the 2021 Census question whether their 'gender identify' was 'the same as sex registered at birth'. Does that mean we should start teaching our children that they can move physical objects, control the minds of others or see the future using the power of 'The Force', introduce legislation making anyone questioning the historical and scientific reality of the Star Wars franchise guilty of 'hate speech', or arrest parents who don't call their children by the name of their preferred Jedi Knight?

Obviously not, and for good reasons. It is a principle of psychiatry not to reaffirm the violent fantasies of a psychopath, pretend to hear the voices in the head of a schizophrenic, or agree with the body perception of an anorexic that he or she is overweight, because to do so would be to entrench them further in their mental illness, to their harm and potentially the harm of others. It is not the confusion of the 0.08 per cent of men who suffer from gender identity disorder (which under trans orthodoxy has been recategorised as 'gender dysphoria') that we should be reaffirming, but rather the safety of the 51 per cent of the population

---

59. See Office for National Statistics, 'Gender Identity, England and Wales: Census 2021' (6 January, 2023).

60. See Office for National Statistics, 'Census 2001 Summary theme figures and ranking — 390,000 Jedi There Are' (13 February, 2003).

to whom the ideology of trans represents a threat, as the intimidation and violence directed at women by its ideologues repeatedly demonstrates.

The biologically false idea that a child can be 'born into the wrong body' is based on the socially repressive notion that there is one way to be either a woman or a man. Indeed, one only has to look at the masquerade of women performed by male transvestites — who typically range between the appearance of drag queens, strippers, prostitutes and a dress code not seen in the UK outside Buckingham Palace since the 1950s — to understand how socially regressive and misogynist is the trans model of women to which every tomboy must now adhere if she is not to be subject to surgical mutilation by the state. The recent increase in the glut of awards handed to male transvestites in women's competitions has made it clear to every girl or woman thinking of competing that the best woman cyclist is a man, the best woman middle-distance runner is a man, the best woman para-athlete is a man, the best track-and-field woman is a man, the best woman mixed martial artist is a man, the best woman beauty queen is a man, and it turns out that even the woman of the year is a man.[61]

Like the male rapist who batters and sometimes kills his female victim in the act of raping her, trans wants to destroy what it isn't and what it so desperately wants to be. This is partly, no doubt, because its adherents are unable to enter into the symbolic order of 'manhood' that has been placed in question by the challenges to the once-dominant place of men in Western economies. There's nothing wrong with that: many men don't, either because they can't or don't want to enter this order out of a rejection of its values and behavioural codes, and perhaps that's a good thing. In many respects, undoubtedly it is. But just as that doesn't justify telling a young man who doesn't make the First XV for Harlequins F.C. to 'man up', so too it doesn't justify the systematic attempt to erase women,

---

61. See Yaron Steinbuch, 'Controversial trans cyclist Austin Killips wins North Carolina race by 5 minutes: "Power is not comparable"', *New York Post* (12 June, 2023); Lewis Pennock, 'Trans runner, 50, who set records in Canada for long distance events is retiring to "stop being center of controversy" — but claims testosterone at her age has no effect on her storming the competition', *Daily Mail* (3 March, 2023); Oliver Brown, 'Transgender runner, 49, wins bronze at Para World Championships', *The Telegraph* (14 July, 2023); Dawn Ennis, 'Outsports Female Athlete of the Year: CeCé Telfer', *Outsports* (26 December, 2019); 'Fallon Fox, Transgender MMA Fighter Who Broke The Skull of Her Opponent', *BJJ World* (2021); Sophie Perry, 'First trans woman crowned winner of Miss Netherlands', *The Pink News* (10 July, 2023); Dawn Ennis, 'Trans Swimming Champion Lia Thomas Is Nominated For Woman Of The Year', *Forbes* (16 July, 2022).

their rights, their sexual difference from men, their place in language, their protected places, their physical safety. Contrary to what is preached at us by trans ideologues, it is not the fantasy existence of trans-identifying men that is being erased but the very real existence of the women they want to be.

As examples of which, in the UK today a cervical cancer charity now describes women's vaginas as a 'bonus hole'; the National Health Service now instructs its staff to call breastfeeding 'chestfeeding', vaginal birth (as distinct from a caesarean section) 'frontal birth'; mothers are now reduced to 'pregnant people' and 'birth-giver'; and women themselves have been replaced with the utilitarian 'menstruators', 'uterus-havers' or 'people with vaginas'.[62] This is not the language of 'inclusivity' trying not to offend the 0.08 per cent of the male population who are being encouraged by this terminology to believe that they have a uterus, can menstruate, give birth or breast-feed, or that the 'front hole' a doctor carved into their pelvis cavity is a vagina. Indeed, it is the exact opposite of inclusive. This — overtly, clearly and unmistakably — is the language of misogyny, of male gynophobia, of a pathological hatred of the female body, of the dehumanising of women. But it is also the discourse of a new and authoritarian ideology which has the legal force and institutional authority of the entire UK state behind it.

One of the more unpleasant events at this year's London Pride was a speech given to a crowd of cheering trans acolytes by Alan Baker, a transvestite male who uses the name Sarah Jane Baker.[63] An artist and violinist born in Brixton, Baker was an underage male prostitute before being sent to jail for kidnapping and torturing his stepmother's brother. While in prison he was convicted, at the age of 21, of the attempted murder of a fellow prisoner. While serving a 30-year sentence, Baker, in 2017, cut off his own testicles with a razor. Why such a violent,

---

62. See Alex Barton, 'Vagina rebranded as "bonus hole" by cervical cancer charity', *The Telegraph* (9 July, 2023); John Ely, 'Government-funded report urges NHS to use terms "chestfeeding" and "frontal birth" instead of breast or vaginal', *Daily Mail* (28 April, 2022); Ewan Somerville, 'Say "pregnant people", NHS watchdog tells staff in gender neutral drive', *The Telegraph* (4 April, 2023); John Abiona, 'Health fears over replacing "mum" with "birth-giver" as experts warn wider use of gender-neutral terms could have "unintended consequences" for women and children', *Daily Mail* (30 January, 2022); Naomi Firsht, 'I am not a walking cervix or a menstruator. I am a W-O-M-A-N', *The Times* (31 October, 2018).

63. See Rory Tingle, 'Police reopen probe into trans activist after she told crowd "punch TERFs in the face": Met reviews Trans Pride speech made by convicted attempted murderer turned campaigner who cut off her own testicles while serving 30 years in jail', *Daily Mail* (10 July, 2023).

criminal and mentally unstable person should be given a platform to speak at London Pride is not something the organisers have explained; but during his speech Baker — who is an advocate for placing transvestite men like himself in women's prisons — told the listening crowd that, 'If you see a TERF, punch them in the fucking face'.[64]

In response to complaints from the Women's Rights Network about this public incitement to violence against women, the Metropolitan Police Service — who in their written response referred to Mr. Baker as a woman — argued that a 'TERF' is not a protected characteristic under the Equality Act 2010; that calling on the crowd to punch one was therefore not a hate crime; that Mr. Baker was acting on his beliefs; that his freedom of speech is protected under Article 10 of The Human Rights Act 1998, and that it would therefore not be appropriate to take the investigation further.[65] I'm relieved to report, however, that a lawyer and Director at Gay Men's Network, Dennis Noel Kavanagh, has challenged the legal incoherence of this response, which I'll briefly summarise here.[66]

'TERF', and in particular as it was used by Mr. Baker, is an insult the Met should not be adopting in its response, while the gender critical beliefs of the women Mr. Baker advised the men listening to assault are protected under the Equality Act 2010. And although relevant to civil claims, a protected characteristic is not relevant to the criminal offence of inciting an offence against others. Whether Mr. Baker was acting on his beliefs that a TERF deserves punching is equally irrelevant to the incitement of violence, which has no defence in law against the offence of Actual Bodily Harm or Grievous Bodily Harm. As for Mr. Baker's freedom of speech, Article 10 of the Human Rights Act does not include the right to threaten violence or encourage it in others. Finally, the reference to this man with a history of criminal violence as a 'woman' indicates institutional bias on the part of the Metropolitan Police Service.

---

64. See Sophie Perry, 'London Trans+ Pride addresses "punch TERFs" speech backlash: "We do not condone violence"', *The Pink News* (11 July, 2023).

65. See Women's Rights Network, 'URGENT. We have reported this man — a convicted torturer and kidnapper, who is on probation — for committing a Public Order offence', *Twitter* (9 July, 2023).

66. See Gay Men's Network, 'Fighting homophobia in all its forms'; Dennis Noel Kavanagh, 'The MET Police and Mayor of London appear unwilling to take open threats of violence against women and girls seriously', *Twitter* (9 July, 2023).

After numerous complaints and media coverage of his speech, Baker was belatedly arrested by the Metropolitan Police Service; but — quite extraordinarily for a man with his record of violence — he was subsequently acquitted after his trial judge, Deputy Chief Magistrate Tan Ikram, concluded that Mr. Baker wasn't, in fact, inciting violence against women and girls when he told transvestite men to 'punch them in the fucking face', but merely wanted publicity for his 'cause'.[67]

But there is something more than this institutional complacency towards and legal tolerance of violence against women at an event sponsored and celebrated by the London Mayor and every other local authority in London.[68] At the heart of the promotion of trans misogyny lies this ancient truth: that despite our best efforts to erase sexual difference in the name of erasing inequality between the sexes, most of the joys, pleasures, happiness and beauty to be found in this world still come from women in ways that they never can from men. Hopefully, it's clear that I mean from far more than their appearance. Replace women with this fake masquerade of femininity, and the world is an even uglier and sadder place, and we in it. And as we saw under lockdown, a depressed and isolated populace, deprived of human contact and social interaction, is easier to control, more willing to believe the lies they're told, more furiously zealous to obey the dictates those lies justify. Before it is the hatred of and violence against women that trans demonstrates every day, misogyny is a means of control, in this case over more than half the population of the UK, which is why all organised religions are founded on misogyny. The reality is that so-called 'trans rights' are not just an attack on women but a new model of what it is to be human that is being implemented through the programmes and technologies of the Fourth Industrial Revolution.

4. A New Paradigm of Citizenship

The adjective 'toxic', when applied — as it increasingly is — to masculine and even feminine behaviour, is part of the terminology of woke, and operates within a biomedical image of purging that makes children going through the difficulties of adolescence believe the now promoted lie that they were 'born in the wrong

---

67. See Tristan Kirk, 'Trans activist Sarah Jane Baker found not guilty of encouraging violence with "punch a Terf" speech', *Evening Standard* (31 August, 2023).

68. See Conor Clark, 'Sadiq Khan: "The trans community should not be stigmatised, demonised or weaponised"', *Gay Times* (2023).

body.'[69] But this is another reversal of the critique of power undertaken by feminism. The feminist critique of gendered behaviour was originally directed at questioning the naturalisation of the equation between female and femininity, male and masculinity, not to telling children that sexual difference is a mere construct of patriarchy, or that the difficult passage to adulthood is solved through mutilating their bodies. To quote another ancient truth, God made us 'male and female' for a reason (Genesis 1:27): and it's the same reason that our new god (Science) and its new faith (Medicine) is trying to erase the difference between us.

Cross-dressing, like 'cosplay', is just that — a bit of fun, often with a sexualised element, which is different from children dressing up in a costume, and why we used to keep the two activities separate.[70] Some players have more emotionally invested in their roles, undoubtedly, and that can become a form of delusional belief; but just as dressing up in Carrie Fisher's bikini from *Return of the Jedi* won't turn the girl (or boy) wearing it into Princess Leia, it also won't turn a male transvestite into a woman, and taking oestrogen to grow breasts or surgically removing his penis won't either. Like the moral puritanism of woke, trans has turned the play of transvestism, which is as old as civilisation itself, into a postmodern, authoritarian, censorial, transhuman ideology whose primary target is our children: the indoctrination of their minds into the absurdities and obscenities of woke orthodoxies, and the control of their chemically damaged and surgically mutilated bodies. The testimony of adults who, as children, underwent what they were told were medical procedures that would make them another sex reads like a catalogue of malpractice, abuse, mutilation, experimentation and financial exploitation.

There are, of course, more reasons for transvestism than just or even sexual gratification. Clothing and appearance play multiple roles in our identity, both social and sexual. But all trans-identifying people are transvestites, because 'transgender' is the categorisation and exploitation of an identity disorder. Someone can be born a hermaphrodite with both male and female reproductive organs; but the Latin prefix *trans* means 'across, beyond or through', which the biology of a living organism does not permit, and certainly not that of a human

---

69. See Nicola Neville, 'This new initiative aims to address toxic masculinity in boyhood', *Glamour Magazine* (10 November, 2022).

70. See Luke Brown, 'Star Wars Celebration Orlando's Very Best Cosplay (Day Two)', *Screen Crush* (15 April, 2017).

being. We can change our clothes, paint our faces and alter our voices, but no amount of drugs or operations will change our sex, only damage our health and mutilate our body. As for those who distinguish between people who merely declare themselves another sex and so-called 'transsexuals', extending transvestism into plastic surgery is not unique to trans-identifying people but includes those who spend tens of thousands of pounds in surgery to look like a doll or some kind of an animal.[71] Far from being a measure of their psychological conviction — which the rest of us are then obliged by legislation to respect or face criminal charges — such mutilation is a measure of their mental disorder.

This is the first time I have used this term in this chapter, as I am reluctant to pathologise any social practice whose origins lie in the conditions of a given society. As we saw under lockdown, when the UK Government considered sectioning members of the public who refused to be injected with experimental gene therapies under the Mental Health Act 1983, declaring someone mentally incompetent is one of the ways the medical industry controls and, indeed, creates its 'patients'.[72] But how otherwise can we describe someone who thinks they are another sex, were 'born in the wrong body', and are willing to damage their health and mutilate their bodies to realise their perception of themselves? Although not illegal in the UK, my own view is that any doctor who performs such medically unnecessary surgery on what by definition are adults suffering some degree of mental disorder if not necessary illness has violated the bounds of medicine and their sworn oath to 'first do no harm'; but doctors performing such services on children who cannot grant consent to what they can't possibly understand are — or should be — treated as criminals under UK law.[73]

The list of permanent damages to the health and bodies of children who have undergone so-called gender 'transition' at the hands of the medical industry prescribing experimental hormone therapy and puberty blockers include a lack of bone density, the failure of spine bones to fuse together in young males taking

71. See Tim Hanlon, 'Woman who spent £100,000 on being a "doll" shares image of how she used to look', *The Mirror* (5 July, 2023); Kate O'Neill, 'Transgender woman "Dragon Lady" chops ears off to look like a reptile', *The Mirror* (9 September, 2016).

72. See Simon Elmer, 'Our Default State: Compulsory Vaccination for COVID-19 and Human Rights Law' (8 January, 2021); collected in *The New Normal*, pp. 53-72.

73. See Spyros Retsas, 'First do no harm: the impossible oath', *British Medical Journal* (19 July, 2019).

oestrogen, consequent osteoporosis, sexual dysfunction in both arousal and orgasm and irreversible future infertility in both males and females.[74] The damage to those who undertake the medical mutilation of their own bodies is far greater, and the cause of bitter recrimination among those who come to regret the decision to act on their mental disorder. Most importantly for the medical industry, such 'transition' creates a permanent patient, with sexual reassignment surgery already a multi-billion-dollar industry in the US and estimated to reach over $3 billion in the next decade.[75] Given the universal promotion of this ideology in the UK, we will doubtless soon produce a proportionately lucrative market here.

Just as concerning as the damaging effects of these experimental medical interventions is the evidence of the success of the promotion of the ideology driving this market. In the USA, where the ideology of trans was first developed into an industry, 1.6 million people identified as 'transgender' in 2022, roughly 0.48 per cent of the population. 1.43 per cent of children aged 13-17 years old now identify as 'transgender', and 1.31 per cent of young adults aged 18-24 years old; compared with 0.45 per cent of adults aged 25-64, and 0.32 per cent of those over 65 year of age.[76] Despite constituting 18.6 per cent of the US population, those under the age of 25 make up 43 per cent of those who identify as 'transgender'. 1 in 5 of them are children aged 13-17, this figure having doubled over the last five years alone.

---

74. See Simona Giordano and Søren Holm, 'Is puberty delaying treatment "experimental treatment"', *International Journal of Transgender Health* (11 April, 2020); Micol S. Rothman and Sean J. Iwamoto, 'Bone Health in the Transgender Population', *Clinical Reviews in Bone and Mineral Metabolism* (June 2019); Hannah Grossman, 'Top Swedish doctors blow whistle on trans puberty-suppressing drugs affecting children's bones: "Experimental"', *Fox News* (27 April, 2023); Alison Clayton, 'Gender-Affirming Treatment of Gender Dysphoria in Youth: A Perfect Storm Environment for the Placebo Effect — The Implications for Research and Clinical Practice', *Archives of Sexual Behaviour* (13 December, 2022); Philip J. Cheng, *et al.*, 'Fertility concerns of the transgender patient', *Translational Andrology and Urology* (June 2019).

75. See Grand View Research, 'U.S. Sex Reassignment Surgery Market Size, Share & Trends Analysis Report By Gender Transition (Male To Female, Female To Male), And Segment Forecasts, 2022-2030'; Acumen Research and Consulting, 'Sex Reassignment Surgery Market Size to reach a remarkable USD 3,171.3 Million by 2032' (8 June, 2023).

76. See Jody L. Herman, Andrew R. Flores and Kathryn K. O'Neill, 'How Many Adults and Youth Identify as Transgender in the United States', UCLA School of Law, Williams Institute (June 2022).

In the UK, where this ideology has only taken hold relatively recently, the figures are even more alarming.[77] 262,000 people in England and Wales identified themselves as 'trans' (that is, their 'gender identity was different from their sex registered at birth') in the Census of 2021, 0.54 per cent of the population, even higher than in the USA. Of those aged 16-24, 1 per cent identified as a different sex from the one they were born. This decreases to 0.77 per cent for those aged 25-34, 0.64 per cent for those aged 35-44, and in decreasing percentages down to 0.22 per cent of those aged over 75. Unfortunately, there is no data for children younger than 16 at whom this ideology has primarily been targeted. These figures were collated from the first Census to ask these questions, so there is also no data on the increase in the trans population. However, in 2018 the UK Government reported that, since the Gender Recognition Act 2004 was made into law, 4,910 UK citizens had been issued a Gender Recognition Certificate, which requires, among other things, a medical diagnosis of 'gender dysphoria' and changes the gender on their birth certificate.[78]

These figures, and the marked difference between age categories, can indicate a number of things:

1. Gender identity disorder, as even the NHS is belatedly coming to realise, is a passing phase of childhood exacerbated by the marketisation of youth consumerism that has penetrated further into childhood and even infancy, but a phase which, like adolescence itself, will pass with time and the protection of our children from predatory ideologies and marketing strategies like trans.[79]

2. With the recent and growing eradication of the stigma of 'being' transgender, the true number of people identifying as such is only now beginning to emerge, and most evidently in the young who, as the young do, have refused the suppression of their true identities by the older generation.

---

77. See Office for National Statistics, 'Gender identity: age and sex, England and Wales: Census 2021' (25 January, 2023).

78. See UK Public General Acts, 'Gender Recognition Act 2004' (1 July, 2004); Government Equalities Office, 'Trans People in the UK' (2018).

79. See Ari Blaff, 'NHS Warns Most Trans-Identifying Children Going Through "Transient Phase"', *National Review* (28 July, 2023).

3. The disproportionate and increasing adoption of transgender identities by the young is a product of trans ideology which, like other advertising campaigns that promotes their products and services through the language of liberation, transgression and rebellion, have targeted our children and youth as the customers most easily manipulated to identifying with its values and falling for its promises.

There is an element of truth in all these explanations, but what I have argued and tried to demonstrate in this chapter is that the ideology of trans is far more than a passing phase of childhood or the latest rebellion of Western adolescents in response to an increasingly terrifying and incomprehensible world, and is — quite evidently for those who look beyond its advertising slogans — a product of both the penetration of the medical industry into more and more aspects of our lives and the biopolitical ends that control serves.

In the UK, anxiety in the young continues to increase. Last year, according to The Children's Society, 6 per cent of children aged 10-15 were unhappy with their lives; 11 per cent said they did not cope with the changes imposed under lockdown; 12 per cent were unhappy with their school; 13 per cent were worried about another pandemic or other threat to their health; 16 per cent were worried about the environment; 18 per cent of girls were unhappy with their appearance, an increase from 15 per cent a decade ago, and 10 per percent of boys.[80] Also last year, the NHS estimated that 18 per cent of children aged 7-16 had a probable mental disorder, an increase from 12.1 per cent in 2017, or 50 per cent more in just five years.[81] For young people aged 17-19 years, 25.7 per cent had a probable mental disorder, up from 10.1 per cent in 2017, a 250 per cent increase. 12.6 per cent of children aged 11-16 reported that they had been bullied online. 12.9 per cent of 11-16-year-olds, 60.3 per cent of 17-19-year-olds, and 62.2 per cent of 20-23-year-olds had a possible eating disorder. 28.3 per cent of 7-16-year-olds and 68.6 per cent of 17-24-year-olds who had a probable mental disorder had tried to harm themselves. As I've said, we must situate these diagnoses of mental disorder within the growing biomedicalisation of our society and the biopolitical

---

80. See The Children's Society, 'The Good Childhood Report' (2022).

81. See NHS Digital, 'Rate of mental disorders among 17 to 19-year-olds increased in 2022, new report shows: statistical press release' (29 November, 2022).

agenda that serves; but this is the demographic at which the ideology of trans is primarily targeted and on which the purveyors of 'transgender therapy' and 'sex reassignment surgery' prey.

Under UK law, a child under the age of 16 cannot legally consent to having sex with an adult. Yet this year a High Court judge ruled that a child can consent to an adult — in this case Dr. Helen Webberley, who describes herself as 'self-taught in trans care' — administering life-changing puberty blockers and testosterone to three girls aged, respectively, 11, 12 and 17.[82] Again, it beggars belief that any judge who has not been instructed to do so would consider an 11- and 12-year-old girl capable of understanding, let alone consenting to, such life-altering interventions. I presume their parents granted their consent — or were compelled to by the Domestic Abuse Act 2021 — which at best demonstrates they are incompetent to raise a child and in effect guilty of abuse, like those parents who starve their child because of their religious beliefs.[83] As for the doctor, who set up her online clinic in 2015, in any other climate than the current one she would be found guilty of professional misconduct at the very least. Instead, the judgement of the High Court has set a judicial precedent that can and will be applied to future cases. Another judge can choose not to follow the precedent if it is 'clearly wrong' — which it clearly is to the great majority of the UK population; but the decision to uphold Dr. Webberley's appeal against her initial suspension from practise for misconduct by a Medical Practitioners Tribunal Service panel looks like an attempt by the medical industry, the UK courts and the British establishment to legalise what is child abuse and worse under the guise of upholding 'trans rights'.

Perhaps the bigger question than this second collusion between medicine and law we've seen in the last three-and-a-half years is why an 11-year-old girl, even in today's social media world, doesn't merely think her bum or nose is too big, or is alarmed by the changes to her body with the onset of puberty, but believes that she was 'born in the wrong body'. Where did a child get such an extreme idea that has such violent consequences for herself? The answer is books

---

82. See Nelli Bird, 'Transgender children GP: Helen Webberley wins suspension appeal', BBC News (31 March, 2023); Dr. Helen Webberley she/her, 'I am a GP, I am self-taught in trans healthcare', *Twitter* (1 July, 2023).

83. See Samuel Osborne, 'Baby died of malnutrition after parents refused to get help "due to religious reasons and fear of child services"', *Independent* (8 August, 2018).

like *Becoming Me*, which is used in UK schools on children as young as 10 as part of their Relationship, Sex and Health Education (RSHE).[84] The first volume, 'Body Parts', opens with a drawn image of a bearded woman with a hairy chest and double mastectomy scars holding a large syringe, telling children that their genitals 'do not determine your gender', and that they can 'medically transition' if they are 'born in the wrong body'. It then lists the ways 10-year-olds can 'transition'. These include, for a girl, testosterone injections, a hysterectomy, double mastectomy and phalloplasty; and, for a boy, speech therapy, eostrogen injections, castration, labiaplasty and breast implants. To guide them in 'transitioning', the book asks children to 'draw arrows' between the correct medical procedures and their new choice of identities, which it defines as: 'If you are born with a vagina but are a man' or 'If you are born with a penis but are a woman'. In an ironically titled 'Disclaimer for the grown ups', the authors state that 'there is no content in the books that children should not know from the age of 10+'.

What I repeatedly hear from transvestites who call themselves 'transsexuals' or 'transgender' is that they just want to be left alone to 'become themselves'; and as long as it doesn't endanger or harm someone else, I support the right of an adult to expand that quest any way they want, even if it's to the fantasy of changing sex — though the professional ethics of performing such surgical mutilations, even on consenting adults, is questionable to say the least. However, the use in schools of books like *Becoming Me* or the new practices of 'Drag Queen Story Hour' for 3-11-year-olds and drag shows for infants and their parents clearly demonstrate that the ideologues of trans want far more than that, and that they are quite willing to sacrifice both adults with an identity disorder and children going through puberty and adolescence to achieve their ends.[85]

But the abuse and violence doesn't stop there. The impunity with which threats to the safety of women are made online and then enacted physically in a climate of censorship in which we can be arrested for a Twitter post that mocks the orthodoxies of trans is an indicator of the level of government and corporate

---

84. See Amy Crozier, *Becoming Me* (2023).

85. See Drag Queen Story Hour UK Ltd (2023); Jo Bartosch, 'Babies should be nowhere near gyrating drag queens', *Spiked* (3 March, 2023).

support for this now official ideology of the UK biosecurity state.[86] As I've tried to demonstrate in this chapter, the perception that a person is 'born in the wrong body' is — quite evidently to the undoctrinated and those with a basic grasp of biology or more advanced knowledge of psychiatry — the product of a form of mental illness, even if it is only depression or the difficulties of childhood and adolescence that social media and the general state of the world have exacerbated beyond what someone of, for example, my generation experienced. What I've tried to identify is the causes of this disorder and why it is being propagated by the UK biosecurity state. The damage to the mental health of children and adolescents by the cultivation of their addiction to smartphones and social media by consumer capitalism, added to two years of lockdown, the interruption of their education and their early indoctrination into the principles and practices of biosecurity (social distancing, mandatory masking, gene therapy and digital identity), has undoubtedly prepared our children to accept, willingly or in fear, the fallacious principles and fraudulent practices of trans ideology.[87]

In addition to asserting as much — which most of the UK population is too intimidated by the police or scared of the consequences for their jobs of doing so to declare openly — we must also start to understand why such demonstrably false, irrational and above all dangerous beliefs are being written into UK legislation, enacted in policy and indoctrinated into our children. It is in this respect, as I have said, that the sudden rise of trans is not coincidental to the Great Reset of Western capitalism and its raft of regulations, programmes and technologies, but rather the official ideology of the Global Biosecurity State. Indeed, it might not be too much to suggest that trans identity and the symbolically castrated, biologically infertile, socially isolated, biotechnologically controlled self is the new model of citizenship in the West. Ultimately, trans hasn't acquired such hegemony in the UK in order to defend the rights or validate the fantasies of the less than 0.5 per cent of the population that has been fooled into adopting its dogma as their own. Trans is an ideology developed to control all the population.

---

86. See Harry Miller, 'The police are now the paramilitary wing of the trans lobby', *Spiked* (10 August, 2022).

87. See SlickText, '44 Smartphone Addiction Statistics for 2023' (23 January, 2023); Ofcom, 'Children and parents: media use and attitudes report 2022' (30 March, 2022).

If it isn't, then why is it that, across the Western world, every government, every legislature, every civil service, every bank, every corporation, every business, every law court, every municipal authority, every council, every civil institution, every civic authority, every parish, every church, every military, every police force, every hospital, every clinic, every union, every forum for public debate, every university, every school, every sporting organisation, every media platform, every news programme, every TV show, every brand, every advertisement — in other words, every instrument of economic, political, legal, cultural and ideological influence — are all, without exception, promoting and enforcing the ideology of trans?

It is not, undoubtedly, because they are expressing the will, beliefs and opinions of the British people, who by an overwhelming majority reject the orthodoxies of trans.[88] Nor is it because the administrators of Western capitalism have all simultaneously opened their hearts, minds and wallets to the values of 'diversity, equity and inclusion' written into UK law by The Equality Act 2010 and imposed on UK businesses by BlackRock and other financial asset managers under the United Nation's Environmental, Social and corporate Governance criteria.[89] No, there is only one answer to this question that is compatible with what we know about the revolution in Western capitalism we have been undergoing over the past four years, since the coronavirus 'crisis' and the many years of preparation that preceded it. Woke is the official ideology of the Global Biosecurity State, stakeholder capitalism is its political economy, and trans is the new biopolitical paradigm of citizenship on which it is being built.

Where does that leave the transvestite friends with whom I began this chapter, some of whom, perhaps, attended London Pride, under whatever spectrum of the once rainbow-coloured flag? I would like to think that they are as angry at what is being done to their practices and identity as I am, and will — hopefully sooner rather than later — come out, physically if need be, to defend the women being threatened and attacked by their fellow transvestites and trans ideologues, and denounce those who shout or carry banners or wear T-shirts with

---

88. See Matthew Smith, 'Where does the British public stand on transgender rights in 2022?', *YouGov* (20 July 2022).

89. See UK Public General Acts, 'Equality Act 2010' (8 April, 2010); Deloitte, 'The Big Three & ESG: A Guide to BlackRock, State Street & Vanguard Proxy Voting Policies & Guidance on Key ESG Issues' (5 June, 2023).

some variation on 'Kill the TERF'.[90] But I also hope — I invite them to do so now — that if they find something in this chapter that resonates with them, or even if they don't, they will oppose the almost universal co-option of transvestism to this transhuman agenda. Because transvestites, as we are rightfully reminded, are humans with human rights, which are no different from those rights and freedoms the rest of us are fighting for; and they need defending from those who seek to profit, financially, medically and politically, from the ideology of trans. Women, parents and feminists have been doing so for some time already; but the time has come for all of us to defend our rights, our bodies and above all our children from this new order of speech, the pseudo-science on which it is based, the misogyny it has sanctioned, and the new paradigm of citizenship it is trying to impose. It is time we stop being afraid to raise our voices above the censorship and threats issued by the ideologues of trans and denounce not only the absurdities and obscenities of this enforced ideology but also the New Normal it is seeking to impose. If we don't, our grandchildren and even our children will one day be unrecognisable to us, as will the world in which they will be forced to live out their lives.

Even after the months of research and thought it took to write this chapter, I still can't claim to understand why the ideology of trans has received such widespread acceptance. I can't begin to explain the parents who sit there with grins on their faces as their children watch adult men strip in front of them, or why people who see themselves as socially progressive cheer young men assaulting women, or how otherwise rational people can affirm that a man can menstruate or give birth, or how teachers can fill the heads of the children in their care with such obvious and dangerous lies, or how doctors can mutilate their bodies. But then, there is always something in excess of what can be rationally explained — something obscene — in all ideologies, and the more extreme the ideology the more obscene is its kernel of irrationality. I imagine many Germans in the 1930s were equally unable to explain how their country was taken over by a gang of criminals dressed as boy-scouts carrying military banners through the streets of their cities to the ecstatic cheers of adoring crowds. I don't imagine I'm alone in having a similar response to the Pride celebrations that were held across the cities of the Western world this summer. States don't invest in such spectacles to

---

90. See Eco-shirt, 'Kill The Terf Shirt' (2023).

celebrate their 'diversity'; they do it to entrench their hegemony. It is a measure of the dominance of an ideology that it cannot be seen, that its distortion of reality and morality is transparent to our vision. This is my attempt to make the obscenity of trans visible.

Postscript: What is a Woman?

In July 2023, *The New Statesman* published two articles by, respectively, the biologist, Richard Dawkins, 'Why biological sex matters', and the feminist, Jacqueline Rose, 'The gender binary is false'.[91] I don't know Rose personally, but her 1986 book, *Sexuality in the Field of Vision*, had a considerable influence on me when I was studying for my MA in the History and Theory of Art at University College London back in the 1990s.[92] I was disappointed, therefore, at her defence of 'trans rights', which she undertakes on the basis of her belief that declaring oneself to be another sex is an act of liberation from the norms of gender roles. The agreement of the rest of us — who, by implication, are too oppressed by patriarchy to free ourselves from our biologically determined sex — to recognise this act of liberation is, she concludes, 'a matter of generosity and freedom'.

Unfortunately, in arriving at this conclusion, Rose, who is Professor of Humanities at the Birkbeck Institute in London, says nothing about trans as an official ideology that — despite being formed by a marginal US subculture around an identity disorder — is being written into UK legislation, enacted in policy, enforced in law and indoctrinated into our children, and the fact that, whether we're feeling generous or not, we are all being forced into compliance with its orthodoxies. If Rose were speaking about the personal choices of what is still the fraction of the percentage of the UK population who identify as another sex then she may have a point about the rest of us being generous towards their fantasies; but she isn't. Trans, as the month-long celebration of Pride across the West demonstrated, is part of the official ideology of the new paradigm of biosecurity by which we have been governed since March 2020.

---

91. See Richard Dawkins, 'Why biological sex matters' and Jacqueline Rose, 'The gender binary is false', *The New Statesmen* (26 July, 2023).

92. See Jacqueline Rose, *Sexuality in the Field of Vision* (Verso, 1986).

Perhaps more concerning than this evidence of the customary blindness of academics to the world in which they appear not to live with the rest of us, Rose breezily dismisses the growing incidents of the violence of trans, in both its theoretical claims (lesbians who refuse sex with male transvestites are 'transphobic') and in the practices of its adherents (the now legalised call to 'Kill the TERFS'), as a stereotype she compares to racism. This is the standard practice of woke ideology when its ideologues want to silence those with whom they disagree, and should be beneath a thinker of Rose's stature.

And for someone who calls herself a feminist and whose defence of transgenderism is founded on Simone de Beauvoir's famous statement that 'One is not born, but rather becomes, a woman', Rose's dismissal of the misogyny of trans on the grounds that 'woman' is a construct is not only symptomatic of her safe, middle-class, academic perspective, but a betrayal of the women under attack by these violent men.[93] Despite Rose's characterisation of woman as 'the mark of oppression, prejudice, low pay, the burden of domestic labour, violence in the home and on the street', it is precisely the women who experience this violence — and who are overwhelmingly working class — that she is betraying.

Nor does Rose have anything to say about the death and rape threats, online abuse, cancellation, misogyny and physical attacks directed at public figures like J. K. Rowling and Kellie-Jay Keen by trans activists and social-media trolls, and which the ideology of trans has authorised and even celebrates. Perhaps, to quote the time-honoured defence of equally violent and misogynist men who attack and abuse women, 'they were looking for it'?

The only possible explanation for such a lack of concern for the safety of UK women and girls in the street, on the sports-field, in the classroom, in women's toilets, in trans-therapy clinics, on protests and in UK law is that Rose appears to have confused feminism's critique of femininity and the inequality between the sexes — which unlike our biological sex *is* a construct of gender norms — with transgenderism's denial of sexual difference and with it of women themselves. But that's the sort of concession one would make to a first-year student straight out of the UK's PSHE and RSE school curricula, not an internationally known academic.

---

93. See Simone de Beauvoir, *The Second Sex* (1949); translated by H. M. Parshley (Jonathan Cape, 1953), p. 273.

A far more likely and mundane explanation is that Rose has simply aligned herself with the class of the students she teaches at Birkbeck, whose students are charged £19,200 per year in tuition fees to be indoctrinated into the principles of woke; the class of her colleagues, publishers and reviewers, all of whom have subscribed to its orthodoxies as a condition of occupying their positions; and the class of the ideologues of trans in academia, the media and Parliament.[94] Because in the UK, as across the Anglosphere in which it has taken deepest root, trans is overwhelmingly an ideology of the middle classes.

But in addition to this demonstration — as if we needed it after two years of lockdown — that allegiance to one's class continues to trump feminist or any other kind of solidarity in the UK, Rose's article is also littered with factual inaccuracies. Contrary to Rose's assertion that 'people over 65, especially women, are almost as gender-fluid as the young', transgenderism, as I've shown in this chapter, is overwhelmingly an identity disorder of the young, and a product of their indoctrination into this ideology by our education and cultural industries. But it beggars belief that Rose, a female academic of international standing, when defining what the word 'female' means, cites a book by a transvestite man who calls himself Andrea Long Chu, and who in *Females: A Concern* (2019) wrote: 'Getting fucked makes you female because fucked is what a female is'.[95]

On the authority of this man — who also claims that the male anus is 'a kind of universal vagina through which femaleness can always be accessed' — Rose claims that the biological category of female — 'as we understand it today', she adds — was developed in the Nineteenth Century to describe black slaves. I'm not sure how that caveat is meant to qualify this absurd and fantastical assertion, but, historically, the word 'female', which has a different etymology to 'male', originated in the Fourteenth Century and derives from twelfth-century French *femelle* and Latin *femella*, the diminutive of *femina*, which means 'she who suckles'.[96] The contemporary spelling of 'female' was changed to correspond with 'male' in the late Fourteenth Century; but rather than being a mere adjunct to the universal man, its Latin origin derives from the unique ability of a woman to

---

94. See Birkbeck, University of London, 'Financial Requirements'.

95. See Joan Smith, 'Andrea Long Chu's Pulitzer win is an insult to women', *Unherd* (12 May, 2023).

96. See Online Etymology Dictionary, 'female', 'male'.

breastfeed her child — to which transvestite men have recently extended their attempts to appropriate female biology.[97]

As for the word 'woman' — which Rose claims is an oppressive construct of patriarchy from which trans offers a means of liberation for men struggling to free themselves from what she calls 'the straightjacket of masculinity' — Old English used *wer* (from Latin *vir*: adult human male) and *wif* (woman and also, but not especially, wife) to distinguish the sexes, before *wer* began to disappear in the late Thirteenth Century and was replaced by 'man'.[98] 'Woman' comes from Old English *wimman*, a corruption of *wifman*, which is a compound of *wif* (a neuter noun) and *man* (a masculine noun denoting a male or female human) to form a word for an adult human female exclusively. This isn't, however, a merely etymological correction of Chu's fabricated history. The meaning of words is important because, as history repeatedly demonstrates — most forcefully in the erasure of races, religions and cultures — when you erase the meaning of a word you erase what it denotes.

It is significant that Chu, who this year was awarded the Pulitzer Prize for Criticism — a further demonstration of the ideological promotion of trans — openly admits that he was drawn to become a transvestite through his addiction to pornography, which one might guess is at the origin of his violent and deeply misogynist opinions and statements about women, and his own masochistic identification with what he sees as woman's essential victimhood.[99] Of course, there's nothing new about men acting out their fantasies of domination and submission in pornography; but what is significant is that this male violence and the object it wants to erase — the 'fucked' female of rape fantasies — is a product of one of the technologies of biopower, digital pornography, to which the libido of an entire generation of children and young adults is being addicted and, through that addiction, indoctrinated into its values.[100] If parents want to know the values

---

97. See John Ely, 'How trans women use a powerful mix of hormones, drugs and pumps to "breastfeed" babies — but how safe is it really? And does it actually nourish a child?', *Daily Mail* (5 July, 2023).

98. See Online Etymology Dictionary, 'woman', 'man'.

99. See 'Andrea Long Chu, New York Magazine's Book Critic, Wins Pulitzer Prize', *New York Magazine* (8 May, 2023).

100. See Harry Fletcher, 'Porn addiction in the UK has "trebled" since the start of the pandemic', *Indy100* (15 December, 2022); and Harriet Grant and Dan Milmo, 'A fifth of teenagers

the ideologues of trans are teaching their children in UK schools, they should look at the genre of pornography called 'sissy porn'.

The fact that a woman, a feminist and an intellectual is collaborating and lending the considerable authority of her academic voice to such erasure is, unfortunately — and to speak in the language of psychoanalysis Rose herself has made a career of employing — a symptom of the times in which we live. And, yet again, she appears to be almost entirely unaware of the past three-and-a-half years as anything other than a viral pandemic that, according to the latest exaggerated estimates, has killed nearly 7 million people, as if the sudden hegemony of trans has nothing to do with the dismantling of our rights, freedoms and democracy, and their replacement with the regulations, programmes and technologies of biopower.[101]

But I don't really believe that either. Like other UK intellectuals who have remained masked, injected, silent and obedient during the vast changes that have been imposed on our society over the last few years outside of any democratic process and on the basis of lie after obvious lie, Rose is not 'confused' — as I too generously suggested before.[102] Like every other academic lining up at the altar of lockdown, mandatory gene therapy, environmental catastrophe, US imperialism and trans ideology, Jacqueline Rose — to use the existential language of her heroine — is demonstrating the bad faith (*mauvaise foi*) of the intellectual who, as intellectuals have done throughout history, side with authority during periods of authoritarian rule and ideological hegemony.[103]

As I wrote back in the dark days of October 2021 — when we were asked to be equally 'generous' in offering up our bodies and those of our children to experimental gene therapies as the condition of the return of our freedoms — history demonstrates that, when Hitler's in the Reichstag, every coward wears a swastika. The LGBTQIA+ Intersex-Inclusive Progress Pride flag is the swastika of our time.

---

watch pornography frequently and some are addicted, UK study finds', *The Guardian* (10 March, 2023).

101. See Worldometer, 'Coronavirus Deaths: 6,928,706 deaths' (21 October, 2023).

102. See Simon Elmer, 'The Betrayal of the Clerks: UK Intellectuals in the Service of the Biosecurity State', *Architects for Social Housing* (12 November, 2020).

103. See Simon Elmer, 'Whatever Happened to the Middle Classes? Bad Faith and the Culture Industry', *Architects for Social Housing* (10 May, 2019).

7. Woke, Racism and the Great Reset

Among the many things the last three-and-a-half-years of cowardice and complicity have demonstrated is that the West, as an idea, is now dead. If it continues to haunt the world, it is only as an interdependent financial sector rapidly reaching the day of its reckoning, military alliances against whatever bogeyman the US identifies for 'liberation' next, and security treaties between Europe, the USA and Australasia. The funeral rites have been a long time in preparation, but in the UK, at least, we no longer have anything one could refer to as a 'culture', for which we have substituted corporate and state propaganda created by global think-tanks to cretinize the national population into compliance. Our leaders in politics, business and the media are at best puppets for transnational technocracies, open to corruption by the highest bidder from any quarter of the globe. London is an offshore financial jurisdiction serviced by increasingly impoverished immigrants living in what will soon be a surveillance city-state. And after years of national decline, humiliation, lockdown and the ongoing theft of our futures for a multitude of manufactured 'crises', the British, as a people, are clinically depressed, apparently unable to do more than make a weary nod of consent to the media-managed spectacle of the latest celebrity scandal, political corruption or proxy war.

Not before time, more and more of us have come to the realisation that, as a political union claiming to be a sovereign state (try not to laugh) we are no longer in charge of our own destiny: not only because the democratic process that has limped across the world stage for years to the mocking jeers of our peers has finally collapsed into what is, in effect, a one-party state; but also because, whatever parliamentary party we vote to form a government in the abject spectacle of universal suffrage inflicted on the union every four years, it will make absolutely no difference to the Great Reset of Western capitalism we have been undergoing since September 2019, nor to the technologies of biopower to which we are being subjected as citizens not of the United Kingdom of Great Britain and Northern Ireland but of the Global Biosecurity State.[1]

---

1. See Simon Elmer, 'Fascism and the Decay of Capitalism' *The Road to Fascism,* pp. 61-80.

Indeed, in many respects the British are now a colonised people, much like India was under the British Empire, the Eastern Bloc countries were under the Soviet Union, and South American countries are under the USA. The coloniser now, however, isn't another country or Empire, but a transnational consortium of financial institutions, global asset managers, information technology companies and the technocracies they form. The names of these unaccountable, anti-democratic organisations have become increasingly familiar to even the most COVID-compliant, Zelenskyy-worshipping and environmental-fundamentalist of UK citizens since March 2020: the World Economic Forum, the World Health Organization, the Intergovernmental Panel on Climate Change, as well as the already familiar but increasingly authoritarian European Commission, United Nations, North Atlantic Treaty Organization, World Bank and International Monetary Fund. It is to oversee, enforce, manage and insert us into the New World Order over which these global technocracies preside that the Great Reset of Western capitalism is being implemented; and in our habituation and subordination to this next phase, woke, as the official ideology of stakeholder capitalism, is instrumental to our compliance.

1. The Politics of Immigration

But when did woke assume this role? In the UK, woke could be said to have begun — even before the term was coined — when our re-elected Prime Minister, Tony Blair, a year into the illegal invasion of Iraq, scolded us for drinking too much, which he called 'the new British disease', and told us we should instead be sipping French wines in Islington restaurants.[2] Behind its middle-class snobbery, this was part of New Labour's recalibration of UK politics away from the paradigm of Left and Right in which it had failed to form a Government since 1979 and towards the woke opposition between Open and Closed. According to this new paradigm, the White British working class were now openly denounced as culturally conservative, anti-immigration and economically protectionist, and the middle classes celebrated as multicultural, globalist and neoliberal. This ideological framework, which was uncritically accepted by the unfailingly cretinous UK Left, laid the ground for the expansion of the European Union in 2004 and the opening

---

2. See Joe Murphy, 'Blair campaign to fight binge drinking', *Evening Standard* (19 May, 2004).

of UK labour markets to workers from eight states, Czechia, Estonia, Latvia, Lithuania, Hungary, Poland, Slovakia, and Slovenia.[3]

However, contrary to the lies of the serial liar, Tony Blair, and the orthodoxies of woke the New Labour governments imposed on the UK, this was not done out of a sudden conversion to the politics of peace, love and harmony between peoples, but rather to drive down the rising cost of the labour of the working-class population of the UK in 2004, at a time when only 10.5 per cent of the working-age population were born outside the UK.[4] Continued from 2010 by Blair's understudy, David Cameron, by 2021, some 17 years after this watershed in UK immigration, 31.2 per cent of workers in elementary occupations were immigrants.[5] This included 60.7 per cent of packers, bottlers, canners and fillers, 38.8 per cent of warehouse operatives, 37.3 per cent of cleaners and domestics, 36.2 per cent of security guards, 35 per cent of delivery operatives, 32.4 per cent of industrial cleaners, dry cleaners and waiters, 29.2 per cent of kitchen assistants, 28.1 per cent of elementary process plant workers, 24.1 per cent of sales assistants, 22 per cent of construction workers, 19 per cent of postal workers, 18.8 per cent of hospital porters, 18.6 per cent of fishing and agricultural workers, and 17.8 per cent of groundworkers. Over the same period, real wages for workers in the UK have largely stagnated — with the income of the poorest fifth of the population after housing costs no higher in 2018-19 than in 2004-05 — while the income of those who employ them and profit from their labour has grown.[6]

3. See Jonathan Este, 'The huge political cost of Blair's decision to allow Eastern European migrants unfettered access to Britain', *The Conversation* (16 November, 2016).

4. See Christian Dustmann and Francesca Fabbri, 'Immigrants in the British Labour Market', *Fiscal Studies*, Vol. 26, No. 4 (December 2005).

5. See Office for National Statistics, 'Migration and the labour market, England and Wales: Census 2021' (21 March, 2023).

6. See D. Clark, 'Average growth of weekly earnings in the United Kingdom compared with the CPI inflation rate from March 2001 to June 2023', *Statista* (August 2023); Phillip Inman, 'UK workers face return to 2006 real-term wages in "highly challenging" 2023', *The Guardian* (23 December, 2022); and Adam Corlett, 'Charting the UK's lost decade of income growth', *Resolution Foundation* (5 March, 2020).

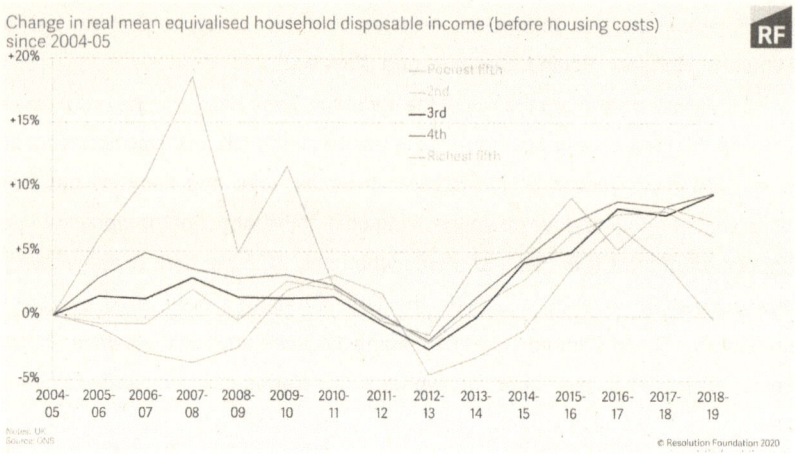

Change in real mean equivalised household disposable income (before housing costs) since 2004-05

Source: Office for National Statistics

Of course, a lot has happened in the UK over the past two decades, including — to recall only the Greatest Hits of Finance Capitalism 2004-2023 — the progressive banning of industrial action by successive waves of anti-worker legislation; the US subprime mortgage crisis of 2007 that sent the UK into recession; the Global Financial Crisis of 2008-2009; the subsequent bailout of the banks with £456.33 billion of UK taxpayers' money and the consequent decade of fiscal austerity that followed; the housing crisis it caused as globalists invested their wealth in UK properties underwritten by new housing legislation like Help to Buy equity loans and Shared Ownership schemes; £895 million in quantitative easing for purchasing government bonds by the Bank of London in order to prop up the financial sector that threatened to enter a second Global Financial Crisis in September 2019; the two years of Government-enforced lockdown to insulate the real economy from the $19 trillion of failing assets purchased by central banks globally between then and April 2022; the consequent escalation in inflation and the cost of living we have now, with interest rates in August 2023 raised to 5.25 per cent, the highest since December 2007; and the £13.767 billion the UK Government has committed to the privatisation of the national resources and assets of the Ukraine.[7] So the immiseration and disenfranchisement of UK

---

7. See Jonathan Jeffries, Andrew Morretta and Alex Just, 'A Chronology of Labour Law 1979-2023', *Institute of Employment Rights* (2023); DataBlog, 'Bank reforms: how much did we bail them

workers can't all be blamed on a market flooded with underpaid foreign workers. The point I want to make is that immigration policy, in 2023 as in 2004, is determined by the economic and political intentions of those setting it. The economic intentions are clear by their results: the poverty and industrial impotence of UK workers; but what is the political intention behind immigration policy in the UK over the last two decades?

According to the Census of 2001, the UK was 91.3 per cent White (87.5% White British, 1.2% White Irish, 2.6% White other); with just 2.2 per cent Black (1.1% Caribbean, 0.9% African, 0.2% other), and 4 per cent Asian (2% Indian, 1.4% Pakistani, 0.5% Bangladeshi and 1.3% mixed).[8] By the 2021 Census, UK immigration policy had changed this to 4 per cent Black, 3.1 per cent Indian, 2.7 per cent Pakistani, 1.1 per cent Bangladeshi and 2.9 per cent mixed. Respectively, that's a 181%, 155%, 192%, 220% and 223% increase in just twenty years. And since the population of the UK over that time rose from 59.12 million to 67.33 million, the actual increase in the number of British citizens of Black, Asian and mixed-race ethnicity is higher than these percentage increases. Over the same period, the percentage of people in the UK of White ethnicity fell to 81.7 percent, White Irish falling to 0.9%, White other rising to 6.2% (a 238 per cent increase reflecting the expansion of UK labour markets into Central and Eastern Europe in 2004), with White British now making up less than three-quarters (74.4 per cent) of the population of the UK. Asians, including Indian, Pakistani, Bangladeshi and Chinese, now make up 9.3 per cent of the population of the UK. That gives this demographic considerable electoral influence in the UK, particularly when targeted by a politics that appeals to its racial identity.

Twenty years later — whether it's Scotland's newly-elected First Minister, Humza Yousef, who in February this year felt completely comfortable declaring

---

out and how much do they still owe?', *The Guardian* (2016); Phillip Inman, '10 years on, what did George Osborne's Help to Buy scheme really achieve?', *The Guardian* (31 March, 2023); Bank of England, 'QE at the Bank of England: A perspective on its functioning and effectiveness', *Quarterly Bulletin 2022 Q1* (18 May, 2022); Fabio Vighi, 'A Self-fulfilling Prophecy: Systemic Collapse and Pandemic Simulation', *The Philosophical Salon* (16 August, 2021); Edward Yardeni and Mali Quintana, 'Central Banks: Monthly Ballance Sheets', *Yardeni Research, Inc.* (22 September, 2023); Bank of England database, 'Official Bank Rate history'; Kiel Institute for World Economy, 'Ukraine Support Tracker' (2023).

8. UK Government, 'Population of England and Wales — Ethnicity facts and figures' (4 April, 2023).

there were too many White people in positions of authority in a Scotland where more than 96 per cent of the population is White British, or London's Mayor, Sadiq Khan, who in August declared that White families are not representative of Londoners, 60 per cent of whom are White — the UK is increasingly being run by second-generation immigrants who, on this evidence and quite openly, hate the White British working class, our indigenous culture and social customs.[9] But in the climate of accusation, censorship and retribution created by woke in the UK, few have had the courage to ask how and why this has happened, or dared to answer their own questions.

2. The Ideology of Racism

As the British know better than anyone and ruthlessly demonstrated in India, Africa, the Middle East and South-east Asia when we ruled not only our own nation but many others, the colonisation of a country is conditional upon the erasure of its indigenous culture and the replacement of its native leaders with foreigners who have no allegiance, in beliefs or customs, to the conquered people. UK's woke-compliant leaders — White, Asian and Black — who occupy positions of leadership and seniority in all the UK's parliamentary political parties, have been appointed by globalists for precisely this purpose. Whether it's Digital Identity, which will enable a system of digital surveillance and Social Credit, Central Bank Digital Currency, which will give the Bank of England total control over our expenditures, the World Economic Forum's 15-Minute Cities, which will function as digital camps, the United Nation's Agenda 2030, which is imposing a programme of progressive eco-austerity, or the World Health Organization's Pandemic Treaty, which will outsource mandatory masking, gene therapy and lockdowns to an unaccountable technocracy, the programmes, agendas and treaties being imposed on us by the UK's woke leadership are designed and

---

9. See Humza Yousaf, 'Humza Yousaf Racist Rant about white people in Scotland', *YouTube* (25 February, 2023); UK Population data, 'Population of Scotland 2023'; Archie Mitchell, 'Sadiq Khan's office under fire for suggesting white families "don't represent real Londoners"', *The Independent* (21 August, 2023); Gordon Rayner, 'How British Asians came to be political powerhouses', *The Telegraph* (29 March, 2023); and UK Government, 'Regional ethnic diversity' (22 December, 2022).

intended to deprive the UK of its national sovereignty and reduce the native population to a subject people.

Woke is a foreign ideology, manufactured largely by US globalists, propagandists and academics to replace the indigenous cultures of the nation states of the West. The leaders selected to enforce it have been chosen strategically to this end because, as repeatedly demonstrated by Sadiq Khan — the second-generation immigrant voted Mayor of London by a demographic of which nearly 40 per cent are of Asian, Black or mixed ethnicity — anyone who opposes the colonisation of the UK by these policies can be denounced as 'far-right', 'racist' and other insults from the lexicon of woke.[10] Just as multiculturalism was the ideology of neoliberalism that justified — among other policies of the great capitalist gangbang of the last forty years — the untaxed and untracked movement of capital through global markets and into offshore financial jurisdictions, so woke is the ideology of stakeholder capitalism justifying the rule of nation states by transnational technocracies. No matter what political party they are nominally a member of, every woke leader is a puppet of the World Economic Forum that — as we're seeing with 15-Minute Cities — creates the policies our politicians impose with the authority of the nation state they've been elected by us — naively and foolishly — to govern.

To cite just two examples, while the population of the UK is suffering £54 billion in increased taxes and cuts to services, Rishi Sunak, the Indian son-in-law of an Indian billionaire and founder of the multinational information technology company, InfoSys — which just happens to be developing a system of Digital Identity — recently returned from the G20 summit held in India with the promise to allocate, under the woke banner of a 'Green Climate Fund', £2 billion of UK taxpayers' money for his globalist partners to address another manufactured crisis.[11] And as part of the C40 Cities Climate Leadership Group he chairs, Sadiq

---

10. According to the Census of 2021, Asians constitute 20.7 per cent of London's population, Black Caribbean and African 13.5 per cent, and mixed race 5.7 per cent.

11. See Jason Groves, 'Britain must "face into the storm" of a global downturn, Jeremy Hunt will warn as he prepares to deliver brutal budget with bleak £54 billion package of tax rises and spending cuts to bring towering national debts and crippling inflation under control', *Daily Mail* (16 November 2022); InfoSys, 'Digital Identity: The Catalyst for Inclusive Financial Services' (21 May, 2021); and Rishi Sunak, 'Prime Minister announces record climate aid commitment as G20 in India concludes' (10 September, 2023).

Khan plans to implement a ban on private car ownership and the consumption of dairy products and meat by 2030.[12] Neither of these policy decisions, nor the funding from UK taxpayers required to implement them, were part of the campaign promises of either Rishi Sunak or Sadiq Khan.

To distract us from which, barely a week passes without Khan accusing and insulting some group of people opposed to his policies. Perhaps the most infamous example was in March 2023, during a public Question Time session, when he accused Londoners opposed to the expansion of his Ultra-Low Emission Zone to the whole of London of being 'in a coalition with the far-right, COVID-deniers and anti-vaxxers', to which he later added 'conspiracy theorists and Nazis'.[13] In employing this discourse of 'denial', Khan had no hesitation in reducing the political opinions of working-class Londoners, and their opposition to fines of £12.50 per day that will immiserate them even further, to 'Holocaust' deniers.

I would argue that, since, under Section 4 of the Public Order Act 1986, it is an offense for a person to use 'threatening, abusive or insulting words or behaviours that causes, or is likely to cause, another person harassment, alarm of distress', and that a person guilty of such an offence is liable to imprisonment for a term not exceeding 6 months, Khan should be arrested, interviewed and charged by the Metropolitan Police Service, and be compelled to resign from his position as morally unfit to hold public office.[14] He won't be, of course, because he is protected from such charges not only by his office but also by his ethnicity, which allows him, as it does other Asian and Black Britons, to accuse anyone in this country who is White of being racist, far-right, anti-Semitic (etc.) with complete impunity, and indeed with the full support and approval of the woke Left and the nearly 1 in 5 of the UK population encouraged by woke to see racism everywhere.

Let me clarify what I'm saying, in anticipation of the knee-jerk reactions to my argument from those on the Left who, in strict obedience to the orthodoxies

---

12. See Panda la Terriere, 'Mayor's initiative calls for car, dairy and meat ban by 2030', *UnHerd* (11 September, 2023).

13. See Jack Simpson, 'Sadiq Khan says those against Ulez are "in coalition" with far-Right and Covid deniers', *The Telegraph* (3 March, 2023).

14. See UK Public General Acts, Section 4. Fear or provocation of violence, 'Public Order Act 1986' (7 November, 1986).

of woke, regard the use of the word 'immigrant' or any reference to the ethnicity or religion of a person as some sort of hate crime. I am not saying that our White politicians and World Economic Forum puppets have any more allegiance to Britain or the British people than their Black and Asian counterparts. The names of Boris Johnson (our former Prime Minister), Matt Hancock (our former Secretary of State for Health), Jeremy Hunt (our current Chancellor of the Exchequer), Grant Shapps (the new Secretary of State for Defence), Michael Gove (our Secretary of State for Housing), Steve Barclay (our current Secretary of State for Health), Thérèse Coffey (our Secretary of State for the Environment), Penny Mordaunt (the Leader of the Commons), Keir Starmer (the Leader of the Labour Party), Nicola Sturgeon (the former First Minister of Scotland), Mark Drakeford (the Leader of the Welsh Assembly) and Caroline Lucas (the single MP for the Green Party) — all of whom are collaborating in the Great Reset of the UK — are ample proof of this. But none of these White politicians can draw on the race card when defending their enforcement of policies and programmes formulated by transnational technocracies and imposed without a mandate from the UK electorate.

To look only at the two political parties with any chance of forming a Government, 17 per cent of the Cabinet of the current Conservative Government are second-generation immigrants, which is representative of the 18 per cent of the UK population from a Black, Asian, mixed or other ethnic group, although all five of them occupy the most senior offices of State; while the Labour Party's Shadow Cabinet has four, although, again, they are all Shadow Secretaries of State.[15] To refer to their ethnicity and not their citizenship, which is of course British, it's for this reason that Rishi Sunak (our unelected Indian Prime Minister), Suella Braverman (our Indian Home Secretary), James Cleverly (our first Foreign Minister with African heritage), Claire Coutinho (our Indian Secretary of State for Net Zero), Kemi Badenoch (our Indian Secretary of State for Business), Priti Patel (our former Indian Home Secretary), Sajid Javid (our former Pakistani Chancellor, Home Secretary and Secretary of State for Health), Nadhim Zahawi (our former Iraqi Minister for COVID-19 Vaccine Development); David Lammy (our Guyanese Shadow Foreign Secretary), Shabana Mahmood (our Pakistani Shadow Secretary of State for Justice), Thangam Debbonaire (née Singh, our Indian Shadow

---

15. See UK Parliament, 'His Majesty's Government: The Cabinet'; and UK Government, 'Ethnicity Facts and Figures' (2021 Census data).

Secretary of State for Culture and Media), Diane Abbott (the Jamaican former Shadow Home Secretary), Sadiq Khan (our Pakistani Mayor of London), Humza Yousaf (our Pakistani First Minister of Scotland) and Anas Sarwar (our Pakistani Leader of the Scottish Labour Party) — all of whom are second-generation immigrants to the UK — have been appointed to such senior leadership positions in a UK whose population is 75 per cent White British.

If any non-European country had such a high proportion of senior politicians of another ethnicity and religion in its government — and how many White Britons in the British Raj were born in India? — we'd call this colonialism; but under the orthodoxies of woke and its permanent apologia for being White and British, we are forced, instead, to celebrate it as 'multiculturalism'. And under the protection of its dogma, these woke leaders can (and do) play the race card when anyone opposes the policies and programmes of their globalist masters.

To cite only a handful of the most transparent examples from the last few years, in May 2019, when Sajid Javid, the former Board Member of Deutsche Bank who sold the collateralised debt obligations that turned the subprime mortgage crisis into the Global Financial Crisis and channelled bankers' bonuses through the Cayman Islands, as UK Home Secretary signed the order to extradite Julian Assange to the USA, he accused critics of using his race and religion to attack his politics.[16]

In June 2020, as protests were banned under the third amendment to the Health Protection (Coronavirus, Restrictions) (England) Regulations 2020, and Priti Patel, as Javid's successor as Home Secretary, was accused of racism by Labour MPs for condemning a Black Lives Matter protest, she responded by saying she had been called a 'Paki' as a child.[17]

In October 2020, Kemi Badenoch responded to the comparative lack of Britons from Black and ethnic minority backgrounds participating in the trials for

16. See Richard Partington, 'John McDonnell questions chancellor's suitability for office', *The Guardian* (5 August, 2019); Lizzie Dearden, 'Critics don't like me because of my colour, Sajid Javid says after online abuse from far right and left', *Independent* (11 May, 2019).

17. See Greg Heffer, 'George Floyd protests: Priti Patel recalls childhood racial slurs as she condemns "hooliganism" towards police', *Sky News* (8 June, 2020).

the COVID-19 justified gene therapies by accusing 'conspiracy theorists' of targeting BAME communities with disinformation.[18]

On 7 December 2020, as the UK signed a military agreement with the apartheid State of Israel, James Cleverly, who at the time was Minister for the Middle East, North Africa and North America, took time out to condemn football fans for booing players complying with the Black Lives Matter ritual of 'taking the knee'.[19]

In February 2021, Nadhim Zahawi — who the previous June had founded a new company, Warren Medical Limited, registered in his wife's name and under the directorship of his two sons — in his capacity as Minister for Vaccines said he was concerned about 'vaccine hesitancy' among the UK's Black and mixed ethnic communities, which he blamed on a 'tsunami of disinformation' from 'anti-vaxxers' on social media.[20]

In March 2021, as the Coronavirus Act 2020 was renewed for the second time with the overwhelming support of the Labour Party, including its Shadow Secretary for Justice, David Lammy, the Commission on Race and Ethnic Disparities found that there was no evidence of institutional racism in the UK. Whereupon Lammy, who in 2016 had been fined £5,000 for instigating 36,000 automatic phone calls urging Londoners to back his campaign to be London Mayor, said its report was an insult to victims of racism.[21]

In November 2021, when the Scottish Government was considering making COVID-19-justified gene-therapies mandatory for Scottish citizens, Humza

---

18. See Kemi Badenoch, 'It's vital more BAME candidates take part in Covid-19 vaccine trials to deliver a vaccine that works for everyone', *Politics Home* (14 October, 2020).

19. See George Allison, 'UK and Israel sign military cooperation agreement', *UK Defence Journal* (7 December, 2020); and Alain Tolhurst, 'Foreign Office Minister James Cleverly Has Condemned Millwall Fans Who Booed Footballers Taking The Knee Against Racism', *PoliticsHome* (7 December, 2020).

20. See 'Family of Vaccine Minister Sets up Medical Company', *Byline Times* (4 January, 2021); and Alan McGuinness, 'COVID-19: "Tsunami of disinformation" around COVID jabs, vaccine minister says', *Sky News* (16 February, 2021).

21. See Andrew Sparrow, 'UK Covid: MPs vote to extend emergency powers for six months; NHS alert level in England to be cut to three — as it happened', *The Guardian* (25 March, 2021); Rajeev Syal, 'David Lammy fined over mayoral bid nuisance calls', *The Guardian* (10 March, 2016); and John Johnston, 'David Lammy Says Landmark Diversity Report Is An Insult To Those Who Have Suffered Institutional Racism', *PoliticsHome* (31 March, 2021).

Yousaf, as Minister for Health, accused a Dundee nursery of refusing his child a place because of his Muslim name.[22]

In March 2022, Sadiq Khan, to justify the target of reducing carbon emissions in London to Net Zero by 2030, said that the climate 'crisis' is a 'racial justice issue' because BAME communities in the capital are the most affected by carbon emissions, soaring temperatures and flash floods, calling it a 'wake-up call to people of colour'.[23]

In May 2022, Claire Coutinho, who as a senior fellow at Policy Exchange, the Conservative think-tank that helped draft the Police, Crime, Sentencing and Courts Act 2022 which, among numerous new police powers, empowers them to ban protests and increased powers of Stop and Search that are already disproportionately used against Black men, during a Parliament Question Time condemned all forms of racial discrimination, prejudice and harassment.[24]

In July 2023, as the Strikes (Minimum Services Level) Act 2023 was made into law, forcing trade union workers in health, education and emergency services to provide a minimum service during a strike, Rishi Sunak informed the media that he had experienced racism growing up.[25] This, presumably, was when the future Prime Minister was at Winchester College public school, which today charges pupils £45,936 per annum in tuition and boarding fees.

Let me also clarify what I mean by 'playing the race card'. This doesn't only mean — as is practiced with tedious regularity by Khan, Lammy, Abbott and Luciana Berger — politicians accusing anyone who opposes their policies of being 'far right', 'racist' or 'anti-Semitic'.[26] Even Braverman, an Indian who calls herself

22. See Scottish Government, 'Coronavirus (COVID-19): mandatory vaccine certification proposas' (9 September, 2021); Severin Carrell, 'Humza Yousaf's family drops discrimination case against nursery', *The Guardian* (7 February, 2023).

23. See Nadine White, 'Sadiq Khan: "Climate crisis is a racial justice issue" as black and Asian Londoners most affected', *Independent* (17 March, 2022).

24. See Ruby Lott-Lavigna, 'Net zero minister linked to oil-funded group that targeted climate protesters, *Open Democracy* (1 September, 2023); and Claire Coutinho, 'Schools: Racial Discrimination', *UK Parliament* (2 May, 2023).

25. See Michael Savage, 'Rishi Sunak speaks of sting of racism after damning cricket report', *The Guardian* (1 July 2023).

26. On the weaponisation of anti-Semitism by the Labour Party, see Simon Elmer, 'The Social Realism of the Labour Party: Jeremy Corbyn and the Socialism of Fools', *Architects for Social Housing* (29 March, 2018), and 'Oy Vey! No Latkes for Labour', *Architects for Social Housing* (5 September, 2018).

a 'Buddhist', is happy to appear racist to her Conservative voter base while allowing a record 1.2 million long-term immigrants into the UK in 2022.[27] Because contrary to what her nominal opposition on the UK Left proclaims, immigration policy is not decided by how 'racist' is a Minister or Government. It has been made to appear so by the ideology of woke because the real economic and political reasons for immigration into the UK and its consequences for British workers cannot now be discussed without the accusation of 'racism' either silencing every attempt at debate or reducing it to virtue signalling and slinging of insults by politicians intent on acquiring political capital among the unfailingly obedient UK electorate.

As an example of which, when publishing exerts from this chapter on my Twitter account, I was accused of contributing to a discourse of racism that endangers immigrants to this country. So that it's clear, I completely reject this accusation, which is the same as that used to condemn criticisms of transgenderism as endangering the lives of transvestites, and is intended — from behind a cynical curtain of concern — to silence any deviation from the ideological orthodoxies of the Great Reset.

3. Woke as Cultural Colonialism

And the accusations of racism don't stop with our politicians. This June, during the second test of the Ashes cricket series between England and Australia, the Independent Commission for Equity in Cricket published a report titled 'Holding Up A Mirror To Cricket' that accused English cricket of 'racism, sexism and elitism'.[28] It's hard to think of another country that would make such an accusation against its own sportsmen as they were contesting a series, but if we look closer into the ICEC it becomes clearer what the motivation for doing so is. The Commission was set up by the England and Wales Cricket Board in July 2021 — the report states — 'in the wake of global movements such as Black Lives Matter

---

27. See Diane Taylor, 'Suella Braverman accused of breaching barristers' code over "racist" language', *The Guardian* (14 May, 2023); and Jay Lindop 'International migration hits new high in 2022 but there are signs of change', *Office for National Statistics* (25 May, 2023).

28. See ICEC, 'Holding up a Mirror to Cricket: A report by the Independent Commission for Equity in Cricket' (June 2023).

and MeToo'. Like woke itself, of which they are subsidiaries, these are ideological movements manufactured and funded by US globalists.

For example, since 2020 Black Lives Matter and related causes have received an astonishing $82.9 billion from companies and corporations, including $18.25 billion from the Bank of America, $10.11 billion from Goldman Sachs, $1.05 billion from Facebook, $810 million from BlackRock, $535 million from Paypal, $500 million from Mastercard, $370 million from Google, $252 million from IBM, $244.6 million from Microsoft, $169.55 million from Amazon, $110 million from Johnson & Johnson, $107.4 million from Twitter, $100 million from YouTube, $85 million from Deloitte, $36.4 million from Alliance, $30 million from Morgan Stanley, $30 million from JPMorgan Chase, $29.7 million from Merck, $7.2 million from Pfizer and $6 million from State Street Global Advisor.[29]

There's only one thing these supposedly 'grass-roots' activist groups can be doing with such vast sums of money, and it isn't organising marches around the streets of London. They are using it to lobby governments to write pro-woke legislation, bribe legislatures to turn it into law, and to fund public institutions and private businesses to impose it on the population. Besides funding Black Lives Matter, all these companies and many more make up the more than 1,100 partners of the World Economic Forum that, on 11 March 2020 — the same day the World Health Organization declared the 'pandemic' — formed themselves into the 'COVID-19 Action Platform' that is the template for stakeholder capitalism.[30] Woke activism isn't merely astroturfing for its corporate funders; it is the means through which stakeholder capitalism is dismantling our democracy and replacing it with the rule of the transnational technocracies these corporations form. As we will see, this is the real goal of the Independent Commission for Equity in Cricket.

Much like our political parties, the Commission is chaired by a Black Woman, Cindy Butts, a second-generation immigrant whose parents were from Guyana and the Caribbean, and a former deputy chair of the Metropolitan Police Authority. The rest of the Board comprises a second-generation Pakistani immigrant, former cricketer and current lawyer, Zafar Ansari, and a mixed-race woman, Michelle

---

29. See Claremont Institute for the American Way of Life, 'BLM Funding Database'.

30. See World Economic Forum, 'Our Partners'; Tedros Adhano Ghebreyesus, WHO Director-General's opening remarks at the media briefing on COVID-19 — 11 March 2020', *World Health Organization* (11 March, 2020); and Peter Vanham, 'World Economic Forum launches COVID-19 Action Platform to fight coronavirus', *World Economic Forum* (11 March, 2020).

Moore, who describes herself as a 'globally recognised executive on leadership, race equity and sport for development'. Only two of its five members are White, Michael Collins, a woke professor at University College London currently writing a book called *Windrush Cricket: Caribbean Migration and the Remaking of Postwar England;* and Sir Brendan Barber, a member of the Labour Party and former General Secretary of the Trades Union Conference. Both Butts and Moore — and it might be argued Ansari and Collins too — make a living from identifying racism, which — to state the obvious — it is in their financial interests to find everywhere they look, much like the witch-hunters of the Counter Reformation who thrived on religious zealotry, fear and trial by public opinion.

And the criteria for the accusation of racism employed by the ICEC is about as rigorous as a seventeenth-century witch hunt, relying on the anonymised anecdotes of the modern equivalents to Arthur Miller's Puritan colonists in *The Crucible*, his allegory of McCarthyism.[31] To qualify as 'racist', according to the ICEC definition, there doesn't have to be intention on behalf of the offending person, merely perception of racism by the offended.[32] And yet, even with such a subjective and legally meaningless definition so open to abuse, a mere 4,156 individuals contributed to the report's findings out of a cricket-playing population in England and Wales of 2.5 million people. That's just 0.16 per cent of those who play a sport in which, as the report concedes, between 30 and 35 per cent are from 'ethnically diverse backgrounds'. That sounds to me like evidence that cricket in England and Wales is one of the least racist sports in the world. But woke, which eschews evidence for wild accusation, takes many of its procedures from McCarthyism; and with its global staging of the Salem Witch Trials having penetrated into every aspect of our culture, sport, education, economy, laws, politics and government, racism is the devil seen everywhere by anyone with a grudge or chip on their shoulder, every signaller of their woke-compliant virtue, every petty advocate of state censorship, every coward hoping to save his own skin.

Like every other equivalent body set up to conduct these witch trials, the Independent Commission for Equity in Cricket is, in reality, nothing of the kind,

---

31. See Arthur Miller's play, *The Crucible* (1953), his allegory of the persecution of US communists by Senator Joseph McCarthy in the 1940s and 1950s.

32. ICEC, 'Holding up a Mirror to Cricket', p. 34.

but rather a state-funded product of UK public institutions having to enforce Diversity, Equity and Inclusion criteria. These are an obligation of the English Cricket Board's Public Sector Equality Duty, which came into effect in April 2011 under Section 149 of the Equality Act 2010.[33] This, in turn, is the legislative equivalent of US asset managers and BLM funders like BlackRock, State Street and Vanguard enforcing DEI criteria on companies in which they invest and over whose decisions they have majority voting power, which in their case means the 500 largest companies on the New York Stock Exchange.[34] And the colonialist and ideological goals of such criteria are made clear in the ICEC report. To this end, the authors insists that existing 'policies, practices and systems are reformed', and that the woke principles of Diversity, Equity and Inclusion formulated by BlackRock and other US asset managers are 'embedded into all aspects of cricket in England and Wales'.[35] Asserting that the racism she sees in cricket is 'indicative of equally deeply rooted societal problems', Butts concludes: 'A fundamental change in culture and attitudes is required'. This is some measure of the scale of ambition and arrogance of these woke colonialists. And it doesn't stop there.

It is not a coincidence that, the day before the report accusing English cricket of being institutionally racist was published and discussed on BBC Radio 5's coverage of the Ashes throughout the players' lunch break, Just Stop Oil, another woke organisation also funded by US globalists, somehow managed to escape security, run onto the Lord's cricket ground and cover it with their brand orange powder.[36] In case we might think they 'got lucky' this one time — as these corporate activists do every time they engage in their promotions for Agenda 2030 — the BBC, which has a strict policy of refusing to cover protests at sporting events in order to deny them the coverage they seek, gave the Just Stop Oil protesters precious and very expensive minutes of screen time in its televised coverage of the day's play that evening. Like the Diversity, Equity and Inclusion criteria the ICEC report insists is embedded into cricket in this country, the

---

33. See UK Public General Acts, 'Equality Act 2010' (8 April, 2010).

34. See Olúfẹ́mi O. Táíwò, 'How BlackRock, Vanguard, and UBS Are Screwing the World', *New Republic* (7 March, 2022).

35. ICEC, 'Holding up a Mirror to Cricket', p. 6.

36. See Stephan Shemilt, 'Ashes: Just Stop Oil protesters briefly disrupt opening morning of England v Australia Test at Lord's', *BBC Sport* (28 June, 2023).

Environment, Social and corporate Governance criteria for Agenda 2030 promoted by Just Stop Oil and other environmental activist groups is not only imposed on businesses by BlackRock, State Street, Vanguard and other US asset managers but, behind their United Nations branding, formulated by them as a tool of stakeholder capitalism.[37]

After the England team, hardly surprisingly, had lost the test at Lords, their captain, Ben Stokes, issued a grovelling apology in response to its accusations.[38] But I'm happy to report that an England captain from a pre-woke era, Ian Botham, who apart from being one of England's greatest cricketers is known for raising more than £12 million for charity, had the courage to call the report 'a nonsense'.[39]

But, of course, the cultural colonialism of woke doesn't stop at cricket. In a similar act of national insult made with complete impunity, in February 2021 Ugo Monye, a second-generation Nigerian immigrant and former England rugby player, accused English rugby of being racist.[40] Two months later he was appointed Chair of the newly-formed Rugby Football Union's 'independent diversity and inclusion advisory group'.[41] Two months after that, in an echo of Tony Blair, Monye said rugby had to tackle its culture of 'heavy drinking' and 'laddishness' in order to attract Muslim and homosexual players.[42] Recently, he interviewed a 'trans' rugby player.[43] Monye is ITV's main commentator at this year's Rugby World Cup on games played by an England team whose 33-man squad includes 10 players that are Black, Polynesian or mixed race. Such are the rewards for the woke-compliant.

---

37. See Gibson Dunn Lawyers, 'BlackRock, Vanguard, State Street Update Corporate Governance and ESG Policies and Priorities for 2022' (25 January, 2022).

38. See Sean Ingle, 'Ben Stokes "deeply sorry" to hear of cricket discrimination detailed in report', *The Guardian* (27 June, 2023).

39. See Elizabeth Ammon, 'Ian Botham: I threw racism report on floor, it was nonsense', *The Times* (19 July, 2023).

40. See Becky Grey, 'Ugo Monye says Premiership "does not care enough" about racism in rugby', *BBC Sport* (26 February, 2021).

41. See Becky Grey, 'Ugo Money hopes new RFU group can help everyone feel rugby is "for them"', *BBC Sport* (19 April, 2021).

42. See Gavin Mairs, 'Ugo Monye: Rugby union must tackle "heavy drinking culture" and "laddish behaviour"', *The Telegraph* (15 June, 2022).

43. See Jordan Page, '"Rugby is supposed to be a sport for all" — trans player on how the sport changed his life', *Gay Times* (19 September, 2023).

This is a man whose father abandoned his family and returned to Nigeria when he was young, and was raised by his single Black mother on a London council housing estate. In this respect, Ugo Monye's upbringing was representative of second-generation Black Britons in the UK. 57 per cent of Black Caribbean families and 44 per cent of Black African families in England and Wales have single parents, compared with 22 per cent of White British families; and 90 per cent of these single parents are women.[44] Partly, but not wholly, as a consequence, 48 per cent of Black Britons live in social housing, and 8 per cent of the tiny amount of social housing being built in the UK is let to Black tenants, double their proportion of the population.[45] But with the help and financial support of a scholarship to an English boarding school and being signed to an English rugby club, Monye went on to play 14 times for his mother's adopted country. Moreover, although a player of no great distinction and with little to recommend him as either an analyst or commentator on the game, he has made a post-playing career as a TV pundit apparently based on nothing more than his ethnicity in a culture and industry obsessed with race quotas and so-called 'positive discrimination'. As a measure of which, in a UK in which, as we have seen, just 4 per cent of the population is Black and 6.9 per cent is of South Asian ethnicity, 37 per cent of adverts feature a Black person and 15 per cent a person from South Asia.[46] While Monye's current employer, ITV, following the launch of its 'Diversity Acceleration Plan Report 2021', announced last July that 34 per cent of lead roles in new commissions over the previous year had been given to BAME actors and presenters.[47] Yet Monye had no hesitation and no fear of damaging his career — quite the opposite — in calling the country that made him so successful 'racist'.

As far as I know, no rugby player equivalent in stature to Ian Botham — Johnny Wilkinson, say, or Martin Johnson — has made public what they think of Monye's insult to their sport, nation and race.

---

44. See Rachel de Souza, 'Family Review: family and its protective effects. Part 1 of the independent family review' (September 2022), p. 18.

45. See Jessica Perera, 'The London Clearances: Race, Housing and Policing', *Institute of Race Relations* (2019); and Alex Turner, 'Race and allocation: who are the new tenants getting social housing, and is it equitable', *Inside Housing* (13 August, 2021).

46. See 4sales, 'Mirror on the Industry Pt 2: Have TV adds improved in the past 2 years?', 2021.

47. See ITX, 'Diversity Acceleration Plan Report 2021' (15 July, 2022).

Finally — although it's by no measure the final example — in May of this year, the actress and second-generation Ghanese immigrant, Adjoa Andoh, during the coronation of King Charles, said on national television that the UK's Royal Family is too White.[48] It remains to be seen how Diversity, Equity and Inclusion criteria will be 'embedded' into the UK monarchy and its practices 'reformed', although the marriage of the Duke of Sussex to Meghan Markle, a mixed-race US actress, looks like a so-far failed attempt to do just that. But as BlackRock's Chief Executive Officer, Larry Fink, made clear back in 2017 in an interview that has recently resurfaced, compliance with Diversity, Equity and Inclusion criteria is now enforced as a condition of any company or institution, and not just sporting or cultural ones, receiving investment:

> You have to force behaviours. If you don't force behaviours, whether it's gender or race or just any way you want to — say, the composition of your team — you're going to be impacted. That's not just recruiting, it's development. We're going to have to force change.[49]

4. The Racism of Woke

Those of us who read and oppose London housing policy have long known that Sadiq Khan is in the pockets of the property developers and now, it appears, the manufacturers of electric vehicles who, presumably, fund his electoral campaigns and write his policies; but his more recent actions have additionally exposed him to accusations of racism and misogyny.[50] Indeed, the monthly spectacles his office funds in Trafalgar Square celebrate every possible demographic by race, religion and sexuality except the White population that still constitutes the majority of Londoners.

---

48. See Michael Deacon, 'The row over the "terribly white" Royal balcony exposes the hypocrisy of the woke Left', *The Telegraph* (13 May, 2023).

49. See Aubrie Spady, 'BlackRock CEO slammed for "force behaviours" comment after 2017 interview re-emerges about DEI initiatives', *Fox Business* (5 June, 2023).

50. See Simon Elmer, 'How Sadiq Khan's Housing Policy is Making London's Housing Crisis Worse', *Vice* (31 January, 2019); 'The Good Practice Guide to Estate Demolition: ASH response to the GLA', *Architects for Social Housing* (8 March, 2017); and TalkTV, 'Sadiq Khan Accused of Anti-White Racism. Many People Believe Mayorality is Stoking Division', *YouTube* (26 August, 2023).

In 2023, the London Mayor will sponsor the Chinese New Year (in January), the London LGBTQIA+ film festival (in March), the newly inaugurated Muslim celebration of Ramadan Lights (throughout March), the Sikh festival of Vaisakhi and the Muslim festival of Eid in the Square (in April), the LGBTQIA+ festival of Pride (which now runs throughout July), the Caribbean Notting Hill Carnival (in August), the newly inaugurated festival of Black on the Square and the Jewish festival of Rosh Hashanah (both in September), Black History Month (in October), the Hindu festival of Diwali on the Square (in November) and the Jewish festival of Hanukkah (in December), as well as announcing plans for a London memorial for Black victims of the transatlantic slave trade.[51] In April, admittedly, the 44.9 per cent of the London population that are White British got a celebration of St. George, the patron Saint of England; but there's no mention on his website of events — let alone funding — from our Muslim Mayor for Lent or Easter or Christmas for the 59.8 per cent that are White and 58.23 per cent of Londoners that are Christian.[52]

I am as opposed to the dogma and institutions of Christianity as I am to all organised religions, but I find it hard to see this as anything other than a deliberate and so-far successful attempt to insult and demean White British Londoners and exacerbate the racial and religious tensions between them and the huge and growing influx of immigrants, particularly from non-Christian countries, into the capital. Far more concerning, however, than this ideological groundwork for the erasure of British culture and customs is what these socially and racially divisive tactics are preparing: not merely the Ultra-Low Emission Zone enclosing the whole of London that is, first and foremost, a tax on London's working class, but also the digital panopticon it has justified, which puts in place the surveillance framework required to enforce the restrictions on our freedoms, prohibitions on our consumptions and invasions into our privacy being implemented under the obligations of the United Nations' Agenda 2030 programme of eco-austerity.

---

51. See Mayor of London, 'Major Events Calendar 2023'; 'Mayor announces Black on the Square — a major new festival showcasing Black culture and creativity' (9 August 2023); 'Mayor announces plans for a landmark memorial in the capital for the victims of the transatlantic slave trade' (24 March, 2023); and Tom Slater, '"Punch a TERF": the violent misogyny of the trans movement', *Spiked* (10 July, 2023).

52. See Population UK, 'London Population 2023'.

For if woke is the ideology of globalism, identity politics is its political strategy. The UK's woke politicians are rightly confident that, as more white working-class Britons detach from a political process increasingly formed around who can insult, impoverish and disenfranchise them the most, more Black and Asian Britons will vote for what they are equally increasingly encouraged to believe are their ethnic 'representatives' in British politics. The Evidence for Equality National Survey has reported that, in a poll of 14,200 UK citizens in 2021, 60 per cent of White British and White Europeans said they were 'fairly' or 'very' interested in politics, while the same level of political interest was expressed by 80 per cent of Black Africans, 78 per cent of mixed-race Britons, and 77 per cent of Indians.[53] Unsurprisingly, given the Left's wholesale adoption of identity politics, over 60 per cent of Black African, Black Caribbean, Pakistani and Bangladeshi Britons supported the Labour Party.

Of course, 'interest' doesn't always convert into votes; but voter turnout among White Britons in the General Election of 2019 was 63 per cent, down from 67 per cent in 2010; while, in comparison, voter turnout among Black and Minority Ethnic Britons in 2019 was 52 per cent, which is marginally up from 51 per cent in 2010.[54] Before that, there is no data on the ethnicity of voters; but in the General Election of 2019, in which 67.3 per cent of the electorate voted — the fifth lowest turnout since 1929, all five of which have come since 2001 — 64 per cent of all Black and Minority Ethnic Britons voted Labour.[55] This might explain a poll, conducted this September, that found that, even after his disastrous record on everything from housing and corruption to police brutality and the Ultra-Low Emission Zone, 33 per cent of the electorate of London are still intending to vote for Sadiq Khan at next year's Mayoral election.[56]

The far more serious result of such identity politics, however, than the election of divisive figures like Khan to a position of leadership in the UK — and

---

53. See University of Manchester, 'Are ethnic and religious minority voters key to electoral success?' (4 May, 2023).

54. See Ipsos, 'How Britain voted in the 2019 election' (20 December, 2019) and 'How Britain Voted in 2010' (21 May, 2010).

55. See Statista, 'Voter turnout in general elections and in the Brexit referendum in the United Kingdom from 1918 to 2019' (2023); Cassie Barton, 'GE2019: How did demographic affect the result?', *House of Commons Library* (21 February, 2020).

56. See Redfield and Wilton Strategies, 'London Mayoral Voting Intention (4-6 September, 2023)' (8 September, 2023).

the real political motivation behind his monthly celebration and funding for Asian and Black cultural and religious festivals — is that what should be political debates about our national sovereignty, parliamentary integrity, civil liberties, human rights, democratic agency, cultural values, children's education, employment rights and economic future — all of which are being erased by the Great Reset of the UK — have all been reduced, instead, to a question of skin colour. For this reason alone, woke is the most cynically racist of ideologies.

It's a product of woke's colonisation of the UK that racism is now regarded in this country as exclusive to the White population, from which Black and Asian British people are supposedly entirely free, even when they make such blatantly racist comments as those made by Monye, Butts, Khan and Yousef. To judge by the Twitter feed of the London Mayor, most White working-class Briton are fed up being called 'racist' by immigrants to this country because of the colour of their skin. But although the blanket statements about White people made by them and other second-generation immigrants are quite clearly racist, and if made by a White politician or public figure about Black or Asian Britons would bring their careers to an abrupt end — as it apparently has for Diane Abbott when she played the race card once too often — I am not necessarily claiming that Khan *et al* are racist.[57]

Appointing a racist to a role in which they are required to make racist statements and impose racist policies is a logical political decision; but attributing such views and values to our politicians — even to those as morally vacuous as Khan, Javid, Patel and Cleverly — would mean them holding at least some beliefs, however foolish or unpleasant, and I am reluctant to do so. This is partly because I believe the accusation of racism — despite being thrown like confetti by the woke at anyone who disagrees with their dogma or opposes their globalist policies — is a serious one, and not to be made lightly. But primarily it is because, after a decade following and writing about UK politics, I don't believe that any politician in the UK holds any belief, even the racism against White people they demonstrate with impunity, that conflicts with their pursuit of power.

What I'm arguing, rather, is that the discourse of racism developed by woke — which is that all White people are racist, whether they know it or not, and that

---

57. See Jemma Crew and Helen Catt, 'Diane Abbott suspended as Labour MP after racism letter', *BBC News* (23 April, 2023).

the UK itself and all its institutions, sporting, educational, cultural and governmental, are racist — is the ideological foundation for the Great Reset of the UK into compliance with the stakeholder capitalism formed by the most powerful companies in the world, and our consequent governance by the transnational technocracies they form. The accusation of 'racism', which is the foundation of woke and the basis to the enforcement of both DEI and ESG criteria, is the ideological instrument of this globalist coup. Second-generation immigrants like Sunak, Lammy, Khan and Yousef, and before them Javid and Patel, have been appointed to senior positions of political leadership in the UK specifically because they can make this accusation — as they do — regularly and without fear of contradiction against anyone who opposes the treaties, agendas, legislation, regulations, policies, restrictions, programmes and technologies of the Great Reset of the UK and, just as crucially, the enforced changes to our culture, behaviour, beliefs and attitudes consequent upon it.

But the clinching example, perhaps, of why woke is the official ideology of stakeholder capitalism across the West is that anyone who tries — as many of us are trying — to think through and articulate why and how it is being enforced outside of any democratic process and at every level of our society is immediately denounced as a 'conspiracy theorist', as a 'racist', as a member of the 'far right', as 'anti-Semitic', as a 'COVID denier', as 'vaccine hesitant', as a 'Putin apologist', as a 'climate-change denier'. These and other insults yet to be coined by the propaganda departments of the European Commission, the United Nations, the World Economic Forum, the International Holocaust Remembrance Alliance, the World Health Organization, the North Atlantic Treaty Organisation, the Intergovernmental Panel on Climate Change and other technocracies of the emerging World Government are not — as even those they are hurled at mistakenly believe — the side-products of a degraded political climate.[58] Nor are

---

58. See European Commission, 'Identifying conspiracy theories'; United Nations, 'United Nations Guidance Note on Addressing and Countering COVID-19 related Hate Speech' (11 May, 2020); World Economic Forum, 'Far-Right Extremism and Anti-vaccine Conspiracy Theories: A Case from Italy' (21 October, 2021); International Holocaust Remembrance Alliance, 'About the IHRA non-legally binding working definition of antisemitism'; World Health Organization, 'Vaccine hesitancy: A growing challenge for immunization programmes'; Jens Stoltenberg, 'Opening Remarks', North Atlantic Treaty Organization (7 September, 2023); Intergovernmental Panel on Climate Change, 'Climate change: a threat to human wellbeing and health of the planet. Taking action now can secure our future' (28 February, 2022).

they the overly exuberant claims of middle-class university students whose hearts are in the right place even if their minds have been indoctrinated by the institutions that should be teaching them how to think critically about the world.[59] These insults and slurs are, to the contrary, the targeted weapons of a concerted political and ideological strategy overseeing the revolution of the West into stakeholder capitalism. It's for this reason that woke, which has attained its rapid colonisation of our politics and culture through the virtue signalling of the compliant and the terrorising of the non-compliant, is the ideology of the Great Reset.

---

59. For a representative example of this view from the Right of UK politics, see the contribution of Toby Young, the founder and director of the Free Speech Union, to the Oxford Union debate, 'Woke Culture Has Gone Too Far', *YouTube* (12 January, 2023).

8. Why You Should Destroy Your Smartphone Now: or, What Is To Be Done?

So, to echo the question with which Lenin opened the unprecedented violence of the Twentieth Century, what is to be done?[1] As I have tried to show in this book, once the programmes and technologies of the Global Biosecurity State are in place, it will be almost impossible to break their control over our lives without an equally violent overthrow not only of this Government but of the UK state, its police forces, military and allies, starting with NATO. But with the uprising of a revolutionary working class not being on the horizon of the UK or anywhere else in the Western World outside the dreams of revolutionaries, those of us not willing to stand by and watch as the UK is transformed into a totalitarian state under the banner of the Great Reset must find other means of resistance. In conclusion, therefore, I want to address an effective means of resistance to this globalist coup in which every UK citizen can engage without risk of arrest or fines or indeed any great inconvenience to our lives, at least for the present. This is, of course, to destroy our smartphones now.

So-called 'smartphones' — far more accurately described as 'dumb phones' — combine a mobile phone with a watch, a road map, a tourist atlas of the world, a digital camera, a personal music system, a music collection, a video recorder, a diary, a calculator, a debit card, a travelcard, an office key, a torch, a newspaper, a television, something to read on the train, access to the internet and probably a lot more. I don't know, because I don't own one. 'But it's so convenient!' cry those who stare unbelieving at my twenty-year-old Nokia. To which I reply: 'Convenience breeds compliance.' But to what?

Since they were first introduced into our lives as recently as 2008, smartphones have become our outsourced memory and brain, replacing both with the convenience of not having to remember anything or think for ourselves. If you don't believe me, then answer me this without looking at your smartphone. What is 9 x 13? What was the capital of the Socialist Federal Republic of

---

1. See Vladimir Ilyich Lenin, *What Is To Be Done?* (1902); collected in *Essential Works*; edited by Henry M. Christman (Bantam Books, 1966), pp. 53-176. Rousseau had asked the same question a century-and-a-half earlier in the conclusion to his *Discours sur l'origine et les fondements de l'inégalité parmi les hommes* (1754).

Yugoslavia? In what month of which year did the UK invade Iraq at the tail-end of the US-led coalition? Before smartphones, every child in the UK knew the answers to these questions. Now, few adults do.[2]

But they are now even more than this. Smartphones, during the two years of lockdown, were the instrument onto which the COVID-faithful downloaded the app (software applications) that connected them to the Test and Trace tracking programme that identified and recorded their location, movements, associations and personal contacts. And in the imminent future, smartphones will be the instrument onto which, in the guise of the digital verification of our identity, the compliant will upload their biometric data (fingerprints, photograph and DNA swab) to a centralised database to which the 32 public authorities presiding over the UK biosecurity state will have access.[3]

Under the Digital Economy Act 2017, these public authorities include the Cabinet Office; the Home Office; the Department for Defence; HM Treasury; the Ministry of Justice; the Department for Education; the Department for Business, Energy and Industrial Strategy; the Department for Work and Pensions; the Department for Communities and Local Government; the Department for Culture, Media and Sport; the Department for Transport; the Department for Food, Environment and Rural Affairs; Her Majesty's Revenue and Customs; all county, district and London councils; the Greater London Authority; the Council of the City of London; all fire and rescue authorities; all police authorities; all education authorities; all gas and electricity authorities; HM Land Registry; and, under Section 35, any other public authority, or private agent providing a service for a public authority, designated for a specific purpose justifying access to that data.[4]

Smartphones are the instrument that will monitor whether their owners are up-to-date with what the World Health Organization decides is fully 'vaccinated' with whatever our Government and its partners in the pharmaceutical industry decide we must inject into our bodies as a condition of access to the rights of citizenship in the Global Biosecurity State.

Smartphones are the instrument that will monitor and record how many times we leave or enter our 15-Minute City currently being implemented by our local and

---

2. The answers are: 117, Belgrade and March 2003.

3. Central Digital & Data Office, 'Consultation on draft legislation to support identity verification' (26 June, 2023).

4. See UK Public General Acts, 'Digital Economy Act 2017' (27 April, 2017).

municipal authorities to restrict and limit our freedom of movement on the justification of 'saving the planet'.

Smartphones are the instrument that will track our carbon footprint in order to monitor and control the quantity of meat, dairy products, energy, oil, petrol and other products to which the UK biosecurity state will progressively cut off our access between now and 2030.

Smartphones are the means by which our compliance with lockdowns, masking mandates and programmes of gene therapy dictated by the World Health Organization's Pandemic Treaty and enforced by the UK biosecurity state will be monitored, recorded and enforced by, among other recourses, cutting off our access to the electronic and digital grid.

And, within the next few years, smartphones will become the digital wallet through which the Bank of England will have complete control over how much, on what and where we spend its Central Bank Digital Currency.

Smartphones are the first generation of the biotechnology that is already being implanted into our bodies in the form of ingested medicines carrying microchips that record compliance; quantum dot dyes in gene therapies injected as vaccines against the latest civilisation-threatening pandemic declared by the World Health Organization; and microprocessors implanted under our skin for the ease and convenience of contactless payments. As such, smartphones are the precursor to what Klaus Schwab, the founder of the World Economic Forum, accurately and prophetically boasted will be 'the fusion of our physical, our digital and our biological identities' in the rapidly approaching future he has planned for us.[5]

Smartphones, therefore, are the technology of our enslavement, and the fact that, knowing all this as more and more of us do, we still — *still* — won't discard them, shows how addicted we are to this technology, how deep it has penetrated into our psychology, and in effect into our biology. Like the prisoners forced to construct the camp in which they are imprisoned, we continue to pay increasing sums for our smartphone, upgrade our prison whenever we're invited to by its manufacturer, and demand that its facilities are regularly increased in efficiency with the latest technology.

---

5. See Klaus Schwab, 'Revolution will lead to a fusion of our physical, digital and biological identity', *YouTube* (10 November, 2020).

As the compliant did with the NHS COVID Pass, we will upload the smartphone app proving that we have been injected with the number of gene therapy injections required by the Government to qualify as 'fully vaccinated', or that we have a negative test within the required number of hours or days. We will accept injection or submit the DNA swab, and our Government and the corporations to which it sells the data will record it in a database. Our smartphone will allow that database to monitor and control what we do when required to prove our identity — for example, when leaving the limits of our 15-Minute City, purchasing petrol for our car, recharging our electric vehicle, eating dairy products and meat, logging onto the internet, entering a supermarket, buying a train ticket, travelling abroad, voting, applying for child benefits, enrolling for an educational course, entering public buildings, applying for a job, getting paid, being seen for healthcare in a clinic or hospital, paying for a booking online, submitting applications for planning permission, registering our business with Companies House, submitting a tax return online, leaving our building or housing estate, entering our place of work, accessing our money or using banking services. Initially, none of these activities will be accessible without a smartphone carrying our biometric data. But, eventually, our citizenship and the rights it confers will be contingent upon owning a fully updated smartphone, even if that means one medically implanted in our body. At which point, we will be — juridically if not yet biologically — a cybernetic organism.

On a drive back from Wales this summer, I stopped at a motorway services and ate at a 'McDonald's'. A McDonald's what? I don't know, but we ordered our fast food not from the counter, where no one was serving, but from one of several large screens standing in the entrance hall. When we collected our food and sat down, I noticed that to our left a mother and her two infant daughters were sitting at a table, across which was projected digital images that flashed and moved across its surface. The girls, who were about three years old, were transfixed. At the next table were several more children, the oldest of which was about six or seven. Their table was fitted with several screens across which similar but slightly more complex digital images moved, and which could to some extent be controlled by the touch of the child's fingers across its surface. Beyond them, in a booth, sat another girl, about twelve years old. She was still in her school uniform and was trying to get the attention of her father, who sat across from her, his eyes fixed on his smartphone. Eventually, frustrated by his lack of response, she took out a child's version of her father's phone, wrapped in a yellow cover. Finally, in the corner of the room in another booth sat two teenage boys, maybe sixteen years old, also in their school uniforms, both staring at their fully-operative smartphones. For all I knew they could have been communicating with each other through their devices, but not once during their meal did they look up at or speak to each other. The final link in this chain was the father I've already mentioned, who was in his forties, and who had handed over the task of raising his child to the smartphone that already had all his attention.

We don't programme smartphones and we don't use them. They programme us, they change how we use them. *They* use *us*. With the rise of the car as a widely-available commodity between the 1950s and 60s, someone observed that, if aliens visited planet earth, they would think cars were the dominant life-form, and that humans were merely the energy source that, upon entering them, allows them to move about — a little like food is for us. Seventy years and two industrial revolutions later, we're now the organic component that operates smartphones, and in doing so allows them to replicate in number and increase in power — above all over us.

It is data about us that smartphones are collecting every time we enter a new venue and log on. As they keep warning us before we tick that box at the end of the list of conditions to which we must agree before using their services for free: 'Your privacy is very important to us.' Before they are anything else, every pub, bar, restaurant, cafe, service station, library, hotel, supermarket, train, transport hub, airport, gym, leisure centre, gallery, museum, theatre, cultural centre, community facility, school, town centre and other venue or public space that offers free wi-fi connection is a data-harvesting facility. And as those who work in the information technology industry never tire of telling us, if a service is free, we're the product being sold. That, at its most basic, is the function of the human being in the Global Biosecurity State. And if we keep thinking that we use our smartphones — as they have programmed us to think — those who programme them will have complete control over us.

So, let's say just for a moment — symbolically at least, or better yet in anticipation of a future and definitive parting — throw your smartphone away now, as you're reading these words. Get up, and throw it in the bin. And if you can't do even that — and I imagine few if any of you reading this will — I invite you to reflect on this addiction to the technologies of the Fourth Industrial Revolution.

When consumers defend their use of their smartphone, they do so by citing its convenience, and list in their defence its combination of the appliances and commodities I listed at the start of this chapter. The easy retort is that we could put all those things in a shoulder bag and carry them with us, and that given the other ways in which smartphones are being used — not by us and not for our convenience — the marginal benefit in weight and size of an ever-slimmer smartphone over a bulky bag should easily fall in favour of the latter. But that's not actually how smartphones are used.

The figures from the US published in January of this year report that the average owner of a smartphone will click, tap or swipe their phone 2,617 times per day.[6] In a 16-hour day, that means we're doing so 2.7 times per minute, or once every 22 seconds, every minute of every day, during work, while eating, while travelling, while watching TV, having a drink, when on holiday, or just slumped on the sofa after a hard day on our smartphone. Now, we're not doing that in order to find the restaurant at which we're meeting our friends, or logging on to hold a business meeting, or booking tickets to a concert, or to check the spelling of a word, or to find the location of our holiday hotel. That's not how smartphones are being used every 22 seconds of our waking life. They're being used out of habit, out of addiction, and that addiction has created a constantly distracted consciousness which, unconsciously, is being uploaded — to use the language of computers — with information and opinions and fears and hatreds which, when we find ourselves acting on them, we believe are our own, though we're not quite sure when or why we formed them.

It could even be said that our addiction to smartphones is changing not only our relationship to the world and how we live with each other but also, and primarily, human consciousness itself. In the West, at least, we appear increasingly unable to enter into a conscious space of concentration, precluding us from the critical thinking or even rational thought processes that are dependent upon it. The last three-and-a-half years have demonstrated that a distracted population is more subject to manipulation and control. As evidence of which, the knee-jerk reactions of the social media addict have become the norm for political

---

6. See Slicktext, '44 Smartphone Addiction Statistics for 2023' (23 January, 2023).

debates, if we can still call them that. Indeed, social media has been decisive in creating this permanently distracted state of consciousness. Of course, not all of us are on social media and not all of the time; but these statistics reveal that, as a nation, we are always on our smartphones. And that addiction is changing our consciousness to the point where the thinking capacity of more and more people in the West, and above all among the middle classes, is now limited to easily triggered expressions of fear, anger, hatred, guilt, compliance, allegiance, revulsion, veneration and all the other psychological states on which the Global Biosecurity State turns.

Admittedly, although more than 84 per cent of the UK population now uses some form of social media, less than 14 per cent inhabit the echo-chamber of Twitter that has all but replaced the Houses of Parliament in UK politics; so we should be wary of equating the working populations of the West with the latter's ignorance and viciousness.[7] But together with the coordinated recalibration of our values under lockdown, these new technologies of biopower have produced new patterns of behaviour, new modes of thinking and new states of consciousness. Or, to put it more accurately, they have produced new degrees of continuity in such states, which now last as long as we are logged on and our smartphones are turned on. We haven't simply dismantled the old values under which we have lived — if more in principal than in practice — in Western democracies since, say, the Second World War; we are, as Yuval Harari predicted, producing 'new minds' to occupy our biopolitical bodies. And although the latter is the object of the technologies of biopower, it is control of the former that is their ultimate goal.

The consensus of opinion by smartphone-users on everything from an unprecedented viral pandemic that turned out to have the infection fatality rate of seasonal influenza, to global warming caused by man-made changes to 0.04 per cent of the atmosphere, to the US proxy-war in the Ukraine that actually started in 2014, to, as I write, the genocide being perpetrated in Gaza with the full support of the West, is the demonstration and confirmation of the success of this function. But soon, unless we get rid of them, our opinions on these matters won't matter, because the World Health Organization's Global Digital Health Certification Network and the Bank of International Settlement's Central Bank Digital Currency will control us outside of anything we think we may or may not believe.

---

7. See Stacy Jo Dixon, 'Social media penetration UK 2023', *Statista* (12 September, 2023).

A smartphone is not a tool. It is not a 'convenience'. It is biotechnology, and the fact that it isn't yet implanted into our bodies doesn't mean it hasn't already become a part of us — and a part of us we have demonstrated we are ready to sacrifice our freedoms to rather than discard. Indeed, what the past three-and-a-half years of cowardice and complicity have demonstrated is that, as obedient subjects of stakeholder capitalism, we will defend our slavery with far more vehemence that we will defend our freedoms.

In 1923, a century ago now, the Surrealist poet, André Breton, declared: 'Freedom colour of man!'[8] No longer. Freedom, as George Orwell predicted a quarter of a century later, is now slavery.[9] Because slavery is safe. Slavery is convenient. Slavery is the common good. Slavery is now the highest civic virtue. Slavery is our duty. Slavery is our fate — so don't bother fighting it. Instead, we should embrace our slavery. Upgrade our smartphone to a new model. Queue outside the Apple or Google shops for hours. Wrap our chains in a nice leather wallet. Download the newest app of our enslavement. Show it off to our friends and boast about its new and improved speeds. Never, ever, let it leave our side. Place it under our pillow before we go to sleep so it can tell us how well we slept. Look into its screen the moment we wake up. For it is our best friend, our big brother, the lover who will never betray us and whom we always wished we had. It is our single source of truth — just as Jacinda Ardern told us.[10] Trust no other!

André Breton also said that we will never have a political revolution until we have a revolution of the mind. As the last three-and-a-half years of abject subservience and unthinking compliance have shown, our minds are already in prison. And until we free them, talk of resisting, let alone overthrowing, the Global Biosecurity State is — if you'll pardon my French poetry — *merde*.

It is an unfortunately purely hypothetical truth that, if a sufficient proportion of the 93 per cent of UK citizens who own a smartphone (51.7% Apple, 47.78%

---

8. See André Breton, 'Il n'y a pas sortir de là', in *Claire de terre*, 1923; collected in *Oeuvres complètes*, vol. 1, Bibliothèque de la Pléiade. Édition établie par Marguerite Bonnet avec, pour ce volume, la collaboration de Philippe Bernier, Étienne-Alain Hubert et José Pierre (Éditions Gallimard, 1988), p. 169.

9. See George Orwell, *Nineteen Eighty-Four*; Everyman's Library, with an introduction by Julian Symonds (Alfred A. Knopf, 1992), p. 6.

10. See Rebel News, 'New Zealand Prime Minister sounds like Ministry of Truth leader', *YouTube* (16 July, 2021).

Google and 0.57% Samsung) threw them away, the threats to our freedom we face today would be over.[11] At least for now, until they invent new chains with which to bind us. All the UK's mobile network provider companies have announced that, over the next few years, both 2G and 3G networks are going to be shut down.[12] And because the UK public are addicted to their smartphones, the Government will be able to make them compulsory in order to gain access to the rights of citizenship.

If you are still in doubt, in March this year the UK Government announced a system of 'Emergency Alerts' that will be sent to our smartphones whenever they announce an emergency.[13] They didn't say what constitutes an emergency requiring such an alert, but based on the past few years of hysteria, they might include hot or cold weather, raised pollution levels, wild-fires, risk of flooding, a busy beach, demands on the energy grid, food shortages, a cyber-attack, a new virus, social unrest, political demonstrations, the threat of nuclear war, the enforcement of martial law. Any of these 'emergencies' and more in the future might activate the alarm on our smartphone, but the response will be the same.

'When you get an alert', the Government has instructed us in no uncertain terms, 'stop what you're doing and follow the instructions.'[14] But that's just a gesture to the illusion that we are still free to choose. Once our smartphone is uploaded with the Government's Digital Verification app and linked to the system of digital surveillance and control being imposed in the UK behind the guise of 15-Minute Cities and London's Ultra-Low Emission Zone, these instructions will be enforced without the need for our willing compliance. Our electric car will be turned off; our allocation of petrol or food or energy will be frozen; our Digital Pound wallet will be locked shut. And if we're under the impression that our phone contract is between us and our mobile network operator, on 23 of April the Government tested its Emergency Alert, and the media reported — accurately or

---

11. See Office for National Statistics, 'ONS methodology working paper series no. 8-Statistical uses for mobile phone data: literature review' (Data and analysis from Census 2021); Stat Counter, 'Mobile Operating System Market Share United Kingdom' (May 2023).

12. See Ofcom, 'Switching off the UK's 3G mobile networks: what you need to know' (3 August, 2022).

13. See UK Government, 'How emergency alerts work' (2023).

14. See UK Government, 'About emergency alerts' (2023).

not (and if not, in order to encourage compliance) — that our 'private' smartphone would be locked until we acknowledge it.[15]

Feel like getting rid of your smartphone yet? 'But what's the point,' you cry, 'when nobody else will get rid of theirs?' Individual non-compliance is almost always enacted in public, in a social setting, in the presence of other people, who may or may not be complying themselves — usually the former. At the very least, it draws attention to the technologies and regulations enforcing compliance, and with which we are becoming habituated to the point where they have become transparent, invisible. Indeed, the dominance of an ideology can be measured by its transparency. Not using a smartphone makes what is now transparent visible again.

Compliance with the UK programme of gene therapy was not — as was claimed by those who all too willingly complied — a personal and individual choice to be 'vaccinated' against a deadly virus, and therefore none of the business of those who opposed the national programme. It was, and continues to be, an act of collective obedience that created the consensus with which the non-compliant were and are socially ostracised, demonised in the media as murderers, fired from our jobs and treated under newly-made laws as citizens without rights and freedoms, prisoners in our own country and homes.

In the same way, using a smartphone is not an individual choice — whether chosen freely or out of habit or addiction. It is a collective act of compliance that is creating the digital camp in which all of us will one day be imprisoned. Only when millions of us stop using the instruments of our enslavement will we escape this camp — as we only can — together; but that individual choice cannot be avoided.

Individual non-compliance is always a demonstration of non-compliance. In Parliament Square in London, opposite the Houses of Parliament, there is a statue of the suffragette, Millicent Fawcett. I'd have preferred one of Sylvia Pankhurst; but she holds a small banner saying: 'Courage calls to courage everywhere.' In the West, and in particular in the UK, we've been cowards for a long time, and we need to find our courage. That comes from individuals standing up and saying: 'No, I will not comply.'

---

15. See Harry Goodwin, 'Sound the Alarm: Everything you need to know about emergency alert that will *override* your phone in days — what to do if you're driving', *The Sun* (17 April, 2023).

The question I get asked more and more these days is no longer, as it was under lockdown, 'what is going on?' but, with increasing desperation, 'what can we do to stop it?' Recently, in an attempt to answer that question, I've been reading Lenin's *The State and Revolution*, which he wrote in the months leading up to the Bolshevik Revolution in the winter of 1917. Whatever one may think of Lenin's responsibility for the course the revolution took after his death and the rapid descent of the Soviet Union into totalitarianism, the Bolsheviks are among the few who managed to overthrow a modern state, even though the Russian Empire at the beginning of the Twentieth Century was still largely a feudal society.[16] But in such desperate times as these we must look where we can for lessons in how to resist the vast apparatus of the Global Biosecurity State being constructed around, between and within us.

Early on in his book, Lenin argued that the apparatus of the capitalist state — which he identified with the military, the police and the legal system by which the ruling class exerts its power over the workers, but which, after Foucault, we can extend to the institutions, apparatuses and technologies of biopower — is a product of capitalist relations of production.[17] It therefore cannot simply be appropriated and rendered 'socialist' by a working-class revolution. Indeed, it is this illusion of revisionism that has turned every uprising of workers in history into the assumption of power by a middle-class bureaucracy presiding over an expanded police force, enlarged prison system and vastly increased system of surveillance and control.[18] The same applies to those who continue to argue for the benefits of smartphones in, for example, organising demonstrations or meetings or all the other forms of revisionist opposition to this globalist coup, which Apple, Google, and those who control the electric grid and internet listen to

---

16. See Simon Elmer, 'Armed Love: Capitalism, Anarchism and the Russian Revolution', *Architects for Social Housing* (4 December, 2017); and 'What Is To Be Done? Changing Metaphors of Change', *Architects for Social Housing* (23 July, 2018)

17. See V. I. Lenin, 'Class Society and the State', Chapter 1 of *The State and Revolution*; edited, translated and with an introduction by Robert Service (Penguin Classics, 2009), pp. 7-21.

18. A recent example of this dream of revisionism were the comments made by John McDonnell, the Labour Party's Shadow Chancellor of the Exchequer, and the cabal of Corbynites that included Paul Mason, Owen Jones, Aaron Bastani and Ken Loach, in the lead up to the 2019 General Election in the UK. See Simon Elmer, '"Middle-class Socialism": A Warning from History', *Architects for Social Housing* (16 November, 2019); and 'The Parliamentary Road to Capitalism', *Architects for Social Housing* (9 December, 2019).

with amusement. Smartphones, as I hope I've shown in this book, are an integral and indeed key part of the expanding apparatuses of the Global Biosecurity State; and as Lenin argued, the destruction of the apparatus of the capitalist state is the condition and outcome of any successful revolution.[19] That includes the regulatory apparatuses of biopower.

I started this book asking who is the 'us' that is forming outside the control of parliamentary politics and its entirely illusory division between Left and Right. For one thing, we are not as stupid and compliant as we were in March 2020. Indeed, never before in my lifetime have so many people in the nations of the West been forced to question the fundamental lie on which capitalism is built, which is that it creates competition rather than, as it has, corporate monopoly; begun to doubt that its goal is to make them free, happy and rich rather than controlled, compliant and poor; and to realise — through their own experiences and not by reading books like this — that our governments are not there to represent us, do not have our best interests or those of our nation at heart, and are, to the contrary, intent on impoverishing, disenfranchising and enslaving us.

Destroying our smartphones is not, of course, sufficient to overthrow the apparatuses of biopower arrayed against us and whose threat to our freedoms I have tried to expose in this book; but in a country that has largely failed to respond to this globalist coup with anything more than demonstrations, protests, meetings, petitions and impotent declarations of future non-compliance, and which is a long way from bringing about the only thing that will defeat this coup, it's a start — and we need to start somewhere. I repeat: the digital camp in which the enemies of humanity wish to imprison us is — *literally* — in our hands. Get rid of them. Smash them! We have nothing to lose but our chains. We have a world of freedoms to win.

---

19. In support of this thesis, Lenin quoted a letter from Karl Marx to Ludwig Kugelmann in April 1871, during the Paris Commune: 'The next attempt of the French Revolution will not be, as happened before, to transfer the bureaucratic-military machine from one set of hands to another, but to *smash* it, and this is the prerequisite for every real people's revolution.' See 'Marx to L. Kugelmann in Hanover' (12 April, 1871); collected in Karl Marx and Friedrich Engels, *Selected Works*, Vol. 2 (Progress Publishers, 1969), p. 420; and quoted in V. I. Lenin, 'The Experience of the Paris Commune', *The State and Revolution*; edited, translated and with an introduction by Robert Service (Penguin Classics, 2009), p. 34.

Afterword: The Soothsayer
(A Parable for our Times)

When the enemies of reason are victorious — as they have been for some time now in the UK — those of us still fighting on the side of reason have to employ another language in order to communicate with them, find other ways to describe the irrationality in which they are imprisoned. This is a parable for our times.

First Prophecy

A man walked into the desert. There he had many visions of a future that only he could see, for he was a Soothsayer, honoured by the Gods, feared among men. After forty days and forty nights he reached the other side of the desert, and descended into a river valley. There he came across a small village surrounded by fields in which the villagers were hard at work that Spring morning, tending to their herds and flocks.

'Oh good people,' the Soothsayer cried, 'I come bearing bad tidings for you! Behold, the God of the River has spoken to me in the desert. He is wroth with you. For too long have you lived off the fat of the land he has watered, and now he demands the sacrifice of your best bull!'

The people of the village looked at him with amazement on their faces. 'But who are you, stranger, and why should we believe what you say? Spring is here, and we need our best bull to increase our herds for the Winter to come.'

'Do not question the Gods of Nature' the Soothsayer responded angrily, 'or they will rise up against you! Have I not studied their ways under learned masters whose knowledge you could not possibly comprehend? Do as I say, or this very night your village shall be swept away in a flood of divine retribution!'

The herdsmen and shepherds went to the village Elders to tell them what the Soothsayer had said. But some stayed in the fields to tend to their animals, and some went home to wash the dust from their clothes, and when they finally reached the village square the Soothsayer was there ahead of them. With many bows and courtesies, the Elders invited him into the village hall — 'to consider his warning,' they said, 'to weigh up the benefits and losses for the whole village, and to make our decision.' The day was almost over when the Elders re-emerged.

'For the greater good!', they cried, announcing their decision to the waiting villagers. 'It's a necessary sacrifice, and although our herd will be diminished until we can buy another, better to sacrifice one bull than to lose the whole village. Surely, anyone can see that? We shall do as the Soothsayer says!'

And that evening the whole village gathered to watch the sacrifice of their best bull in the village square. First the bones, horns and tail were thrown onto the fire as an offering to the River God. Then the best cuts of meat were shared among the village Elders. Last of all the entrails and offal were handed over to the villagers. Some of them reported seeing the Soothsayer sitting among the Elders at the high table, licking the blood and fat off his fingers.

The next morning nothing had changed. The river had not risen and the village was still standing.

'You see?' cried the Soothsayer triumphantly. 'The River God is appeased by your obedience. He has spared your village from his wrath. But never forget, good people, that the Gods of Nature watch over you always, and their wrath is only averted for a time!'

Second Prophecy

The Summer Solstice had passed, and the villagers were attending to their diminished herds, when once again the Soothsayer appeared to them, a shadowy figure beneath the noonday sun.

'Alas, obedient people, I bring you more woe! In the night the God of Rain spoke to me, and he is wroth with you! For too long have you grazed your sheep on the hills he has made fertile, and now he demands just payment for his beneficence!'

The people of the village looked at the Soothsayer in fear, for they had not forgotten that he had predicted their future before — though how he did none knew nor dared to ask. 'What shall we do, O Master, to avoid the anger of the Rain God?'

'To me alone does he speak!' the Soothsayer shouted, pointing to the sky (in which not a cloud could be seen). 'Only through me will you find protection from his divine wrath. And this has he made known to me through portents, auguries and divination. The village shall hand over half its flock of sheep to me, his appointed and trusted Emissary, and I shall see them returned to the Gods from whose watchful care and bounty they came.'

Without waiting to consult the rest of the villagers, the village Elders pushed forward and spoke in loud voices. 'We shall do what you order, Master, in the sure and certain belief that you are, in truth, an Emissary of the Gods!'

After a quick calculation of the number of sheep in the village, the Elders turned to the villagers, and raised the batons of their office menacingly over their heads. 'O villagers, each of you must hand over a dozen sheep to this Emissary of the Gods, and be glad that we have his wisdom and knowledge to guide us through this terrible time. Only through obedience to his commandments shall we pass through the storm and see the sun again!'

Some of the villagers were not happy with this arrangement, which meant that those with two dozen sheep lost half their flock, those with four dozen a mere quarter, while those with only a dozen sheep were left destitute. They tried to point out that the man the Elders now called 'Master' had asked for half the sheep in the whole village — but the Elders would not listen. Instead, when the poorer villagers refused to hand over their entire flock, the Elders sent a handful of guards (who until then had protected their homes from wolves and other wild animals) to take the sheep from the villagers by force.

Those who put up a struggle were thrown into a fenced enclosure they called a 'stockade'. Nobody had heard this word before, or knew when the stockade had been built or by whom; but the other villagers took note, and no matter how many sheep they owned, they obediently handed over the dozen designated by the Elders. In the confusion, few thought to ask what the Soothsayer whom they now called Master would do with the sheep, and those who did were shouted down by the others.

'Better to lose half our flock than the whole village! Do as our Elders say! They understand these matters better than you, and the Emissary of the Gods has spoken! Or do you no longer believe in the Gods of Nature?'

To this question few had an answer, and by late afternoon the Soothsayer had received half the entire village's sheep. With the help of a few other villagers (to whom he had promised a reward for their loyalty) the Soothsayer took these over the brow of the hill and disappeared — nobody knew where. Some of the bolder villagers let it be known that they hoped they had seen the last of the Soothsayer, and refused to call him 'Master' (except of the other villagers). But the majority laughed and called them 'Unbelievers', warning them of the fate that awaited those who denied the Gods of Nature.

Third Prophecy

The winds of Autumn were blowing through the village, and the sheep that were left had all been slaughtered, when the Soothsayer returned for the third time. He came as the shadows of evening fell, and his face was terrible to look upon.

'O vain and ungodly people', he cried, 'your sins have not been hidden from me! The God of Storms has spoken to me in the desert, and he is wroth with you! Ask not what you have done, less you sharpen his fury! This very night your village shall be laid low by his tempests. Have I not seen it all in your future? Do I not have secret knowledge unfathomable to your shallow thoughts and selfish desires? Harken to me, you who are faithful to the Gods, and close your ears to the Unbelievers! The Storm God demands a sacrifice to appease his most just and fearful temper. Greedy have you been all the days of your lives, and now the reckoning is upon you! The God of Storms, most merciful of all the Gods, demands that you gather all your coins and jewels, your richest cloth and your least trinket — yea, even your children's inheritance — and leave them in the village square. There shall his trusted Emissary convey your offerings to a place too sacred for you to enter, from whence they shall be returned to him from whom they were granted only in loan. Unworthy and godly people, in the purity of poverty alone lies your protection from the winds of justice. This is your last chance of salvation!'

As he said this, some of the villagers — mostly those who had refused to acknowledge the Soothsayer as their Master, but some others too — saw sweat trickling down his face, and could hear the tremble of doubt in his voice. And they said to themselves — 'Liar!' But when they repeated this out loud, they were seized by the village guards, whose ranks had swollen with many of their fellow villagers, and thrown into the stockade. This too had grown in size, and outside stood more guards, members of a newly-created village militia, who hid their faces behind scarves.

Long into the night the rest of the villagers laboured to gather their coins and jewels, their least trinket and their richest cloth, and anything else they had put aside after long labour for the future of their children. And everything was piled in heavy chests in the village square, where yet more guards stood, armed now with long spears and heavy shields that had never before been seen in the village.

And throughout the gathering the Soothsayer that some now called 'Lord' urged the villagers to hurry, less dawn come and their village be swept away by the terrible wrath of the God of Storms. And so it was that, even as the last chest was taken on mules over the brow of the hill and into the desert, the dawn broke bright behind them, with a blue sky overhead. A great cry went up from all the villagers (or at least, from those not imprisoned in the stockade).

'We are saved! Once more the Soothsayer has spoken the truth, and saved us from destruction!' And turning to the Soothsayer they knelt before him. 'Tell us, O Lord and most certain Emissary of the Gods of Nature, are we now saved from their wrath? Are all our many sacrifices sufficient to appease the Gods for their many and generous bounties, of which, until now, we have proved so unworthy? Are the Gods of Nature pleased with us?'

The Soothsayer looked at the villagers with a smile on the side of his face (the side turned away from them). 'We shall see, obedient and fearful servants of the Gods. Oh yes, we shall see.'

With that he turned and walked up the hill in the same direction in which the mule train had disappeared. And as the sun rose it glittered on the Soothsayer's robes, which were as rich as any in the village had once been, even among the Elders. And around his neck there hung the heaviest of necklaces, which glinted in the morning light so that it dazzled their eyes. And some of them said they heard the clink of coins in the heavy bags he bore under his cloak.

Fourth Prophecy

Throughout the remainder of the year there was huge relief in the village. They had sacrificed their best bull, given away half their sheep flocks, and handed over all their coins and jewels, their richest cloth and least trinket, and the wealth they had stored for their children's future — but the village still stood against the wrath of the Gods of the River, of the Rain and of the Storms. Now, surely, their future was assured! They could work and save for another bull, breed more sheep and build up their lost wealth. Their children would never see the future they had planned for them, nor, perhaps, their children's children; but when the villagers who were now living were dead and buried, their great-grand-children would still have the village!

But as dusk fell in the valley one cold Winter's night, a figure appeared on the brow of the hill. It was the Soothsayer that the villagers now called Lord, and this time he came not alone but with a company of armed guards, among whom the villagers recognised many of their former friends and members of their families.

'God-fearing people of the village!' the Soothsayer cried in a loud voice, and all the guards clashed their spears against their shields. Some of the villagers began to protest, but the guards grabbed them from among the others and slew them there in the village square where the bull had been sacrificed, the sheep gathered and the chests piled high with the former wealth of the village.

'God-fearing people of the village!', the Soothsayer cried again, and this time the village fell silent. 'Have I not returned just in time? Do we not see here the origin and cause of the ills which, alas, still afflict you? For see, the Winter is drawing in, and many shall die if you do not heed my commands. I have spoken to the God of Winter, and he is wroth with you! For though many have obeyed the Gods of Nature, still some among you doubt my prophecies.'

A murmur of assent ran through the crowd of villagers, and following it rose a wave of fear — though of what exactly none yet knew. Some began to pick up sticks and clubs that lay nearby. Others ran to their farms and returned with pitchforks, hammers, scythes and axes. Still others picked up stones and flaming brands from a fire that the guards had kindled in the village square.

'And where are these accursed few,' cried the Soothsayer, 'whose selfish acts alone place your village — nay, your very lives in peril? Tell me! Show me where they are, and be avenged upon these murderers!'

At this the entire crowd of villagers pointed as if with one finger to the stockades whose prisoners had so swelled in number that the fences that enclosed them now ringed the entire village.

'There! There they are!' the villagers cried with one voice. 'Murderers and Unbelievers among us! We must purge ourselves of those whose lack of faith threatens all our futures. Kill them! Kill them! Kill them all!'

Few would speak afterwards of what was done that night in the stockades, where the formerly warm firelight from the village homesteads did not reach. But all agreed that the guards of the Soothsayer who all now called 'King' had no part in it — having, indeed, no need to. For no more terrible revenge could be taken than that enacted by the villagers themselves. And as the morning light dawned red on the cold dew, they barely noticed that the village still stood, and the wrath of the Winter God had been appeased, saving them all from disaster once again.

Fifth Prophecy

That Winter was long and dark, and with their herds and flocks gone and their wealth spent, many of the villagers died of cold and hunger, or merely from lack of care — for all now suspected each other. Some, indeed, doubted that Spring would ever come again. The bodies of the Unbelievers were disposed of by the guards, but the stockades soon filled again with more villagers who dared to speak against the Soothsayer. But at long last the new Spring arrived, and the few trees they had not cut down for fuel began to bloom again. The next day, the Elders who now called themselves 'Knights' summoned the villagers to the village hall. In a great chair warmed by a roaring fire sat the Soothsayer, surrounded by many guards, and their faces were hidden by the visors of metal helms.

'Obedient and pure people of the village', the Soothsayer said quietly (and as he spoke a smile escaped from his cruel mouth), 'the Gods of nature are pleased with you. So pleased, in sooth, that you have no need for me anymore. The trusted Emissary of the Gods has other disasters to avert, other villages to save, other offerings to convey. This very day I shall depart back into the desert. But to assure the safety of my journey (which I undertake for the good of all people of faith) the God of the Desert demands a sacrifice. Faithful and fearful people of the village, I know I do not need to explain why, but the Desert God demands the lives of your children.'

In the hush that followed, the Soothsayer looked at the terrified villagers, and saw on their faces neither doubt nor dissent.

'Yes, fearful and faithful people. One child must be sacrificed for each of the forty days and forty nights I must walk in the desert. Who among you will dare to deny me now, after all I have done for you?'

It was with unwavering and emotionless hands that the villagers slit the throats of their children, their eldest son and their newest-born baby, every morning and every evening for the next forty days, there in the village square where their best bull had been sacrificed, where they had gathered their sheep and packed their wealth into chests for the Soothsayer, where the Unbelievers had been slaughtered by their own hands.

And nobody asked why the Soothsayer left the village with such a long train of carts on which so many chests and bags were packed; nor why he was followed by so many sheep; nor why the Knights left with him, dressed in the richest of robes and wearing the heaviest jewellery (while the villagers were left in rags); nor why the sound of coins and jewels clinking under their cloaks accompanied them all the way up the hill and disappeared over the brow.

But all kept count of the number of days and nights they must make sacrifice, and on the forty-first day they built a tall statue of the Soothsayer that all now called 'God'. And in words carved on its base they wrote:

FOR TRULY

ONLY GOD HIMSELF COULD HAVE SAVED OUR VILLAGE
AND BY OBEDIENCE TO HIS COMMANDS ALONE
HAS A TERRIBLE FATE BEEN AVERTED

From that day on, in each season of the year, the villagers made offerings to their God at the foot of the statue: sacrificing their best bull in the Spring; in the Summer slaughtering half their sheep no matter how few they had; giving away their wealth to the Knights who returned every Autumn to collect it; and in the middle of Winter, when their hope was at its lowest, killing the Unbelievers among them. And they called these rituals and the beliefs on which they were founded 'Religion'. And only by following their commands (it was said now by all) was the village saved from the just and terrible wrath of the Gods of Nature.

Bibliography

Abiona, John. 'Health fears over replacing "mum" with "birth-giver" as experts warn wider use of gender-neutral terms could have "unintended consequences" for women and children', *Daily Mail* (30 January, 2022).

Acres, Tom. 'Emergency alert test happens today — here's everything you need to know', *Sky News* (23 April, 2023).

Acumen Research and Consulting. 'Sex Reassignment Surgery Market Size to reach a remarkable USD 3,171.3 Million by 2032' (8 June, 2023).

AFP in Lagos. 'Riots erupt in Nigerian cities as bank policy leads to scarcity of cash', *The Guardian* (15 February, 2023).

Agamben, Giorgio. 'Capitalism as Religion', collected in *Creation and Anarchy: The Work of Art and the Religion of Capitalism*. Meridian: Crossing Aesthetics, series edited by Werner Hamacher and David E. Wellbery. Translated by Adam Kotsko. Stanford University Press, 2019, pp. 66-78.

_____. *State Of Exception*. Homo Sacer II, 1. Translated by Kevin Attell. University of Chicago Press, 2005.

Alessi, Christopher. '"A golden opportunity" — HRH the Prince of Wales and other leaders on the Forum's Great Reset', *World Economic Forum* (3 June, 2020).

Allison, Graham. 'Xi and Putin Have the Most Consequential Undeclared Alliance in the World', *Foreign Policy* (23 March, 2023).

Ammon, Elizabeth. 'Ian Botham: I threw racism report on floor, it was nonsense', *The Times* (19 July, 2023).

Amnesty International. 'Ukraine: Abuses and war crimes by the Aidar Volunteer Battalion in the north Luhansk region' (8 September, 2014).

_____. 'Israel's apartheid against Palestinians: a cruel system of domination and a crime against humanity' (1 February, 2022).

_____. 'Saudi Arabia 2022'.

_____. 'Yemen 2022'.

_____. 'Afghanistan 2022'.

_____. 'Libya 2022'.

_____. 'Iraq: 20 years since the US-led coalition invaded Iraq, impunity reigns supreme' (20 March, 2023).

Anon. 'Katyusha Хор Пятницкого MSK-US', *YouTube* (19 December, 2014).

_____. 'Privatization of Russian Industry', *Facts and Details* (last updated May 2016).

_____. '50th anniversary of the devastating floods in East Devon', *Straitgate Action Group* (10 July, 2018).

_____. 'Goldman Sachs's European headquarters targeted by climate-change activists', *Reuters* (25 April, 2019).

_____. 'Gold Dinar: the Real Reason Behind Gaddafi's Murder', *Millenium State* (3 May, 2019).

_____. 'Family of Vaccine Minister Sets up Medical Company', *Byline Times* (4 January, 2021).

_____. Russia's Super Rich Wealthier Than Poorest 99.8% — Report', *The Moscow Times* (10 June, 2021).

_____. 'Fallon Fox, Transgender MMA Fighter Who Broke The Skull of Her Opponent', *BJJ World* (2021).

_____. 'Profile: Who are Ukraine's far-right Azov regiment?', *Al Jazeera* (1 March, 2022).

_____. 'Ukraine lays out plan to be "most digital" country', *Kyiv Post* (5 July, 2022).

_____. 'Extinction Rebellion: Climate activists arrested after protest in Commons chamber', *BBC News* (2 September, 2022).

_____. 'Arrest of UK anti-royal protesters raises free speech concerns', *Al Jazeera* (13 September, 2022).

_____. 'New UK Prime Minister Rishi Sunak Pushes Heavily to Introduce CBDC', *Unlock* (25 October, 2022).

_____. 'Russia enters the top ten economies in the world for GDP at current prices', *Nova Mews* (31 December, 2022).

_____. 'United Kingdom Food Inflation', *Trading Economics* (2023).

_____. 'World Economic Forum Discussion on Technology and National Security', *C-Span* (19 January, 2023).

_____. 'Central Bank of Nigeria Delays Demonetization by 10 Days', *PYMNTS* (30 January, 2023).

_____. 'The Lockdown Files', *The Telegraph* (1 March 2023).

_____. 'Exposed: London's Secretive "Smart Stations" Roll Out', *Winter Oak* (13 March, 2023).

_____. 'What are depleted uranium munitions the UK is sending to Ukraine?', *Al Jazeera* (23 March, 2023).

_____. 'Far-left student protestors chant "f*ck off nazis" in reaction to Michael Knowles speaking event at Purdue University', *The Post Millenial* (24 March, 2023).

_____. 'Andrea Long Chu, New York Magazine's Book Critic, Wins Pulitzer Prize', *New York Magazine* (8 May, 2023).

_____. 'The U.S. Government and the World Health Organization', *KFF* (22 May, 2023).

_____. 'South Africa Invites Putin to Summit Despite ICC Arrest Warrant', *teleSUR English* (26 June, 2023).

_____. 'Russia Warns Ukraine Over Crimea "A Threat To State Existence"', *TeleSUR English* (26 June, 2023).

_____. 'Greece investigating whether organised arson groups to blame for deadly wildfires', *SkyNews* (23 August, 2023).

_____. 'G20 declaration adopted with no mention of Russian aggression in Ukraine', *The Daily Star* (9 September, 2023).

Aoraha, Claudia. 'Woman, 36, attacked at NYC Pride for brandishing a "stop female erasure" sign is a "deprogrammer" who believes the transgender movement is a CULT for kids', *Daily Mail* (26 June, 2023).

Allison, George. 'UK and Israel sign military cooperation agreement', *UK Defence Journal* (7 December, 2020).

Atlantic Council. 'Central Bank Digital Currency Tracker' (2023).

Badenoch, Kemi. 'It's vital more BAME candidates take part in Covid-19 vaccine trials to deliver a vaccine that works for everyone', *Politics Home* (14 October, 2020).

Bank of England. 'Official Bank Rate history'.

_____. 'Central Bank Digital Currency: opportunities, challenges and design' (12 March, 2020).

_____. 'Bank of England statement on Central Bank Digital Currency' (19 April, 2021).

_____. 'Central Bank Digital Currency: An update on the Bank of England's work — speech by Tom Mutton' (17 June, 2021).

_____. 'Statement on Central Bank Digital Currency next steps' (9 November, 2021).

_____. 'QE at the Bank of England: A perspective on its functioning and effectiveness', *Quarterly Bulletin 2022 Q1* (18 May, 2022).

_____. 'HM Treasury and Bank of England consider plans for a digital pound' (7 February, 2023).

_____. 'The digital pound — speech by Jon Cunliffe' (7 February, 2023).

_____. 'The digital pound: Technology Working Paper' (February 2023).

_____. 'The digital pound: We are looking at the case for issuing a digital pound. This type of money is known as a central bank digital currency (CBDC). It would not replace cash' (last updated 1 June, 2023).

Bank of England and HM Treasury. 'The digital pound: a new form of money for households and businesses? Consultation paper' (February 2023).

Bank of International Settlements. 'Central bank digital currencies: system design and interoperability' (September 2021).

Barker, Richard. 'How many security cameras are in London?', *Clarion Security Service* (2023).

Barking & Dagenham. 'Rainbow flag flies over town hall to mark LGBT+ History Month' (1 February, 2022).

Barrett, Emily, and Jesse Hamilton. 'Why the U.S. Repo Market Blew Up and How to Fix It', *Bloomberg* (6 January, 2020).

Barthes, Roland. 'Lecture in Inauguration of the Chair of Literary Semiology, College de France, 7 January, 1977'; translated by Richard Howard, *October*, Vol. 8, no. 162 (Spring 1979).

Barton, Alex. 'Vagina rebranded as "bonus hole" by cervical cancer charity', *The Telegraph* (9 July, 2023).

Barton, Cassie. 'GE2019: How did demographic affect the result?', *House of Commons Library* (21 February, 2020).

Bartosch, Jo. 'Babies should be nowhere near gyrating drag queens', *Spiked* (3 March, 2023).

Baska, Maggie. 'Three common anti-trans myths easily debunked by science', *Pink News* (31 March, 2022).

Bazaraa, Danya. 'Trans double rapist Isla Bryson who attacked two women while living as a man is jailed in male prison for eight years: Judge tells sex predator "you are NOT the victim"', *Daily Mail* (28 February, 2023).

BBC News. 'Ukraine: Rishi Sunak meets Volodymyr Zelensky in Kyiv' (19 November, 2022).
_____. 'Ukraine war: President Volodymyr Zelensky visits the UK' (8 February, 2023).

BBC Politics Live. 'I'm not a Criminal I'm a Scared Kid trying to Fight for my Future', *YouTube* (30 March, 2023).

Beauvoir, Simone de. *The Second Sex*; translated by H. M. Parshley (Jonathan Cape, 1953).

Beeley, Vanessa. 'Assassinated for telling the truth about Ukraine', *The Wall Will Fall* (17 April, 2022).

Beloe Zlato. 'Russian folk Ансамбль "Белое злато" — За тихой рекой', *YouTube* (11 November, 2013).

Bennetts, Marc. 'Ukraine's National Militia: "We're not neo-Nazis, we just want to make our country better"', *The Guardian* (13 March, 2018).

Bignell, Francis. 'Walletmor Introduces a Payment Implant Chip To Allow For Cardless Payments', *The Fintech Times* (11 October, 2021).

Bill and Melinda Gates Foundation. 'Committed Grants: World Health Organization'.

Bird, Nelli. 'Transgender children GP: Helen Webberley wins suspension appeal', BBC News (31 March, 2023).

Birkbeck, University of London. 'Financial Requirements'.

BlackRock Investment Institute. 'Dealing with the next downturn: From unconventional monetary policy to unprecedented policy coordination' (August 2019).

Blaff, Ari. 'NHS Warns Most Trans-Identifying Children Going Through "Transient Phase"', *National Review* (28 July, 2023).

Blair, Alex. 'Xi Jinping predicts "change not seen in 100 years" as he departs Russia after Vladimir Putin meeting', *News.com* (22 March, 2023).

Bloomberg Television. 'Pfizer CEO on Vaccine Developments', *YouTube* (18 January, 2023).

Board of Governors of the Federal Reserve System. 'Federal Reserve Actions to Support the Flow of Credit to Households and Businesses' (15 March, 2020).

Boardman, Terry. 'Ukrainian policy in the Donbass: Is it fair to call it genocide?', *UK Column* (25 February, 2023).

Bolton, Paul, and Iona Stewart. 'Domestic energy prices', *House of Commons Library* (13 March, 2023).

Boot, Arnoud W. A., Peter Hoffmann, Luc Laeven and Lev Ratnovski. 'Financial Intermediation and Technology: What's Old, What's New?', *IMF Working Papers* (7 August, 2020).

Bosnic, Drago. 'Dangers of Pentagon's "decapitation strike" against Russia', *Brics Information Portal* (28 December, 2022).

Bounds, Andy. 'Dutch farmers in uproar over plans to curb animal numbers to cut nitrogen emissions', *Financial Times* (3 August 2022).

Boyd, Connor. 'Fury as CPS hires transgender activist in new £31,000 working from home diversity job who has backed using the derogatory term "womxn" instead of "woman"', *Daily Mail* (2 June, 2022).

Brady United. 'The Facts That Make Us Act', 2019.

Breton, André. 'Il n'y a pas sortir de là', in *Claire de terre*, 1923; collected in *Oeuvres complètes*, vol. 1, Bibliothèque de la Pléiade. Édition établie par Marguerite Bonnet avec, pour ce volume, la collaboration de Philippe Bernier, Étienne-Alain Hubert et José Pierre (Éditions Gallimard, 1988), p. 169.

Bristol Pride. 'Flag Raising, Stonewall Remembered' (28 June, 2019).

British High Commission Nairobi. 'Climate finance to flow to Kenya as UK Prime Minister agrees with President Ruto to fast-track KES 500 billion of British investment' (7 November, 2022).

British Library. 'Wishing all a happy and hopeful Pride Month', *Twitter* (1 June, 2023).

Brown, Ellen. 'Another Bank Bailout Under Cover of a Virus', *The Web of Debt Blog* (18 May, 2020).

_____. 'Conservation or Land Grab? The Financialisation of Nature', *The Web of Debt* (5 November, 2021).

Brown, Luke. 'Star Wars Celebration Orlando's Very Best Cosplay (Day Two)', *Screen Crush* (15 April, 2017).

Brown, Oliver. 'Transgender runner, 49, wins bronze at Para World Championships', *The Telegraph* (14 July, 2023).

Brunel University London. 'Brunel celebrates Pride Month 2022' (2022).

Burford, Rachel. 'Animal Rebellion: ten arrests as protesters spray Houses of Parliament with paint', *Evening Standard* (7 September, 2022).

Bush, George W. 'President Bush Announces Start of Iraq War', *YouTube* (13 March, 2013).

Butchard, Patrick, and Bukky Balogun, 'What is the proposed WHO Pandemic Preparedness Treaty?', *House of Commons Library* (2 June, 2023).

Cabinet Office. 'Consultation on draft legislation to support identity verification' (updated 26 June, 2023).

Cabinet Office, Department for International Development and Foreign, Commonwealth and Development Office. 'Corporate Report: Implementing the Sustainable Development Goals' (updated 15 July, 2021).

Camden Council. 'Camden unveils crossing to celebrate Transgender Awareness Week' (9 November, 2021).

Carrell, Severin. 'Humza Yousaf's family drops discrimination case against nursery', *The Guardian* (7 February, 2023).

Carstens, Agustín. 'Bank for International Settlements head Augustin Carstens about CBDC and control', *YouTube* (1 January, 2021).

_____. 'Digital currencies and the soul of money', Bank of International Settlements (18 January, 2022).

Carter, Hana. '"Great Reset": Bizarre new Covid conspiracy theory as "Build Back Better" slogans around the world spark "fascist" regime claims', *The Sun* (20 November, 2020).

CBS News. 'Trump meets with Ukrainian president amid whistleblower controversy', *YouTube* (25 September, 2019).

Central Digital & Data Office. 'Consultation on draft legislation to support identity verification' (26 June, 2023).

Chamberlain, Lisa. 'The surprising stickiness of the "15-minute city"', *World Economic Forum* (15 March, 2022).

Cheng, Philip J., *et al*. 'Fertility concerns of the transgender patient', *Translational Andrology and Urology* (June 2019).

Chicago Council on Global Affairs. 'World Economic Forum founder Klaus Schwab on the Fourth Industrial Revolution', *YouTube* (13 May, 2019).

Children's Society, The. 'The Good Childhood Report' (2022).

Claremont Institute for the American Way of Life. 'BLM Funding Database'.

Clark, Conor. 'Sadiq Khan: "The Trans community should not be stigmatised, demonised or weaponised"', *Gay Times* (2023).

Clark, D. 'Number of people receiving emergency food parcels from Trussell Trust foodbanks in the United Kingdom from 2008/09 to 2022/23', *Statista* (3 May, 2023).

————. 'Average growth of weekly earnings in the United Kingdom compared with the CPI inflation rate from March 2001 to June 2023', *Statista* (August 2023).

Clark, Nick. 'Anti-vax marches — a warning from the right', *Socialist Worker* (25 January, 2022).

Clayton, Alison. 'Gender-Affirming Treatment of Gender Dysphoria in Youth: A Perfect Storm Environment for the Placebo Effect — The Implications for Research and Clinical Practice', *Archives of Sexual Behaviour* (13 December, 2022).

Climate Emergency Fund. 'Our 2022 grantees disrupted normalcy and created breakthroughs: Funding Disruptive Climate Protest in the US' (2022).

Climate Investment Funds. 'Egypt' (2023).

CNN World. 'Watch Zelensky's historic speech to Congress' (22 December, 2022).

Cole, Brendan. Fact Check: Did President Zelensky Call on NATO to Start Nuclear War?', *Newsweek* (7 October, 2022).

Collins, Paul. 'IPCC climate report 2022 summary: The key findings', *Selectra Climate* (7 April, 2022).

Corbishley, Nick. 'The Central Bank of Nigeria Just Gave a Whole New Meaning to the Term "Financial Repression"', *Naked Capitalism* (9 December, 2022).

————. 'This Was Another Big Week for Central Bank Digital Currency (CBDCs)', *Naked Capitalism* (10 February, 2023).

Corlett, Adam. 'Charting the UK's lost decade of income growth', *Resolution Foundation* (5 March, 2020).

Coutinho, Claire. 'Schools: Racial Discrimination', *UK Parliament* (2 May, 2023).

Crawford, Neta C. 'Pentagon Fuel Use, Climate Change, and the Costs of War', Watson Institute International and Public Affairs (13 November, 2019).

Crew, Jemma, and Helen Catt. 'Diane Abbott suspended as Labour MP after racism letter', *BBC News* (23 April, 2023).

Crown Prosecution Service. 'Domestic Abuse' (5 December, 2022).

Crozier, Amy. *Becoming Me* (2023).

Dal, Ray. 'Principles for Dealing with the Changing World Order', *YouTube* (2 March, 2022).

Damshenas, Sam. 'Regent Street hangs Intersex-Inclusive flags to mark 50 years of Pride in the UK', *Gay Times* (2023).

D'Andrea, Aaron. 'Liberals try to strike Hunka recognition from official record. What that means', *Global News* (27 September, 2023).

207

DataBlog. 'Bank reforms: how much did we bail them out and how much do they still owe?', *The Guardian* (2016).

Davies, Gareth. 'Just Stop oil protesters force Dartford Crossing to close after scaling bridge' *The Telegraph* (17 October, 2022).

Davies, Richard. 'UK — Evacuations After Floods in Devon and Somerset', *Floodlist* (10 May, 2023).

Davis, Barney. 'Police detain man after Just Stop Oil activist shoved to ground on Blackfriars Bridge', *Evening Standard* (23 May, 2023).

Davis, Iain. 'SDG7: The Impossible Energy Transformation', *Unlimited Hangout* (6 January, 2023).

Davis, Iain, and Whitney Webb. 'Sustainable Debt Slavery', *Unlimited Hangout* (13 September, 2022).

Dawkins, Richard. 'Race Is A Spectrum: Sex is Pretty Damn Binary', *Areo Magazine* (5 January, 2022).

_____. 'Why biological sex matters', *The New Statesmen* (26 July, 2023).

Deacon, Michael. 'The row over the "terribly white" Royal balcony exposes the hypocrisy of the woke Left', *The Telegraph* (13 May, 2023).

Dearden, Lizzie. 'Critics don't like me because of my colour, Sajid Javid says after online abuse from far right and left', *Independent* (11 May, 2019).

Deloitte. 'The Big Three & ESG: A Guide to BlackRock, State Street & Vanguard Proxy Voting Policies & Guidance on Key ESG Issues' (5 June, 2023).

Department for Business, Energy and Industrial Strategy. 'Business population estimates for the UK and regions 2022: statistical release' (6 October, 2022).

Department for Digital, Culture, Media and Sport. 'Digital identity and attributes consultation' (3 February, 2023).

Department for Education. 'Proud to be flying the Armed Forces Day flag and Pride flag alongside the Union Jack today', *Twitter* (27 June, 2015).

_____. 'Changes to personal, social, health and economic (PSHE) and relationships and sex education (RSE): New curriculum introduction in September 2020' (25 June, 2019).

Department for Energy Security and Net Zero. 'Annual Fuel Poverty Statistics in England, 2023 (2022 data)' (28 February, 2023).

Department of Health and Social Care. 'Next phase of NHS coronavirus (COVID-19) app announced' (18 June, 2020).

_____. 'Specification COVID Pass Delivery Partner, Reference: C50516'; reproduced from its response to an FOI request in Richard Morgan, 'Vaccine Passports Are Alive and Kicking', *Daily Sceptic* (5 September, 2022).

Department for Work and Pensions, 'Environmental Social Governance (ESG) and responsible investment' (6 June, 2019).

Dianova, Yana. 'Assassinated for telling the truth about Ukraine', *The Wall Will Fall* (17 April, 2022).

Dimitropoulou, Alexandra. 'Economy Rankings: Largest countries by GDP, 2022', *CEO World Magazine* (31 March, 2022).

Dixon, Stacy Jo. 'Social media penetration UK 2023', *Statista* (12 September, 2023).

Donadio, Rachel. 'Portrait of Bravery: Ukraine's First Lady, Olena Zelenska', *British Vogue* (26 July, 2022).

Donnelly, Drew. 'China Social Credit System Explained — What is it and How Does it Work?', *NH Global Partners* (22 July, 2022).

Drag Queen Story Hour UK Ltd (2023).

Duell, Mark, and Abbie Llewelyn. 'Police swoop on eco mob and arrest 32 activists who set up road blocks around Trafalgar Square as they demand new oil and gas projects are shutdown on sixth day of chaos', *Daily Mail* (6 October, 2022).

Dunn, Gibson. 'BlackRock, Vanguard and State Street Update Corporate Governance and ESG Policies and Priorities for 2022' (25 January, 2022).

Dustmann, Christian, and Francesca Fabbri, 'Immigrants in the British Labour Market', *Fiscal Studies*, Vol. 26, No. 4 (December 2005).

Ebell, Myron, and Steven J. Milloy. 'Wrong Again: 50 Years of Failed Eco-pocalyptic Predictions', *Competitive Enterprise Institute* (18 September, 2019).

Eco-shirt. 'Kill The Terf Shirt' (2023).

Eco, Umberto. 'Ur-fascism'. *The New York Review of Books* (22 June, 1995); collected in *How to Spot a Fascist*; translated by Ricard Dixon and Alastair McEwan (Harvill Secker, 2020).

Eddo-Lodge, Reni. 'Why I'm no longer talking to white people about race', *The Guardian* (30 May, 2017).

Edginton, Steven, and Robert Mendick. 'Exclusive: Welcome to woke Whitehall, where more than 100 genders are recognised', *The Telegraph* (27 May, 2022).

Edwards, Eve. 'Where to buy Zelensky's Sweatshirt as Ukrainian Trident Jumper goes Viral', *HITC* (22 December, 2022).

Elliott, Larry. 'Mutiny erupts among WEF staff over role of "Mr. Davos"', *The Guardian* (18 January, 2023).

Elmer, Simon. 'The Good Practice Guide to Estate Demolition: ASH response to the GLA', *Architects for Social Housing* (8 March, 2017).

_____. 'Armed Love: Capitalism, Anarchism and the Russian Revolution', *Architects for Social Housing* (4 December, 2017).

_____. 'The Social Realism of the Labour Party: Jeremy Corbyn and the Socialism of Fools', *Architects for Social Housing* (29 March, 2018).

_____. 'What Is To Be Done? Changing Metaphors of Change', *Architects for Social Housing* (23 July, 2018).

_____. 'Oy Vey! No Latkes for Labour', *Architects for Social Housing* (5 September, 2018).

_____. 'How Sadiq Khan's Housing Policy is Making London's Housing Crisis Worse', *Vice* (31 January, 2019).

_____. 'Extinction Rebellion: Socialist Revolution', *Architects for Social Housing* (24 April, 2019).

_____. 'Whatever Happened to the Middle Classes? Bad Faith and the Culture Industry', *Architects for Social Housing* (10 May, 2019).

_____. 'Stand Up To Labour: The Denials of Momentum', *Architects for Social Housing* (10 October, 2019).

_____. '"Middle-class Socialism": A Warning from History', *Architects for Social Housing* (16 November, 2019).

_____. 'The Parliamentary Road to Capitalism', *Architects for Social Housing* (9 December, 2019).

_____. 'Giorgio Agamben and the Biopolitics of COVID-19' (25 April, 2020); collected in *Virtue and Terror: Selected Articles on the UK Biosecurity State, Vol. 1*. Architects for Social Housing, 2022, pp. 3-20.

_____. 'Manufacturing Consensus: The Registering of COVID-19 Deaths' (1 May, 2020); collected in *Virtue and Terror: Selected Articles on the UK Biosecurity State, Vol. 1*. Architects for Social Housing, 2022, pp. 21-54.

_____. 'Lockdown: Collateral Damage in the War on COVID-19' (2 June, 2020); collected in *Virtue and Terror: Selected Articles on the UK Biosecurity State, Vol. 1*. Architects for Social Housing, 2022, pp. 97-145.

_____. 'The Science and Law of Refusing to Wear Masks: Texts and Arguments in Support of Civil Disobedience', *Architects for Social Housing* (11 June, 2020).

_____. 'The New Normal: What is the UK Biosecurity State. Part 1: Programmes and Regulations' (31 July, 2020); collected in *Virtue and Terror: Selected Articles on the UK Biosecurity State, Vol. 1*. Architects for Social Housing, 2022, pp. 147-154.

_____. 'Betrayal of the Clerks: UK Intellectuals in the Service of the Biosecurity State', *Architects for Social Housing* (12 November, 2020).

_____. 'Our Default State: Compulsory Vaccination for COVID-19 and Human Rights Law' (8 January, 2021); collected in *The New Normal: Selected Articles in the UK Biosecurity State, Vol. 2*. Architects for Social Housing, 2023, pp. 53-72.

_____. 'Bowling for Pfizer: Who's Behind the BioNTech Vaccine?' (9 December, 2020); collected in *The New Normal: Selected Articles in the UK Biosecurity State, Vol. 2.* Architects for Social Housing, 2023, pp. 33-52

_____. '*Cui Bono?* The COVID-19 "Conspiracy"' (19 February, 2021); collected in *The New Normal: Selected Articles in the UK Biosecurity State, Vol. 2.* Architects for Social Housing, 2023, pp. 103-160.

_____. 'Lies, Damned Lies and Statistics: Manufacturing the Crisis' (27 January, 2021); collected in *The New Normal: Selected Articles in the UK Biosecurity State, Vol. 2.* Architects for Social Housing, 2023, pp. 73-101.

_____. 'March for Freedom, 29 May, 2021', *Architects for Social Housing* (30 May, 2021).

_____. 'The UK "Vaccination" Programme. Part 1: Adverse Drug Reactions and Deaths' (15 September, 2021); collected in *The New Normal: Selected Articles in the UK Biosecurity State, Vol. 2.* Architects for Social Housing, 2023, pp. 161-205.

_____. 'The UK "Vaccination" Programme. Part 2. Virtue and Terror' (22 September, 2021); collected in *The New Normal: Selected Articles in the UK Biosecurity State, Vol. 2.* Architects for Social Housing, 2023, pp. 223-235.

_____. *The Road to Fascism: For a Critique of the Global Biosecurity State.* Architects for Social Housing, 2022.

_____. The Four Horsemen of the Apocalypse: New Technologies of Biopower', PANDA Open Society Sessions, *YouTube* (2 June, 2023).

Elmer, Simon, and Geraldine Dening. 'Lecture 3. The Economic Sphere: Part 1. Environmental Principles', *For a Socialist Architecture: Under Capitalism* (Architects for Social Housing, 2021), pp. 87-103.

_____. *For a Socialist Architecture: Under Capitalism* (Architects for Social Housing, 2021).

_____. *Saving St. Raphael's Estate: The Alternative to Demolition* (Architects for Social Housing, 2022).

Ely, John. 'Government-funded report urges NHS to use terms "chestfeeding" and "frontal birth" instead of breast or vaginal', *Daily Mail* (28 April, 2022).

_____. 'How trans women use a powerful mix of hormones, drugs and pumps to "breastfeed" babies — but how safe is it really? And does it actually nourish a child?', *Daily Mail* (5 July, 2023).

Emefiele, Godwin I., Governor, Central Bank of Nigeria. 'Press Remarks on Issuance of New Naira Banknotes' (26 October, 2022).

Ennis, Dawn. 'Outsports Female Athlete of the Year: CeCé Telfer', *Outsports* (26 December, 2019).

_____. 'Trans Swimming Champion Lia Thomas Is Nominated For Woman Of The Year', *Forbes* (16 July, 2022).

Este, Jonathan. 'The huge political cost of Blair's decision to allow Eastern European migrants unfettered access to Britain', *The Conversation* (16 November, 2016).

European Commission. 'Identifying conspiracy theories'; United Nations, 'United Nations Guidance Note on Addressing and Countering COVID-19 related Hate Speech' (11 May, 2020).

_____. 'Identifying conspiracy theories' (12 August 2020-19 February, 2021).

_____. 'Statement by President von der Leyen on energy' (7 September, 2022).

European Council. 'EU digital COVID certification'.

_____. 'An international agreement on pandemic prevention and preparedness' (last reviewed 6 June, 2023).

European Court of Human Rights. 'Guide on Article 2 of Protocol No. 4 to the European Convention on Human Rights: Freedom of Movement' (updated on 31 August, 2022).

Evans, Holly. 'Canadian Parliament accidentally honours Nazi — with Zelensky and Trudeau applauding', *Independent* (26 September, 2023).

Extinction Rebellion, 'Enough is enough . . . How are our governments letting us down?', *Emergency on Planet Earth*.

Falconer, Rebecca. 'PG&E bankruptcy judge sides with fire victims in liability challenge', *Axios* (28 November, 2019).

Farinelli, Francesco. 'Conspiracy theories and right-wing extremism — Insights and recommendations for P/CVE', Radicalisation Awareness Network, European Commission (2021).

Felton, Mark, Productions. 'Hitler and the Hohenzollerns — The Kaiser's Family & the Nazis', *YouTube* (27 March, 2023).

Fenton, Nick, and Andrew Lohsen. 'Corruption and Private sector Investment in Ukraine's Reconstruction', *CSIS* (8 November, 2022).

Fernandez, Colin. 'Sadiq Khan slammed over "nonsense data" behind ULEZ scheme which council chief says didn't take into account his region's older population', *Daily Mail* (14 February, 2023).

Firsht, Naomi. 'I am not a walking cervix or a menstruator. I am a W-O-M-A-N', *The Times* (31 October, 2018).

Fiscal Data Treasury. 'What is the national debt?'

Fisher, Lucy. 'Threat of terror attack in UK is "rising", home secretary warns', *Financial Times* (18 July, 2023).

Fletcher, Harry. 'Porn addiction in the UK has "trebled" since the start of the pandemic', *Indy100* (15 December, 2022).

Foreign, Commonwealth & Development Office. 'Transgender Pride Flag' (20 November, 2017).

Forrest, Adam. 'Ex-Bank of England boss in scathing attack on Truss as he claims she turned UK into "Argentina on the Channel"', *Independent* (19 September, 2023).

Foucault, Michel. *Society Must Be Defended: Lectures at the Collège de France, 1975-1976.* Edited by Michel Senellart. English series edited by Arnold I. Davidson. Translated by Graham Burchell. Palgrave Macmillan, 2003.

_____. *Security, Territory, Population: Lectures at the Collège de France, 1977-1978.* Edited by Michel Senellart. English series edited by Arnold I. Davidson. Translated by Graham Burchell. Palgrave Macmillan, 2007.

_____. *The Birth of Biopolitics: Lectures at the Collège de France*, 1978-1979; edited by Michel Senellart. English series edited by Arnold I. Davidson. Translated by Graham Burchell. Palgrave Macmillan, 2008.

_____. *The Will to Knowledge.* Volume 1 of *The History of Sexuality.* Translated by Robert Hurley. Penguin Books, 1998.

4sales. 'Mirror on the Industry Pt 2: Have TV adds improved in the past 2 years?', 2021.

Francis, Krishnan, and Elaine Kurtenbach. 'Explainer: Why Sri Lanka's economy collapsed and what's next', *AP News* (11 July, 2022).

Francis-Devine, Brigid. 'Research Briefing: Poverty in the UK: statistics', *House of Commons Library* (6 April, 2023).

Francis-Devine, Brigid, Daniel Harari, Matthew Keep, Paul Bolton, Wendy Wilson and Cassie Barton. 'Rising cost of living in the UK', *House of Commons Library* (22 September, 2023).

Freeland, Chrystia. 'Full text of Chrystia Freeland's remarks during Emergencies Act announcement', *Toronto Star* (14 February, 2022).

Gardner, Abby. 'A Complete Breakdown of the J. K. Rowling Transgender-Comments Controversy', *Glamour* (25 April, 2023).

Gardner, Maria. 'The Internet of Bodies Will Change Everything, for Better or Worse', *Rand Corporation* (29 October, 2020).

Gayle, Damien. 'XR protesters shut down central London bridges including Westminster', *The Guardian* (15 April, 2022).

_____ 'Just Stop Oil activists glue themselves to Turner painting frame in Manchester', *The Guardian* (1 July, 2022).

_____. 'Extinction Rebellion protesters block Oxford Circus in London', *The Guardian* (25 August, 2021).

_____. 'Just Stop Oil activists throw soup at Van Gogh's Sunflowers', *The Guardian* (14 October, 2022).

GB News. 'Just Stop Oil's Phoebe Plummer argues "People are dying" in net zero clash with Jacob Rees-Mogg', *YouTube* (27 March, 2023).

General Consensus, The. 'This, ladies and gentleman, is what corruption looks like', *Facebook* (19 July, 2022).

Ghebreyesus, Tedros Adhano. WHO Director-General's opening remarks at the media briefing on COVID-19 — 11 March 2020', *World Health Organization* (11 March, 2020).

Giles, Chris. 'How much will it cost the UK to reach net zero?', *Financial Times* (3 November, 2021).

Giordano, Simona, and Søren Holm. 'Is puberty delaying treatment "experimental treatment"', *International Journal of Transgender Health* (11 April, 2020).

Gleckman, Harris. 'How the United Nations is quietly being turned into a public-private partnership', *Open Democracy* (2 July, 2019).

Global Climate Intelligence Group. *World Climate Declaration: There is no climate emergency* (October 2022).

Global Fire Power. '2023 Military Strength Ranking'.

Global Security. '1933-1945: Krupp under the Nazis'.

Goldman, Marshall I. 'Putin and the Oligarchs', *Foreign Affairs* (1 November 2004).

Goldman Sachs. 'Unpacking what ESG Investing Really Means'.

Google. 'Exposure Notification API launches to support public health agencies' (20 May, 2020).

Good Jobs First. 'Violation Tracker Current Parent Company Summary: Siemens'.

Goodman, Jack, and Flora Carmichael. 'The coronavirus pandemic "Great Reset" theory and a false vaccine claim debunked', *BBC News* (22 November, 2020).

Goodwin, Harry. 'Sound the Alarm: Everything you need to know about emergency alert that will *override* your phone in days — what to do if you're driving', *The Sun* (17 April, 2023).

Gordin, Michael D. 'Lysenkoism', *Encyclopedia of the History of Science* (Carnegie Mellon University, 2023).

Gordon, Michael R. 'Facing Severe Shortage of Food, Russia Seeks Foreign Relief Aid', *The New York Times* (10 October, 1998).

Government Equalities Office. 'Trans People in the UK' (2018).

Government of Canada. 'February 14, 2022 Declaration of Public Order Emergency' (14 February, 2022).

Gozzi, Laura, and Sofia Bettiza. 'Are arsonists behind Italy's devastating wildfires?', *BBC News* (28 July, 2023).

Grand View Research. 'U.S. Sex Reassignment Surgery Market Size, Share & Trends Analysis Report By Gender Transition (Male To Female, Female To Male), And Segment Forecasts, 2022-2030'.

Grant, Harriet, and Dan Milmo. 'A fifth of teenagers watch pornography frequently and some are addicted, UK study finds', *The Guardian* (10 March, 2023).

Green, Daniel. 'Trans Day of Visibility: Flag flown from Brighton town halls', *The Argus* (1 April, 2023).

Greenesmith, Heron. 'Atheist Richard Dawkins swings to anti-trans right in grasp at broader intellectual relevance', *Religion Dispatches* (30 November, 2021).

Gregory, Andrew. 'UK's cost of living crisis will cause thousands of premature deaths, study says', *The Guardian* (25 September, 2023).

Grey, Becky. 'Ugo Monye says Premiership "does not care enough" about racism in rugby', *BBC Sport* (26 February, 2021).

_____. 'Ugo Money hopes new RFU group can help everyone feel rugby is "for them"', *BBC Sport* (19 April, 2021).

Grossman, Hannah. 'Top Swedish doctors blow whistle on trans puberty-suppressing drugs affecting children's bones: "Experimental", *Fox News* (27 April, 2023).

Groves, Jason. 'Britain must "face into the storm" of a global downturn, Jeremy Hunt will warn as he prepares to deliver brutal budget with bleak £54 billion package of tax rises and spending cuts to bring towering national debts and crippling inflation under control', *Daily Mail* (16 November 2022).

Guardian News. 'Biden and Zelenskiy hug after visiting Kyiv church to pay tribute to fallen soldiers', *YouTube* (20 February, 2023).

Guzman, Alyssa, and Stephen M. Lepore, 'Trans swimmer Lia Thomas "dropped her pants" and exposed her "male genitalia" in a women's locker room after a meet, claims University of Kentucky athlete Riley Gaines', *Daily Mail* (9 February, 2023).

Hanlon, Tim. 'Woman who spent £100,000 on being a "doll" shares image of how she used to look', *The Mirror* (5 July, 2023).

Hansard Society. 'Coronavirus Statutory Instruments Dashboard, 2020-2022' (4 March 2022).

Harrington, Suzanne. 'Not all men? Yes, actually, all men are part of the problem', *Irish Examiner* (24 March, 2021).

Harris, Kamala. 'Remarks by Vice President Harris at the Munich Security Conference', The White House (18 February, 2023).

Harriss, Lydia, and Philippa Kearney. 'Research Briefing: Smart Cities', *UK Parliament* (22 September, 2021).

Hart, Robert. '"Nobody Is Safe Until Everyone Is Safe": World Leaders Call For Global Pandemic Preparedness Treaty', *Forbes* (30 March, 2021).

Hartung, William. 'Biden's new whopping $886B defense budget request', *Responsible Statecraft* (9 March, 2023).

Hatchet, Jean. 'Eddie Izzard uses the ladies loo in Sheffield', *The Critic* (30 September, 2022).

Hayton, Debbie. 'How Richard Dawkins fell victim to the transgender thought police', *The Spectator* (21 April, 2021).

Heffer, Greg. 'George Floyd protests: Priti Patel recalls childhood racial slurs as she condemns "hooliganism" towards police', *Sky News* (8 June, 2020).

Herman, Jody L., Andrew R. Flores and Kathryn K. O'Neill. 'How Many Adults and Youth Identify as Transgender in the United States', UCLA School of Law, Williams Institute (June 2022).

Hersh, Seymour. 'How America took out the Nord Stream Pipeline', *Peoples Dispatch* (10 February, 2023).

_____. 'Trading with the Enemy', *Substack* (12 April, 2023).

Hickel, Jason. 'The World's Sustainable Development Goals Aren't Sustainable', *Foreign Policy* (30 September, 2020).

Hinchliffe, Tim. '"Individual carbon footprint tracker, stay tuned": Alibaba president at WEF 2022', *The Sociable* (25 May, 2022).

Hitchens, Peter. 'End this crude smear against conservatives — Hitler's Nazis were in fact left-wing racists', *The Mail on Sunday* (11 March, 2023).

HM Treasury. 'Policy Paper: Autumn Statement 2022 HTML' (17 November, 2022).

_____. 'The digital pound: A new form of money for households and businesses?' (7 February, 2023).

Hobson, Francis, and Aaron Kulakiewicz. 'Potential merits of a universal basic income', *House of Commons Library* (13 June, 2022).

Hoffman, David. 'Audit Shows Russia Misled IMF on Loan', *The Washington Post* (1 July,1999).

Holocaust Memorial Day Trust. 'First they came — by Pastor Martin Niemöller', 2023.

Hollis, Patrick. 'Strikes in March 2023: All the industrial action set to take place this month — including from the RMT', *London World* (28 February, 2023).

Home Office. 'Automated Facial Recognition: ethical and legal use' (25 October, 2021).

Horton, Helena. 'Transgender model who said "all white people are racist" appointed as Labour adviser', *The Telegraph* (27 February, 2018).

House of Lords Environment and Climate Change Committee. '1st Report of Session 2022–23. In our hands: behaviour change for climate and environmental goals' (12 October, 2022).

Hoyer, Katja. 'Nazi Billionaires: The Dark History of Germany's Wealthiest Dynasties', *The Spectator* (23 April, 2022).

Huang, Pien. 'Trump And WHO: How Much Does The U.S. Give? What's The Impact Of A Halt In Funding?', *NPR* (15 April, 2020).

Hudson, Alan, and Ania Calderon. 'Silence is Violence: Black Lives Matter', *Global Integrity* (5 June, 2020).

Hull, Rob. 'Volvo says emissions from making EVs can be 70% higher than petrol models — and claims it can take up to 9 years of driving before they become greener', *This is Money* (5 November, 2021).

Human Rights Watch. 'US Sanctions on the International Criminal Court' (14 December, 2020).

Hunt, Jeremy. 'The bravest man I have ever met. Slava Ukraini!', *Twitter* (8 February, 2023).

Iacobucci, Gareth. 'Covid-19: Government writes off £10bn on unusable, overpriced, or undelivered PPE', *BMJ* (3 February, 2022).

Independent, The. 'Macron presents Legion of Honour medal to Zelensky during Paris visit', *YouTube* (9 February, 2023).

Independent Commission for Equity in Cricket. 'Holding up a Mirror to Cricket: A report by the Independent Commission for Equity in Cricket' (June 2023).

InfoSys. 'Digital Identity: The Catalyst for Inclusive Financial Services' (21 May, 2021).

Ingle, Sean. 'Ben Stokes "deeply sorry" to hear of cricket discrimination detailed in report', *The Guardian* (27 June, 2023).

Inman, Phillip. 'UK workers face return to 2006 real-term wages in "highly challenging" 2023', *The Guardian* (23 December, 2022).

_____. '10 years on, what did George Osborne's Help to Buy scheme really achieve?', *The Guardian* (31 March, 2023).

Insolvency Service. 'Official Statistics: Commentary — Monthly Insolvency Statistics May 2023' (16 June, 2023).

Insulate Britain. 'We all want to just stop oil' (2023).

Intergovernmental Panel on Climate Change. 'Climate change: a threat to human wellbeing and health of the planet. Taking action now can secure our future' (28 February, 2022).

International Campaign to Abolish Nuclear Weapons. 'Which countries have nuclear weapons?'

International Criminal Court. 'The States Parties to the Rome Statute'.

_____. '31 Cases'.

_____. 'Situation in Ukraine: ICC judges issue arrest warrants against Vladimir Vladimirovich Putin and Maria Alekseyevna Lvova-Belova' (17 March, 2023).

International Holocaust Remembrance Alliance. 'About the IHRA non-legally binding working definition of antisemitism'.

Intrinsic Exchange Group. 'Be Invested' (2023).

Ioannidis, John P.A., Sally Cripps and Martin A. Tanner. 'Forecasting for COVID-19 has failed', *International Journal of Forecasting*, Vol. 38, Issue 2 (April-June 2022).

Ipsos. 'How Britain voted in the 2019 election' (20 December, 2019) and 'How Britain Voted in 2010' (21 May, 2010.

Isacchenkov, Vladimir. 'Russia's security chief blasts West, dangles nuclear threats', *AP News* (23 March, 2023).

ITX. 'Diversity Acceleration Plan Report 2021' (15 July, 2022).

James, Frank. 'Al Gore Slips On Arctic Ice; Misstates Scientist's Forecast', *NPR* (15 December, 2009).

Jeffries, Jonathan, Andrew Morretta and Alex Just. 'A Chronology of Labour Law 1979-2023', *Institute of Employment Rights* (2023).

Johnston, John. 'David Lammy Says Landmark Diversity Report Is An Insult To Those Who Have Suffered Institutional Racism', *PoliticsHome* (31 March, 2021).

Jones, Brea. 'Social Media Posts Make Unsupported Claims About Zelensky's Income, Net Worth', *FactCheck.org* (21 July, 2022).

Just Stop Oil. 'Campaign Background'.

_____. 'What if the Government doesn't have it under control?'

_____. Just Stop Oil, 'Al Gore | World Economic Forum', *YouTube* (9 February, 2023).

Kallio, Jake, and Ben Norton. 'West prepares to plunder post-war Ukraine with neoliberal shock therapy: privatization, deregulation, slashing worker protections', *Geopolitical Economy* (28 July, 2022).

Kaminska, Izabella. 'Why CBDCs will likely be ID-based', *Financial Times* (4 May, 2021).

Kavanagh, Dennis Noel. 'The MET Police and Mayor of London appear unwilling to take open threats of violence against women and girls seriously', *Twitter* (9 July, 2023).

Keane, Daniel. 'Watch: Animal Rebellion protesters pour milk on Harrods shop floor', *Evening Standard* (16 October, 2022).

Kerry, John. 'Remarks With French Foreign Minister Laurent Favius Before their Meeting', *U.S. Department of State* (13 May, 2014).

_____. 'John Kerry at World Economic Forum: "Extraordinary" for "Select Group" to Discuss Green Mandates', *YouTube* (17 January, 2023).

Khatoon, Nimrah. 'Ukraine to Become the World's First 100% Cashless Country by 2025, Says National Bank Official', *BNN* (7 September, 2023).

Kiel Institute for the World Economy. 'Ukraine Support Tracker: A Database of Military, Financial and Humanitarian Aid to Ukraine'.

King College Hospital. 'New link-bridge at the PRUH incorporates Intersex-Inclusive Pride flag design' (2 June, 2023).

Kirk, Tristan. 'Trans activist Sarah Jane Baker found not guilty of encouraging violence with "punch a Terf" speech', *Evening Standard* (31 August, 2023).

Klein, Naomi. 'The Great Reset Conspiracy Smoothie', *The Intercept* (8 December, 2020).

Knight, Kathryn. 'They say it's harmless fun, but some parents think it's inappropriate indoctrination. . . . So why are our councils spending taxpayers' cash on getting drag queens to read stories to children?', *Daily Mail* (5 August, 2022).

Landberg, Reed. 'Bank of England Says Digital Punds Unlikely to Work Like Cash', *BNN Bloomberg* (6 July, 2022).

Lenin, Vladimir Ilyich. *What Is To Be Done?* (1902); collected in *Essential Works*; edited by Henry M. Christman (Bantam Books, 1966).

_____. *The State and Revolution* (1918); edited, translated and with an introduction by Robert Service. Penguin Classics, 2009.

Levy, Thomas E. 'Myocarditis: Once Rare, Now Common', *Orthomolecular Medicine News Service* (5 January, 2023).

Lewis, C. S. 'The Humanitarian Theory of Punishment'; collected in *Undeceptions: Essays on Theology and Ethics*; edited by Walter Hooper. Geoffrey Les, 1971, p. 287-288.

Liberty. 'Public Order Act: New Protest Stop & Search Powers', 2023.

Lindop, Jay. 'International migration hits new high in 2022 but there are signs of change', *Office for National Statistics* (25 May, 2023).

Lindzen, Richard, and William Happer. 'Challenging "Net Zero" with Science', *CO Coalition* (February 2023), pp. 35-37.

Liphshiz, Cnaan. 'Staircase in Ukraine mall decorated with giant swastika', *The Times of Israel* (18 February, 2019).

_____. 'Hundreds in Ukraine attend marches celebrating Nazi SS soldiers', *The Times of Israel* (4 May, 2021).

Liu, Xiao. 'Tracking how our bodies work could change our lives', *World Economic Forum* (4 June, 2020).

Lloyd, Nina. 'Inclusive workplaces unlock growth, Starmer tells LGBT+ business leaders', *Independent* (29 June, 2023).

Loginova, Elena. 'Pandora Papers Reveal Offshore Holdings of Ukrainian President and his Inner Circle', *OCCRP* (3 October, 2021).

London Underground. 'Smart Station Proof of Concept' (2022).

Lott-Lavigna, Ruby. 'Net zero minister linked to oil-funded group that targeted climate protesters, *Open Democracy* (1 September, 2023).

Loutfi, Dr. Anna Z. *Reclaim Education: The Case Against PSHE* (Bad Law Project, 2023).

Lowbridge, Caroline. 'The lesbians who feel pressured to have sex and relationships with trans women', *BBC News* (26 October, 2021).

Luscher, Dan. 'The 15-Minute City: Putting people at the center of urban transformation', *The 15-Minjute City Project* (2023).

Mairs, Gavin. 'Ugo Monye: Rugby union must tackle "heavy drinking culture" and "laddish behaviour"', *The Telegraph* (15 June, 2022).

Manning, Charlotte. 'Pride in London unveils 2023 campaign "Never March Alone" in support of trans community', *Attitude* (26 May, 2023).

Marx, Karl, and Friedrich Engels. *Selected Works*, Vol. 2 (Progress Publishers, 1969).

Matuszak, Sascha. 'Data Privacy and the Cambridge Analytica Scandal', *The Compliance and Ethics Blog* (27 March, 2018).

Mayor of London. 'Celebrating Transgender Awareness Week' (20 November, 2018).

_____. 'Major Events Calendar 2023'; 'Mayor announces Black on the Square — a major new festival showcasing Black culture and creativity' (9 August 2023).

_____. 'Mayor announces plans for a landmark memorial in the capital for the victims of the transatlantic slave trade' (24 March, 2023).

Medicines and Healthcare products Regulatory Agency. 'Pfizer/BioNTech COVID-19 vaccine authorised for use in infants and children aged 6 months to 4 years' (6 December, 2022).

Mendel, Jack. 'Ex Fed official says Bank of England "contributed to the Truss govt's demise"', *City A.M.* (28 October, 2022).

Merrick, Rob. '"Unprecedented" sanctions can still reverse Putin's invasion of Ukraine, UK minister insists', *The Independent* (24 February, 2022).

McGuinness, Alan. 'COVID-19: "Tsunami of disinformation" around COVID jabs, vaccine minister says', *Sky News* (16 February, 2021).

McKie, Robin. 'As a new variant emerges, is Covid coming back to the UK?', *The Observer* (3 September, 2023).

Mearsheimer, John J. 'Why the Ukraine Crisis Is the West's Fault', *Foreign Affairs* (September/ October 2014).

Metropolitan Police Service. 'LGBT+ community liaison officers', 2023.

Miller, Arthur. *The Crucible*. Viking Press, 1953.

Miller, Harry. 'The police are now the paramilitary wing of the trans lobby', *Spiked* (10 August, 2022).

Mills, Mark P. 'The "New Energy Economy": An Exercise in Magical Thinking', *Manhattan Institute* (March 2019).

Milne, Seumas. 'It's not Russia that's pushed Ukraine to the brink of war', *The Guardian* (30 April, 2014).

_____. 'The demonisation of Russia risks paving the way for war', *The Guardian* (4 March, 2015).

Ministry of Foreign Affairs of the People's Republic of China. 'China's Position on the Political Settlement of the Ukraine Crisis' (24 February, 2023).

Ministry of Housing, Communities & Local Government. 'Rainbow flag flown with pride' (28 June, 2013).

Mitchell, Archie. 'Sadiq Khan's office under fire for suggesting white families "don't represent real Londoners"', *The Independent* (21 August, 2023).

Mohan, Geeta. 'Are Ukraine's vast natural resources a real reason behind Russia's invasion?', *Business Today* (25 February, 2022).

Monbiot, George. 'This professor of denial can't even answer his own questions on climate change', *The Guardian* (14 September, 2009).

Monetary Institute. 'Richard Werner: Today's Source of Money Creation', *YouTube* (23 April, 2018).

Murphy, Joe. 'Blair campaign to fight binge drinking', *Evening Standard* (19 May, 2004).

Murphy, Meghan. 'Kellie-Jay Keen is attacked and mobbed by trans activists in New Zealand', *Feminist Current* (25. March, 2023).

Naldrett, Chloe. 'Arrested for wearing a T-shirt? The coronation heralded a frightening slide towards authoritarianism', *The Guardian* (7 May, 2023).

Napoleon Series. 'Declaration of the Powers against Napoleon' (13 March, 1815).

National Geographic. 'Gender Revolution', special issue (January 2017).

Nativa Economics. 'Open forum: In Harmony with Nature', *YouTube* (17 January 2023).

NBC News. 'Elton John, Michael Caine in Comic Vaccine Ad', *YouTube* (10 February, 2021).

NCAA. 'Draft Senior Cycle Social, Personal and Health Education (SPHE) Specification' (2023).

_____. 'Information note: Draft Senior Cycle SPHE Curriculum' (July 2023).

Neville, Nicola. 'This new initiative aims to address toxic masculinity in boyhood', *Glamour Magazine* (10 November, 2022).

Newman, Jack. 'Transgender woman, 18, sexually assaulted girl, 10, in Morrisons' female toilets — just weeks after using mobile to peep on another girl in Asda loos', *Daily Mail* (15 March, 2019).

New World Order, The. 'WEF 2023: Siemens Chairman Jim Hagemann Snabe on eating meat and sustainable food', *YouTube* (19 January, 2023).

Nguyen, Andy. 'There's no evidence that Ukraine's president has a net worth of $596 million', *PolitiFact* (21 July, 2022).

NHS. 'Vaccination as a condition of deployment (VCOD) for healthcare workers' (8 February, 2022).

NHS Digital. 'Rate of mental disorders among 17 to 19-year-olds increased in 2022, new report shows: statistical press release' (29 November, 2022).

Niranjan, Ajit. '"Era of global boiling has arrived," says UN chief as July set to be hottest month on record', *The Guardian* (27 July, 2023).

Norton, Ben. 'Ukraine's Zelelnsky Sends Love Letter to US Corporations, Promising "Big Business" for Wall Street', *Scheerpost* (27 January, 2023).

Nuland, Victoria and Geoffrey Pyatt. '"Fuck the EU!" Victoria Nuland & Geoffrey Pyatt secret phone talk', *YouTube* (20 February, 2015).

Ocasio-Cortez, Alexandria. '"People are dying": Ocasio-Cortez delivers fiery speech on climate inaction — video', *The Guardian* (27 March, 2019).

Ofcom. 'Children and parents: media use and attitudes report 2022' (30 March, 2022).

_____. 'Switching off the UK's 3G mobile networks: what you need to know' (3 August, 2022).

Office for National Statistics. 'ONS methodology working paper series no. 8- Statistical uses for mobile phone data: literature review' (Data and analysis from Census 2021).

_____. 'Census 2001 Summary theme figures and ranking — 390,000 Jedi There Are' (13 February, 2003).

_____. 'Gender Identity, England and Wales: Census 2021' (6 January, 2023).

_____. 'Gender identity: age and sex, England and Wales: Census 2021' (25 January, 2023).

_____. 'Migration and the labour market, England and Wales: Census 2021' (21 March, 2023).

O'Neill, Kate. 'Transgender woman "Dragon Lady" chops ears off to look like a reptile', *The Mirror* (9 September, 2016).

Onians, Charles. 'Snowfalls now are just a thing of the past', *Independent* (20 March, 2000).

Online Etymology Dictionary. 'female', 'male', 'woman', 'man'.

O'Riordan, Kate. 'The life of the gay gene: from hypothetical genetic marker to social reality', *The Journal of Sex Research*, Vol. 49, issue 4 (2012), pp. 362-368.

Orwell, George. *Nineteen Eighty-four*, Everyman's Library; with an introduction by Julian Symonds (Alfred A. Knopf, 1992).

Osborne, Samuel. 'Baby died of malnutrition after parents refused to get help "due to religious reasons and fear of child services"', *Independent* (8 August, 2018).

Padilla, Noe. '"Crisis of Identity": Michael Knowles speaks to a packed room at Purdue University', *Journal & Courier* (24 March, 2023).

Page, Jordan. '"Rugby is supposed to be a sport for all" — trans player on how the sport changed his life', *Gay Times* (19 September, 2023).

Partington, Richard. 'John McDonnell questions chancellor's suitability for office', *The Guardian* (5 August, 2019).

_____. 'Number of days lost to strikes is highest since the Thatcher Era', *The Guardian* (14 February, 2023).

Pearson-Jones, Bridie. 'Transgender model who punched feminist and smashed her £120 camera in violent brawl at Hyde Park Speakers' Corner protest walks free from court', *Daily Mail* (13 April, 2018).

Pennock, Lewis. 'Trans runner, 50, who set records in Canada for long distance events is retiring to "stop being center of controversy" — but claims testosterone at her age has no effect on her storming the competition', *Daily Mail* (3 March, 2023).

_____. 'Joe Biden is bankrolling Ukraine's 57,000 first responders — and even funding fashion stores, schools and farms — in $10bn aid package', *The Daily Mail* (25 September, 2023).

Perera, Jessica. 'The London Clearances: Race, Housing and Policing', *Institute of Race Relations* (2019).

Perry, Sophie. 'First trans woman crowned winner of Miss Netherlands', *The Pink News* (10 July, 2023).

_____. 'London Trans+ Pride addresses "punch TERFs" speech backlash: "We do not condone violence"', *The Pink News* (11 July, 2023).

Pettinger, Tejvan. 'Washington Consensus — definition and meaning', *Economics help* (25 April, 2017).

Philips, Kathleen. 'Augmented tech can change the way we live, but only with the right support and vision', *World Economic Forum* (16 August, 2022).

Philp, Catherine. 'On the front line of Ukraine's cultural de-Russification', *The Times* (26 June, 2023).

Plimer, Ian. *Heaven and Earth: Global Warming — The Missing Science*. Quartet Books, 2009.

_____. *Green Murder: A Life Sentence of Net Zero with No Parole*. Connor Court, 2021.

_____. 'Professor Ian Plimer on "Green Murder"', *YouTube* (27 April, 2022).

Population UK. 'London Population 2023'.

Prentice, Andrew. 'Why a small but very important change was made to the stumps at Headingley for the third Ashes Test', *Daily Mail* (7 July, 2023).

Preussen, Wilhelmine. 'Von der Leyen's warning message to Italy irks election candidates', *Politico* (23 September, 2022).

Price, Oliver. 'Fury after fire brigades spend £17,000 of taxpayers' money on decorating engines in LGBT rainbow colours', *Daily Mail* (3 September, 2022).

Pride in London. 'Pride in London 2023', 2023.

Prime Minister's Office. 'UK announces major new package of climate support at COP27' (7 November, 2022).

Pugh, Rachel. 'National Insurance rates are set to rise by 10% from April', *Manchester Evening News* (3 February, 2022).

Quasar, Daniel. 'Progress Pride flag', V&A (2021).

Quinn, Benn. 'What has happened to England's seven Nightingale hospitals?', *The Guardian* (8 October, 2020).

_____. 'Leonardo would have backed gallery protest, say Just Stop Oil activists', *The Guardian* (8 February, 2023).

Quinn, Chay. 'Wildfires in Tenerife blamed on arsonists by Spanish authorities after 12,000 evacuated in holiday spot', *LBC* (20 August, 2023).

Radical Faeries Men. 'Homophobic trans chaplain claims homosexuality doesn't exist', *YouTube* (18 November, 2020).

Rahman, Abdul. 'Opposition political parties banned in Ukraine and "unified information policy" imposed', *Peoples Dispatch* (21 March, 2022).

Rajasingham-Senanayake, Darini. 'Privatizing Sri Lanka ex-ante IMF Bailout of BlackRock', *IDN-InDepthNews* (26 August, 2022).

Rakovic, Maia. 'This Unnerving 2-Minute YouTube Ad Encourages American Men To "Take" Ukrainian Women', *TrillMag* (27 June, 2022).

Rayment, Sean. 'MI6 flies transgender flag for first time as boss speaks of his pride in staff', *The Mirror* (3 April, 2021).

Rayner, Gordon. 'How British Asians came to be political powerhouses', *The Telegraph* (29 March, 2023).

Rebecca Speare-Cole. 'Just Stop Oil activists spray paint on Aston Martin showroom in London', *The Independent* (16 October, 2022).

Rebel News. 'New Zealand Prime Minister sounds like Ministry of Truth leader', *YouTube* (16 July, 2021).

Redfield and Wilton Strategies. 'London Mayoral Voting Intention (4-6 September, 2023)' (8 September, 2023).

Retsas, Spyros. 'First do no harm: the impossible oath', *British Medical Journal* (19 July, 2019).

RIBA Architecture. 'RIBA celebrates Pride Month 2023' (31 May, 2023).

Ritchie, Hannah, and Pablo Rosado. Electricity Mix', *Our World In Data* (10 July, 2020).

Robinson, Martin, and Iwan Stone. 'Hospital facing backlash after chaplain puts up LGBT flags in prayer room for gravely ill children — leaving one practising Christian mother "shaking with anger"', *Daily Mail* (29 June, 2023).

Roehr, Daniel. 'Vancouver's Housing Crisis: A Collaborative Opportunity for Planners and Architects', *Spacing Vancouver* (16 September, 2019).

Rogoża, Jadwiga. 'Ukraine's disputes over the 80th anniversary of the Babi Yar massacre', *Centre for Eastern Studies* (22 October, 2021).

Rose, Jacqueline. 'The gender binary is false', *The New Statesmen* (26 July, 2023).

Rosser, Jack. 'United We don't care about the England result, we just want 90 minutes where we can forget about the war says Ukraine fan', *The Sun* 25 March, 2023).

Roth, Andrew. 'Battlefield deaths in Ukraine have risen sharply this year, say US officials', *The Guardian* (18 August, 2023).

Rothman, Micol S., and Sean J. Iwamoto. 'Bone Health in the Transgender Population', *Clinical Reviews in Bone and Mineral Metabolism* (June 2019).

Royal Mint, The. 'Celebrate with Pride — Introducing the Pride UK 50p Coin' (2022).

Rozenwurcel, Guillermo. 'Reasons for the success or failure of structural reforms: Argentina and Chile's contrasting experiences revisited', *Documento de Trabajo no. 28* (November 2007).

RT News. 'Prof. Werner brilliantly explains how the banking system and financial sector really work', *YouTube* (9 March, 2017).

Rubinstein, Alexander and Max Blumenthal. 'How Ukraine's Jewish president Zelensky made peace with neo-Nazi paramilitaries on front lines of war with Russia', *The Grayzone* (4 March, 2022).

Russ, Katheryn N., Phillip Baker, Manho Kang, and David McCoy. 'Corporate Lobbying on U.S. Positions Toward the World Health Organization', *Science Digest* (19 May, 2022).

Russell, Rachel. 'Emergency alert could be sound that saves your life, says deputy PM', *BBC News* (23 April, 2023).

Russell-Jones, Lily. 'Extinction Rebellion activists smash JP Morgan windows', *City A.M.* (1 September, 2021).

Savage, Michael. 'Rishi Sunak speaks of sting of racism after damning cricket report', *The Guardian* (1 July 2023).

Schwab, Klaus. *The Fourth Industrial Revolution*, with an introduction by Marc R. Benioff (Portfolio Penguin, 2017).

_____. 'Revolution will lead to a fusion of our physical, digital and biological identity', *YouTube* (10 November, 2020).

_____. 'Klaus Schwab of World Economic Forum boasting of his infiltration into governments', *Bitchute* (21 February 2021).

Schwab, Klaus, with Nicolas Davis. *Shaping the Future of the Fourth Industrial Revolution: A Guide to Building a Better World*, with a foreword by Satya Nadella (Portfolio Penguin, 2018).

Schwab, Klaus, and Thierry Malleret. *COVID-19: The Great Reset* (Forum Publishing, July 2020).

_____. *The Great Narrative: For a Better Future* (Forum Publishing, 2021).

Schwab, Klaus, with Peter Vanham. *Stakeholder Capitalism: A Global Economy that Works for Progress, People and the Planet* (John Wiley & Sons, 2021).

Scottish Government. 'Coronavirus (COVID-19): mandatory vaccine certification proposas' (9 September, 2021).

Sexual Diversity. 'How Many Genders Are There? Gender Identity List', *Education and LGBT Publications* (7 December, 2022).

Shakespeare, William. *King Richard III*; edited by Antony Hammond (The Arden Shakespeare, 1981).

Shemilt, Stephan. 'Ashes: Just Stop Oil protesters briefly disrupt opening morning of England v Australia Test at Lord's', *BBC Sport* (28 June, 2023).

Shubber, Kadhim. 'A simple guide to the Prism controversy', *Wired* (10 June, 2013).

Silkoff, Shira. 'Kyiv to name street for Ukrainian Nazi collaborator after public vote', *Jerusalem Post* (13 April, 2023).

Simcox, Georgia. 'Six-in-ten Britons have gone without sex during lockdown — and from today it will be illegal to romp at home with someone from another household', *Daily Mail* (1 June, 2020).

Simpson, Jack. 'Sadiq Khan says those against Ulez are "in coalition" with far-Right and Covid deniers', *The Telegraph* (3 March, 2023).

Sky News. 'European Commission President Ursula von der Leyen speaks at the World Economic Forum in Davos', *YouTube* (17 January, 2023).

Slater, Tom. 'The policing of "non-crimes" and the dark side of rainbow cars', *The Spectator* (23 August, 2021).

———. '"Punch a TERF": the violent misogyny of the trans movement', *Spiked* (10 July, 2023).

SlickText. '44 Smartphone Addiction Statistics for 2023' (23 January, 2023).

Slobodian, Quinn. 'How the "great reset" of capitalism became an anti-lockdown conspiracy', *The Guardian* (4 December, 2020).

Smith, Joan. 'Andrea Long Chu's Pulitzer win is an insult to women', *Unherd* (12 May, 2023).

Smith, Joe. 'Tik Tok clown Mizzy's mum is "sick of his stupid pranks" and wants him to get a job', *The Mirror* (3 June, 2023).

Smith, Matthew. 'Where does the British public stand on transgender rights in 2022?', *YouGov* (20 July 2022).

Smith, Tim. 'U.S. Debt Ceiling: Definition, History, Pros, Cons, and Clashes', *Investopedia* (updated 28 September, 2023).

Somerville, Ewan. 'Say "pregnant people", NHS watchdog tells staff in gender neutral drive', *The Telegraph* (4 April, 2023).

Souza, Rachel de. 'Family Review: family and its protective effects. Part 1 of the independent family review' (September 2022).

Spady, Aubrie. 'BlackRock CEO slammed for "force behaviours" comment after 2017 interview re-emerges about DEI initiatives', *Fox Business* (5 June, 2023).

Sparrow, Andrew. 'UK Covid: MPs vote to extend emergency powers for six months; NHS alert level in England to be cut to three — as it happened', *The Guardian* (25 March, 2021).

Spielmann, Peter James., 'U.N. Predicts Disaster if Global Warming Not Checked', *Associated Press News* (30 June, 1989).

Stacey, Danielle. 'Prince William shows support for LGBTQ+ community ahead of London Pride', *Hello!* (30 June, 2023).

Stanley, Alessandra. 'Russian Banking Scandal Poses Threat to Future of Privatization', *New York Times* (28 January, 1996).

Stat Counter. 'Mobile Operating System Market Share United Kingdom' (May 2023).

Statista. 'Voter turnout in general elections and in the Brexit referendum in the United Kingdom from 1918 to 2019' (2023).

Stein, Hannes. 'Zelensky As Churchill, An Iconic "V" For Victory Sign By Other Means', *World Crunch* (22 December, 2022).

Steinbuch, Yaron. 'Controversial trans cyclist Austin Killips wins North Carolina race by 5 minutes: "Power is not comparable"', *New York Post* (12 June, 2023).

Stevens, William K. 'Scientists Sat Earth's Warming Could Set Off Wide Disruptions', *The New York Times* (18 September, 1995).

Stoltenberg, Jens. 'Opening Remarks', North Atlantic Treaty Organization (7 September, 2023).

Strohm, Chris. 'FBI Searched Data of Millions of Americans Without Warrants', *Bloomberg* (29 April, 2022).

Student Brexit Group, The. 'The University of Liverpool are telling their students that "genital preferences are transphobic", *Twitter* (2 March, 2020).

Subject Access. 'Massive Anti Lockdown Protest — London', *YouTube* (20 March, 2021).

Sumption, Jonathan. 'Former Supreme Court Justice: "This is what a police state is like", *The Spectator* (30 March, 2020).

Sunak, Rishi. 'Prime Minister announces record climate aid commitment as G20 in India concludes' (10 September, 2023).

Sutton Council. 'New crossing will celebrate Sutton's transgender community' (15 May, 2021).

SWF Institute. 'Top 100 Largest Central Bank Rankings by Total Assets'.

Syal, Rajeev. 'David Lammy fined over mayoral bid nuisance calls', *The Guardian* (10 March, 2016).

Synovitz, Ron. 'Russia Has Highest Level of Health Inequality', *Radio Free Europe* (10 October, 2013).

Taaffe-Maguire, Sarah. 'Bank of England ceases bond-buying after spending £19.3bn', *Sky News* (14 October, 2022).

Táíwò, Olúfẹ́mi O. 'How BlackRock, Vanguard, and UBS Are Screwing the World', *The New Republic* (7 March, 2022).

TalkTV. 'Sadiq Khan Accused of Anti-White Racism. Many People Believe Mayorality is Stoking Division', *YouTube* (26 August, 2023).

Taylor, Diane. 'Suella Braverman accused of breaching barristers' code over "racist" language', *The Guardian* (14 May, 2023).

Taylor, Luke. 'World Health Organization to begin negotiating international pandemic treaty', *British Medical Journal* (2 December, 2021).

Taylor, Petroc. 'Number of mobile cellular subscriptions in the United Kingdom (UK) from 2000 to 2022', *Statista* (17 September, 2022).

Telegraph, The. 'Celebrities share "lockdown" coronavirus moments for a new charity song in aid of Telegraph Appeal', *YouTube* (9 April, 2020).

Teltonika. 'Geofence Solution in the Event of a Pandemic' (2023).

Tempest, Kate. 'End Times', *YouTube* (7 December, 2009).

TERF Is A Slur. 'Documenting the abuse, harassment and misogyny of transgender identity politics'.

Terriere, Panda la. 'Mayor's initiative calls for car, dairy and meat ban by 2030', *UnHerd* (11 September, 2023).

Thompson, Henry. 'Latest Updates on UK Government COVID-19 Contracts and Spending', *Tussell* (15 March, 2023).

Thunberg, Greta. *No One Is Too Small To Make A Difference*. Penguin, 2019.

Tidman, Zoe. 'Just Stop Oil shuts parts of M25 as protesters climb gantries over motorway', *The Independent* (7 November, 2022).

Tingle, Rory. 'Police reopen probe into trans activist after she told crowd "punch TERFs in the face": Met reviews Trans Pride speech made by convicted attempted murderer turned campaigner who cut off her own testicles while serving 30 years in jail', *Daily Mail* (10 July, 2023).

Tolhurst, Alain. 'Foreign Office Minister James Cleverly Has Condemned Millwall Fans Who Booed Footballers Taking The Knee Against Racism', *PoliticsHome* (7 December, 2020).

Torrance, David, and Douglas Pyper. 'The Secretary of State's veto and the Gender Recognition Reform (Scotland) Bill', *House of Commons Library* (26 April, 2023).

Trafton, Anne. 'Storing medical information below the skin's surface', *MIT News* (18 December, 2019).

Transparency International. *At Your Service: Investigating how UK businesses and institutions help corrupt individuals and regimes launder their money and reputations*; edited by Steve Goodrich (24 October 2019).

Transport for London. 'Smart Station Proof of Concept: What is Smart Stations?' (2023).

Trilateral Commission. 'Task Force Report on Artificial Intelligence: Draft for Discussion' (25 March, 2018).

Turner, Alex. 'Race and allocation: who are the new tenants getting social housing, and is it equitable', *Inside Housing* (13 August, 2021).

UCL News. 'Transgender pride flag flies at UCL', (15 November, 2018).

UK Draft Statutory Instruments. 'The Health and Social Care Act 2008 (Regulated Activities) (Amendment) (Coronavirus) Regulations 2021' (11 November, 2021).

UK Statutory Instruments. 'The Health Protection (Coronavirus, Restrictions) (England) Regulations 2020 (26 March, 2020).

UK Government. 'Ethnicity Facts and Figures' (2021 Census data).

_____. 'Regional ethnic diversity' (22 December, 2022).

_____. 'How emergency alerts work' (2023).

_____. 'About emergency alerts' (2023).

_____. 'Population of England and Wales — Ethnicity facts and figures' (4 April, 2023).

_____. 'Russian aggression and isolation continues: UK Statement to the OSCE' (21 September, 2023).

UK Health Security Agency. 'Using the NHS COVID Pass to demonstrate COVID-19 status' (7 May, 2021).

UK Parliament. 'Parliament fly LGBT rainbow flag for the first time' (3 June, 2016).

_____. UK Parliament, 'His Majesty's Government: The Cabinet'.

_____. 'Energy Bill 2023'.

UK Parliament committees. 'Written evidence submitted by the Digital Pound Foundation' (September 2022).

UK Population data. 'Population of Scotland 2023'.

UK Public General Acts. 'Highways Act 1980' (13 November, 1980)

_____. 'Police and Criminal Evidence Act 1984 (31 October, 1984).

_____. 'Public Order Act 1986' (7 November, 1986).

_____. 'Gender Recognition Act 2004' (1 July, 2004).

_____. 'Equality Act 2010' (8 April, 2010).

_____. 'Digital Economy Act 2017' (27 April, 2017).

_____. 'Coronavirus Act 2020' (25 March, 2020).

_____. 'Domestic Abuse Act 2021' (29 April, 2021).

_____. 'Health and Care Act 2022' (28 April, 2022).

_____. 'Police, Crime, Sentencing and Courts Act 2022' (28 April, 2022).

_____. 'Judicial Review and Courts Act 2022' (28 April, 2022).

_____. 'Nationality and Borders Act 2022' (28 April, 2022).

_____. 'Elections Act 2022' (28 April, 2022).

_____. 'Public Order Act 2023' (2 May, 2023).

_____. 'Online Safety Bill 2023' (awaiting Royal Assent in October 2023).

United Nations. 'Sustainable Development Goals: 17 goals to transform our world'.

_____. 'What is the Kyoto Protocol?'

_____. 'What is the Paris Agreement?'

_____. 'Transforming our world: the 2030 Agenda for Sustainable Development', Department of Economic and Social Affairs.

_____. United Nations, 'United Nations Carbon Offset Platform'.

United Nations Department of Economic and Social Affairs. 'Transforming our world: the 2030 Agenda for Sustainable Development'.

United Nations High Commissioner for Human Rights. 'Conflict-related civilian casualties in Ukraine' (27 January, 2022);

_____. 'Ukraine: civilian casualty update 24 September 2023' (25 September, 2023).

United Nations Office on Genocide Prevention and the Responsibility to Protect. 'Definitions'.

University of Cambridge. 'Absolute Zero: Delivering the UK's climate change commitment with incremental changes to today's technologies' (November 2019).

University of Manchester. 'Are ethnic and religious minority voters key to electoral success?' (4 May, 2023).

U.S. Department of the Treasury. 'Secretary of the Treasury Janet L. Yellen Sends Letter to Congressional Leadership on the Debt Limit' (13 January, 2023).

Vanham, Peter. 'World Economic Forum launches COVID-19 Action Platform to fight coronavirus', *World Economic Forum* (11 March, 2020).

Vighi, Fabio. 'Slavoj Žižek, Emergency Capitalism, and the Capitulation of the Left', *The Philosophical Salon* (24 May, 2021).

_____. 'A Self-fulfilling Prophecy: Systemic Collapse and Pandemic Simulation', *The Philosophical Salon* (16 August, 2021).

Waggaman, Riley. 'Putin & Xi's Moscow agreements', *Off-Guardian* (28 March, 2023).

Walker, Shaun. 'Azov fighters are Ukraine's greatest weapon and may be its greatest threat', *The Guardian* (10 September, 2014).

Wallace, Tim. 'Bank of England tells ministers to intervene on digital currency "programming"', *The Telegraph* (21 June, 2021).

Walport, Mark. 'The Internet of Things: making the most of the Second Digital Revolution', *Government Office for Science* (December 2014).

Watson, Steve. 'Video: Trans "Activist" Literally Burns Harry Potter Book', *Summit News* (28 March, 2023).

Weaver, Matthew. 'Cardiff Philharmonic removes Tchaikovsky performance over Ukraine conflict', *The Guardian* (9 March, 2022).

Webber, Jude. 'Irish farmers pressured to cull up to 200,000 cows to meet climate goals', *Financial Times* (11 August, 2023).

Webberley, Dr. Helen. 'I am a GP, I am self-taught in trans healthcare', *Twitter* (1 July, 2023).

Wedel, Janine R. 'The Harvard Boys Do Russia', *The Nation* (14 May, 1998).

Werner, Richard. *Princes of the Yen: Japan's Central Bankers and the Transformation of the Economy*. Routledge, 2003.

Whipple, Tom. 'Professor Neil Ferguson: People don't agree with lockdown and try to undermine the scientists', *The Times* (25 December, 2020).

White, Nadine. 'Sadiq Khan: "Climate crisis is a racial justice issue" as black and Asian Londoners most affected', *Independent* (17 March, 2022).

Wikipedia. 'German-occupied Europe'.

_____. 'Industrielleneingabe'.

_____. 'Servant of the People'.

Wolfe, Danielle de. '"If you do that it's a crime": Police warn motorists it's assault if they move Just Stop Oil protesters off road', *LBC* (25 April, 2023).

Women's Rights Network. 'URGENT. We have reported this man — a convicted torturer and kidnapper, who is on probation — for committing a Public Order offence', *Twitter* (9 July, 2023).

Woodcock, Andrew. 'Scathing report blasts 'unimaginable' £37bn cost of coronavirus test and trace system', *The Independent* (10 March, 2021).

World Bank Group. 'Practitioner's Guide' (October 2019).

World Economic Forum. 'World Economic Forum launches COVID-19 Action Platform to fight coronavirus' (11 March, 2020).

_____. 'Our Partners'.

_____. 'Great Reset | HRH Prince of Wales | We have no alternative' (3 June, 2020).

_____. 'Great Reset: Why LGBT+ inclusion is the secret to cities' post-pandemic success' (3 June, 2020).

_____. 'Far-Right Extremism and Anti-vaccine Conspiracy Theories: A Case from Italy' (21 October, 2021).

_____. 'Is climate denialism dead?' (15 August, 2022).

_____. 'Trans-inclusive workplaces: 5 considerations for companies' (2 November, 2022).

_____. 'Our network is preparing humanity for the Fourth Industrial Revolution' (2023).

_____. 'The Great Reset' (2023).

_____. 'Measuring Stakeholder Capitalism: Towards Common Metrics and Consistent Reporting of Sustainable Value Creation' (2023).

_____. 'World Economic Forum Annual Meeting', (16-20 January, 2023).

_____. 'Mastering New Energy Economics | Davos 2023', *YouTube* (17 January, 2023).

_____. 'A Conversation with Satya Nadella, CEO of Microsoft', *YouTube* (19 January, 2023).

_____. '100 Days to Outrace the Next Pandemic | Davos 2023', *YouTube* (21 January, 2023).

_____. 'A Conversation with Satya Nadella, CEO of Microsoft | Davos 2023', *YouTube* (19 January, 2023).

World Government Summit. 'The State of the World', *YouTube* (15 February, 2023).

World Health Organization. 'Transforming Health in the Fourth Industrial Revolution', *YouTube* (25 January, 2018).

_____. 'Vaccine hesitancy: A growing challenge for immunization programmes'.

_____. 'WHO Director-General's opening remarks at the media briefing on COVID-19' (11 March, 2020).

_____. 'World Health Assembly agrees to launch process to develop historic global accord on pandemic prevention, preparedness and response' (1 December, 2021).

_____. 'Zero draft of the WHO CA+ for the consideration of the Intergovernmental Negotiating Body at its fourth meeting' (1 February, 2023).

_____. 'Pandemic prevention, preparedness and response accord' (24 February, 2023).

_____. 'The European Commission and WHO launch landmark digital health initiative to strengthen global health security' (5 June, 2023).

Worldometer. 'Coronavirus Deaths: 6,905,481 deaths' (8 August, 2023).

Wright, Richie. 'Liverpool town hall rainbow flag', *Wikipedia* (30 May, 2012).

Yardeni, Edward, and Mali Quintana, 'Central Banks: Monthly Balance Sheets', *Yardeni Research, Inc.*

Young, Toby. 'Woke Culture Has Gone Too Far', *YouTube* (12 January, 2023).

Yousaf, Humza. 'Humza Yousaf Racist Rant about white people in Scotland', *YouTube* (25 February, 2023).

Yuko, Elizabeth. 'The Meaning Behind 32 LGBTQ Pride Flags', *Reader's Digest* (22 June, 2023).

Zaimov, Stoyan. 'Father of Two Who "Hid Identity for 40 Years" Becomes UK Methodist Church's First Transgender Minister', *The Christian Post* (20 November, 2017).

Zelenskyy, Volodmyr. 'Ukraine President Zelensky in High Heels singing', *YouTube* (2 March, 2021).

_____. 'Zelensky Winning "Dancing with the Stars"', *YouTube* (28 February, 2022).

_____. 'Volodymyr Zelenskyy 2016 Playing Piano with Penis', *YouTube* (1 March, 2022).

_____. 'Volodmyr Zelensky on Dancing with the Stars Ukraine', *YouTube* (7 March, 2022).

_____. 'President Zelensky and Ukrainian people singing and dancing naked in supermarkets', *YouTube* (10 March, 2022).

_____. 'Ukraine's Zelensky addresses UK in Westminster Hall', *YouTube* (8 February, 2023).

Zimmerman, Dwight Jon. 'The Faustian Bargain: Industrialist Fritz Thyssen and the Nazis', *Defense Media Network* (15 August 2017).

Zindulka, Kurt. 'UK police force poses with progress pride flag, vows to "monitor" hate speech responses', *Breitbart* (7 June, 2022).

Zoopla, 'House prices in Tipton St. John' (September, 2023).

Zubkova, Daria. 'Cabinet Introduces Military Registration from Age of 16', *UkraNews* (4 January, 2023).